HOW TO TEACH
FOREIGN LANGUAGES
EFFECTIVELY

How to Teach Foreign Languages Effectively

REVISED EDITION

by **THEODORE HUEBENER**

*Formerly Director of Foreign Languages in the Schools of the
City of New York
Professor of Languages, Fairleigh Dickinson University*

NEW YORK UNIVERSITY PRESS · 1965

Preface

The aim of this book is to provide the classroom teacher of modern languages with practical aids in the teaching of his subject. It devotes itself, therefore, primarily to the description of various methods of instruction and to the presentation of a generous collection of illustrations, examples, model lessons, suggested procedures, games, and devices.

Over forty complete lessons in French, German, Italian, and Spanish to illustrate the various phases of language instruction have been included. These lessons are eminently practical, for they have all been tried out in the classroom and found successful. They are culled largely from the daily observation notes of a supervisor in a foreign language department of over a thousand teachers, who give instruction in nine foreign languages to 185,000 pupils. To many years of experience in the New York school system may be added the fruits of observation at various times in hundreds of classrooms in foreign countries.

Since the book is to be a practical guide, no attempt has been made to present the historical development and the psychology of language teaching. Only such theoretical material has been introduced as has a direct bearing on the daily classroom activities of the teacher. It is hoped that the description in nontechnical language of effective methods of teaching the student to hear, speak, read, and write a foreign tongue will prove helpful to the teacher.

Various types of teaching procedures are described in this book, for there is no one best method for all lessons and all teaching situations. The method will be effective to the degree that it is adjusted to the various factors involved. These will include the personality, experience, and background of the teacher; the type of material to be taught; the nature of the textbook used; the age, intelligence, and scholarship of the pupils; and the aims of the course of study. The skillful teacher is the one who knows how to adapt himself adequately to the circumstances.

Methods of teaching the various school subjects change from decade to decade. In foreign language teaching the direct method, stimulated by the Reform Movement in Europe, was more or less advocated, although not universally practiced, in the United States from the 1870's to about 1910. From 1910 to about 1918, that is, up to World War I, the grammar-translation method was widely used. Then followed the reading method, the conversational method, the intensive method, and the eclectic method with its fourfold aim. Within the last few years an entirely new procedure—strictly not a method—has been developed, namely, the audio-lingual approach. Since this approach is being introduced in many schools on an experimental basis, its theoretical foundation and its practical application are described in considerable detail.

Under normal conditions the teacher is, in the final analysis, the most important factor in the learning process. Although it has been said that good teachers are born, not made, and although natural endowment is undoubtedly basic in the case of the inspired teacher, anyone who is willing to learn may be taught how to teach an effective lesson. We cannot all be gifted artists, but we can all be skilled craftsmen. The less experienced can always profit by observing the work of the more experienced.

"Let him who dares to teach never refuse to learn."

In making his acknowledgments the author wishes to express first and foremost his appreciation of the generosity of so many able members of the foreign language staff of the New York City Schools who have provided the basis for most of the model lessons.

He is very grateful to Miss Renée J. Fulton, Director of In-Service Training, New York City Board of Education, for her careful reading of the original manuscript, of which the present volume is a revision.

The author is particularly and deeply indebted to two other faithful colleagues who have gone over much of the material presented here and who have made many valuable suggestions. They are Dr. Emilio Guerra, Acting Director of Foreign Languages in the New York City Schools, and Professor at New York University, and Dr. Maxim Newmark, Coordinator and Editor of the Foreign Language Revision Program, in the New York City Schools.

Finally, the author wishes to express his gratitude to his wife Elizabeth, also a teacher of foreign languages, for her untiring and conscientious service in the preparation of the manuscript.

T.H.

Contents

III The Audio-Lingual Activities—*Continued*

ditory Comprehension—Illustrative Lessons—Topics for Audio-Lingual Experiences—Examples of Dialogues

IV Reading

Importance of Reading—Types of Reading—Pleasurable Reading—What Is Reading?—Reading a Foreign Language—Fundamental Considerations—Introduction to Reading—Reading Should Be Properly Motivated—Reading Aloud—Choral Reading—Intensive Reading—Silent Reading—Comprehension Should Be Tested—Visual and Aural Aids Should Be Studied—Review Through Oral Activities—Extensive Reading—Supplementary Reading—Illustrative Lessons

V Writing

Values—Introducing Writing—Imitative Writing—Dictation—Guided Writing—Controlled Writing—Composition—Controlled Composition—Directed Composition—Free Composition—Illustrative Lessons

VI Vocabulary

Subject Matter—What Words Should Be Taught?—Vocabulary Range—Topics That Determine a Vocabulary—Learning Vocabulary—Effective Practice—Habit Formation—Word-Study Techniques—Inferring Meanings—Practice—Illustrative Lessons

VII Grammar

Need for Grammar—Language Learning of the Child—Audio-Lingual Approach to Grammar—Change of Emphasis—Analysis and Explanation—Terminology—Conventional Approach to Grammar—Structures To Be Taught during the First Two Years—French—Spanish—Italian—German

I ʼ Introduction

Why Learn Foreign Languages?

Or rather, since this is a book for teachers of foreign languages, why teach foreign languages?

Although in most American schools foreign languages are an elective subject, and although their value has been questioned at various times in the past, they are basically one of the soundest subjects of our curriculum. When properly taught, foreign languages are, next to English, the most broadening and the most cultural elements of a liberal education.

Fundamentally, language is man's unique accomplishment. More than anything else, it sets man apart from the animal world. It is the vehicle of communication and speech; it makes possible the keeping of records and the creation of a store of knowledge; it is the basis of all creative thought. Without language there would be no progress, no civilization, no culture. The cultural heritage of mankind resides in language.

In the language and literature of every people are preserved its hopes, its aspirations, and its thinking. Through the learning of a foreign tongue we gain a better insight into human relations and a deeper appreciation of man's struggles and achievements. In setting up as its ultimate aim the better understanding of a foreign

1

people and of its culture, the study of foreign languages belongs essentially to the social sciences.

A foreign language presents so many interesting facets that it is the best medium for introducing the student to the history, civilization, and cultural achievements of the foreign people. It is so many-sided that, in the hands of a skillful teacher, it easily becomes a genuine "core subject" through which the fields of English, art, architecture, music, literature, history, and geography can be correlated. The study of a foreign language then becomes a course in civilization and the humanities. In fact, until very recently, cultural rather than practical values are what have justified the inclusion of foreign languages in the curriculum of the American secondary school.

The distinction between the cultural and practical, as related to school subjects, is at best artificial. Almost any subject can be taught so that the emphasis falls on either the cultural or the practical aspects or on the educational or vocational phase. Certain subjects, because of their very nature, have been taught in but one way: stenography is regularly treated as practical, music as cultural. French is offered in an academic high school because of its educational value, but in a commercial language school for its vocational value. Viewed in the broadest educational perspective, the "cultural" is always more important than the "practical," for it involves permanent life values, character qualities, attitudes, and ideals.

Despite the brevity of the foreign language course, the type of instruction can and should be such that a firm foundation is laid, upon which the student will be able later to build up ease and facility in speaking, if the need and desire therefor should arise. Thousands of Americans who travel in foreign countries every year derive greater enjoyment from their trips because they have some knowledge of a foreign tongue. For the businessman, whether he is engaged in the export trade or whether he deals with large numbers of persons in our metropolitan areas who speak a foreign tongue, an acquaintance with one or more foreign languages is a valuable asset.

The school, in fact, in such foreign communities renders a real service by teaching the children the language of their parents and by preserving the better features of the foreign culture. Understanding, respect, and goodwill may be established in this way between the older and the younger generations, between the foreigner

2

and the American school. Indeed, one may say that the teaching of the foreign language has sociological value here.

Constantly improving means of communication have contracted the world so much that the most distant peoples have become our neighbors. Radio and television bring the cultures and the languages of other nations into our very homes. In the metropolitan areas one may hear programs in as many as seven different languages. And travel to foreign countries has expanded enormously within recent times. In one year alone seventy million persons were transported by airplane throughout the world.

There was a time when much emphasis was placed on the claim that the study of foreign languages promotes international peace. This beautiful ideal appears to be hopelessly lost in a world suffering acutely from political rivalries, economic distress, and social ills. Yet, fundamentally, most of our troubles are due to prejudice and hatred based on misunderstanding. A better acquaintance with the psychology and with the problems of other nations would help to remove some of the discord.

Especially now that the United States has assumed the political, military, scientific, and cultural leadership of the Western world, a knowledge of foreign languages is imperative for our youth. Large staffs of representatives of our country are stationed all over the world. In one year alone over a million Americans were stationed abroad. Highly significant, too, is the fact that the UN has its headquarters in the United States. The center of gravity—political, economic, and scientific—has swung to the United States.

This change has a vital implication for American education. We can no longer ignore the languages of other nations. Experts in many fields, who are called upon to act as leaders, must be equipped with foreign languages. The average citizen must be given some knowledge of foreign languages so that he may cope more intelligently with international problems.

The extreme importance of foreign languages in the international role which America has assumed was given official recognition and active support in the National Defense Education Act (1958 et seq.). Through this act almost a billion dollars were alloted for the promotion of the teaching of science, mathematics, and foreign languages. With respect to the latter the development of the ability to speak was given primary consideration.

3

Aims

The major objective, then, for teaching a foreign language is to provide the student with an additional medium of communication. This objective may be subdivided into general aims and specific aims.

The general aim of language teaching is to equip the student with the knowledge and skills required for effective communication in the foreign language. To this may be added the aim of imparting to the learner an understanding of the foreign people and its culture.

More specifically the linguistic aim includes the following objectives:

1. The ability to comprehend the foreign language when spoken at normal speed and when concerned with ordinary, nontechnical subject matter.

2. Facility in the use of the spoken language with acceptable standards of pronunciation and grammatical correctness.

3. Ease in reading and comprehending printed material of ordinary difficulty.

4. The ability to write with acceptable standards of correctness on topics within the learner's experience.

The cultural objectives may be summarized as follows:

1. An understanding of the everyday life of the foreign people, including customs, family life, work and play, and typical reactions.

2. Knowledge of the main facts concerning the geography and history of the foreign country, together with its economic and political development.

3. Appreciation of the art, music, literature, and science of the foreign people and its contributions to world civilization.

4. The promotion of international amity through a consideration of the foreign people's contribution to the development of the United States.

5. A growth in understanding of the value of language as a basic factor in culture, in general, and specifically of the relationship of the foreign language to English.

The Learning of a Foreign Language

Learning is essentially the process of change in mental and physical behavior induced in a living organism by experience. Formal learning is the total of experiences to which the child is subjected in school. The final stage of learning is habit; the result of habit is skill. Learning, then, is basically habit formation.

To learn a new language means simply to acquire another set of speech habits. We learn through the observance of rules; we have mastered the language when the rules have been forgotten and speech has become spontaneous.

Sounds are the basis of speech. The printed word merely represents the symbol of a combination of sounds which carries meaning.

Effective learning takes place when a response becomes automatic. It will do so if the laws of learning are observed. Essentially these are:

1. *A vivid impression.* The learner must have presented to him a definite impression of what he is to learn.

2. *Intense motivation.* Effective learning will take place only if the learner is eager to acquire the new knowledge.

3. *Complete comprehension.* The learner must understand clearly what is involved and required.

4. *Focus of consciousness.* The more fully the learner concentrates his attention, the more readily he will learn.

5. *Frequent, lively practice* at ever-widening intervals. This is necessary to counteract the tendency to forget.

6. *A feeling of satisfaction* to accompany achievement. The learner will be more eager if he likes what he does, and if he has pleasurable sensations in doing it.

In addition to these factors, there are favorable conditions that will increase readiness to learn and practices to offset monotony. Among the latter are speed, changing of form, multiple sense appeal, and the use of variety.

Since school subjects differ in objectives, methods, and values, the types of learning which are the outcomes of any given lesson will vary. However, in any formal learning situation five basic factors should be clearly in evidence. Depending upon the type of lesson, they will differ in degree, but the good teacher will provide for them quite unconsciously at times. These five learning outcomes are:

1. *Increased knowledge.* Learning, except in purely imitative or

mechanical operations, is chiefly an intellectual, a cognitive process. An effective lesson will result in greater knowledge of subject matter. In a language lesson this means the acquisition of new vocabulary, idioms, points in grammar, or cultural facts.

2. *Improved skill.* In a subject like a foreign language various skills are the concomitants of increased knowledge. The vocabulary and the idioms are to be practiced and the grammatical facts are to be applied. The exercises and activities should be such that the skill of the student in manipulating language facts is improved. The acquisition of knowledge falls under *presentation;* the improvement of skill is essentially *application.*

3. *Strengthened attitudes.* Through the activities provided and by means of the example of the teacher, the students' formation of wholesome habits and reactions should be encouraged. Some of the attitudes may be related specifically to the subject; others will be of a general nature, such as open-mindedness, receptivity, and scholarliness. Or it may be good character traits that are developed, such as cooperativeness, courtesy, cheerfulness, and honesty.

4. *Deepened interests.* If there is one aim that the teacher should continually keep in mind, it is to strengthen the pupil's interest in the subject. This means enlisting the student's active participation in the immediate situation, and also building up a permanent, lifelong interest.

5. *Enriched ideals.* If our ultimate aim is to provide a better understanding of the foreign people and its civilization, the language lesson should result in clearer ideals of tolerance and international friendliness. This should be true particularly of the cultural lesson.

Aside from the knowledge, skills, attitudes, ideals, and interests, certain insights and appreciations, which may be termed "imponderables," should be the outcomes of a language lesson. Some of these are:

1. A general insight into the psychology of language structure and modes of expression.
2. An appreciation of the beauties of language.
3. An enrichment of English vocabulary.
4. Scholarly standards in the approach to all cultural and scientific subjects.
5. Standards of neatness, accuracy, and precision in the preparation of all written and spoken material.

6. Efficient habits of study.
7. Ideals of courage, integrity, loyalty, and humanitarianism.
8. An abiding interest in the foreign language and its literature.

Aspects of Language Learning

There are four aspects to a language: listening, speaking, reading, and writing. This is the exact order in which the learner picks up his native tongue as a child and, later on, the way he approaches a foreign language. First, he hears sounds and tries to understand them; then, he attempts to reproduce them. Next, he learns to read the written and printed symbols of the language, and finally, he expresses himself in written form. Or, broadly speaking, there is the passive or receptive phase, and there is the active or reproductive phase.

All four phases are closely interdependent, for hearing is related to silent speaking; silent reading to inner hearing and speaking; and oral reading is controlled speaking. Writing implies speaking, hearing, and reading, for an inner voice is dictating to the writer. The constant problem of the teacher is to integrate these phases into a unified whole by the separate and successive training of each phase.

The elements learned in one phase of language learning do not always carry over automatically to another phase. We learn only those applications that we practice. Hence, transfer must be enforced by specific exercises with specific aims. Essentially, there is transfer through identical elements if they are pointed out and if the method of learning is the same.

Hagbolt makes the following observation:

> Hearing facilitates reading in proportion to the number of sounds, words, etc. learned and spontaneously recognized in reading. Oral exercises facilitate speaking and writing. Silent reading helps comprehension only if the student pronounces correctly. Writing and speaking also aid comprehension. In brief, transfer from the receptive phases (hearing and reading) to the reproductive phases (speaking and writing) is far less likely to occur than the reverse. (Peter Hagbolt: *Language Learning*, University of Chicago, 1935.)

The emphasis on one particular phase of language learning has led to the setting up of different aims.

The Reading Aim

Largely through the implementation of the so-called Coleman Report ("The Teaching of Modern Foreign Languages in the United States"), published in 1929, the reading aim was accepted throughout the country. In view of the fact that most students pursued the study of a language for only two years, it seemed to be a reasonable objective. There were undoubted advantages, as for example:

1. Reading is an attainable goal.
2. The ability to read is more lasting than the ability to speak or to write.
3. In presenting masterpieces, or selections from them, to the student, reading acquaints the learner with the life and culture of the foreign people.
4. For the teacher who is not so well grounded in the language, reading is easier to handle.
5. In the long run reading is of greatest utility to the student.

There were, however, many language teachers who did not approve, insisting that the spoken language was the important thing. They pointed to obvious disadvantages in the reading method, such as:

1. Pronunciation gets scant attention.
2. Unless the teacher is resourceful, reading lacks vivacity.
3. It is stultifying for the teacher unless relieved by conversation and other activities.
4. It is inadequate preparation for travel or for practical situations.
5. In the final analysis, it is unsatisfying to the student and to the public. The question always is, "What languages do you *speak*?" not "What languages do you read?"

Dissatisfaction with the reading aim was brought to a head by the outbreak of World War II, when it became apparent how few Americans, despite years of study in school, knew any foreign language. The vaunted success of the A.S.T.P. (Army Specialized Training Program) in the teaching of languages strengthened the insistence on speaking rather than reading.

The Conversational Aim

The enthusiasm for oral practice was formulated as the "conversational aim." Experimentation with it soon showed, however, that it, too, had certain disadvantages. Some of the factors that had to be considered were:

1. The primary aim of foreign language instruction in the schools has always been educational and cultural. The ability to speak fluently is not acquired primarily in the classroom, but through much additional practice on the outside.
2. Real conversation is difficult to achieve in the classroom because the time to develop it is insufficient.
3. Conversation must not be confused with oral practice. Conversation involves the free, spontaneous discussion by two or more persons of any topic of common interest. Part of its effectiveness is due to facial expression and gestures.
4. Speaking ability is the most difficult phase of a foreign language to teach and to acquire.
5. This ability is least likely to be retained, for it depends on constant practice.
6. It is difficult to teach because it requires unusual resourcefulness, skill, and energy on the part of the teacher. No textbook can make up for the originality of an everyday-life situation.
7. Conversational competence depends essentially on an extensive vocabulary, the memorization of numerous speech patterns, and the automatic control of structures.

The Fourfold Aim

In view of the close interrelation of the various phases of language, it is unwise to stress any one of them, unless a specific objective has been set up for attainment (for example, the aim of the A.S.T.P. for immediate practical use in speaking). Otherwise, and especially for classroom instruction, all of the aspects of language learning should, in the long run, receive equal attention. This is achieved best through the pursuit of the so-called fourfold aim, which endeavors to provide for the progressive development of the learner's power

1. To understand the spoken language
2. To express himself orally in it
3. To read the foreign language, and
4. To employ the language in written form within the range of his ability.

The above objectives are attainable on different levels, depending upon the pupil's ability and the time devoted to the subject. Within the short time generally allotted to foreign language study, the fourfold aim does not imply that the student will achieve even near-native fluency. It does, however, mean that the learner can be provided with an acceptable pronunciation, that he will be able to express himself with reference to everyday subjects of conversation in a fairly correct and intelligible manner, that he will be able to understand the foreign language when spoken at a moderate tempo, and that he will be able to read printed matter of average difficulty. Complete mastery of a foreign tongue requires years of practice, preferably in life situations in the foreign country.

Even if the course were lengthened, the most that can be expected of classroom teaching is the laying of a foundation on which the student can build further competence as the need arises.

The Cultural Aspect. What has been said above has been concerned primarily with the linguistic aspect of language teaching. This is and must remain foremost in any foreign language course.

Closely linked with the language is the civilization of the nation whose tongue is being studied. In fact, the language serves as a vehicle for the study of the culture of the foreign people. The ultimate aim of our instruction should be to acquaint students with the literature, art, music, history, and scientific achievements of the other country. This seems like a vast body of knowledge. However, its highlights can be brought into the picture by constant reference to the foreign scene from the very first day. Even the simplest words have cultural significance, as, for example, *fenêtre*, for a French window is quite different from an American window.

Furthermore, because of the large numbers of our fellow-citizens who are of foreign origin and who continue to speak their mother tongue, an awareness of the contributions of various racial stocks to the history and development of the United States must be included. This, we hope, will strengthen the ideal of tolerance and lead to a more sympathetic attitude toward our minorities.

Recent Trends. The A.S.T.P. was influential in introducing the intensive method in the colleges and universities and in stressing the spoken aim. The latter gathered momentum through the studies and projects of the National Association of Secondary School Principals, the findings of the Modern Language Association, the pronouncements of Dr. Conant and the construction by the College Entrance Board of tests in listening comprehension. Classroom experiments in Glastonbury, Connecticut, resulted in the so-called Glastonbury method. Based on the contributions of the comparative linguists, the "new key," the new method, the audio-lingual approach was evolved. Not only were the procedures different from the traditional teaching methods, but the entire philosophy of language learning and teaching was completely changed.

The new method immediately received powerful support from three sides. Financially and morally it was aided by the Federal government, which gave it semiofficial sanction and allotted millions of dollars through the National Defense Education Act (N.D.E.A.) for a program extending over a number of years. On the secondary level money has been spent for equipment, chiefly language laboratories and mechanical aids; in the colleges and universities it has paid for the setting up of summer institutes for the training of teachers.

Technically the new method was supported by the appearance on the market of a large variety of mechanical teaching aids, such as tape recorders, teaching machines, and language laboratories. Numerous audio-lingual films and programed courses for the teaching of foreign languages were published. There is a veritable *embarras de richesses* in the field of audio-visual aids.

Thirdly and theoretically, the new method was based on the findings of the structural linguists, who developed a psychology and a philosophy of language learning quite different from the traditional.

Problems and Questions for Discussion

1. Draw up a brief which justifies the inclusion of your major language in the high school curriculum.
2. Present arguments for the teaching of foreign languages in the elementary grades.

11

3. What should be the basic criteria for the inclusion of a foreign language in the American school curriculum?

4. In what way may foreign languages be thought of as a social science?

5. Tell what factors have helped to establish the audio-lingual approach in foreign language teaching.

I I ⁄ The Audio-Lingual Approach

Theory. The new conception of teaching foreign languages, known as the audio-lingual approach, is based on the following assumptions.

Language is the everyday spoken utterance of the average person at normal speed. This oral communication usually consists of talk between two or more persons; that is, conversation. The subject matter is primarily concerned with the common facts and occurrences of life; it is not literature. The speakers express their thoughts freely, without thinking of verb forms, idioms, or syntax. The spoken language is purely an instrument of communication, used in given situations. Hence the dialogue should form the basis of every language lesson.

In the approach to any language, listening and understanding come first. Almost immediately oral utterance follows; an attempt is made to reproduce vocally what has been heard, primarily through imitation.

In the case of the individual, as in the history of the race, speech comes first; reading and writing come later. The graphic symbols do not represent the sounds of any language accurately, even though some languages are highly phonetic, for example,

13

Spanish. In other languages, on the other hand, for example, English, the disparities between the written and the spoken language are great. Letters stand for different sounds; a given sound may be spelled in a variety of ways. Hence the learner should not see printed forms of the foreign language in the beginning stages, for he is likely to be confused and give the graphic symbols the values they have in his native tongue.

Every speaker uses a language in a slightly different, personal manner. But to make himself understood he has to conform almost exactly to the requirements of the standard, the communal language. The latter does change gradually, although it is fairly well fixed. Technically, it is known as the *langue,* whereas the individual's use of it is called *parole.* The two are interdependent and are termed *langage.*

New Terminology. The comparative linguists have developed a large number of new terms to express their ideas or have given different meanings to those already in use. In fact, the new expressions have grown so voluminous that several handbooks have appeared defining them. If the more recent literature on language learning is to be at all intelligible to the average foreign language teacher, he must acquaint himself with some of the basic terms. A summary of these terms is presented here.

Language consists of meaningful sounds produced by the human voice. Any sound made by the vocal apparatus is known as a *phone.* The utterance of sounds is called *phonation;* hearing them is *audition.* A word or a series of words functioning as a unit is an *utterance.*

The number of sounds made by the vocal apparatus and distinguishable by the human ear is great. These sounds differ from language to language; they are not identical. Although the number of sounds is great, only a certain number is employed in any one language. Furthermore, only a smaller number of sounds make a difference in meaning. Certain sounds tend to occur more frequently than others in any one language. Certain sounds combine into *clusters.*

A word is made up of a sequence of *phonemes.* A *phoneme* is not a sound but a class of sounds. A phoneme is made up of *allophones.* The *allophone* is the smallest unit of sound.

A language usually has at least twenty but no more than fifty phonemes. English has thirty-two phonemes—nine vowels and twenty-three consonants.

Although a phoneme by itself does not carry meaning, it indicates a difference of meaning in words. For example, in *cop, top, pop, sop* the changes in meaning are effected by the phonemes *c, t, p,* and *s*. Allophones are unlike one another phonetically, but they do not indicate a change in meaning. A phoneme may be represented by different letters, as for example, the hard *k* sound in English by *c* and *k* and *ch,* or the *ou* of *route* by *oo, u,* and *ou*.

Phonemes, by their contrast in sound, indicate changes in meaning. The sounds that make the distinction do not, however, carry meaning in themselves; for example, *big* and *bag, fit* and *fat, hot* and *hit*.

There are sounds that do convey meaning, for example, the plural ending *s* or *es*. Such a unit of sound is called a *morpheme*. A morpheme may be an entire word, a prefix, a suffix, a tense ending, or the possessive case (*'s*). The members of a given morpheme are called *allomorphs*. When separated from the utterance in which they occur, they are known as *morphs*.

The speech sounds or phones that are combined to form the words of a language are known as *segmental* phonemes. Another class of phonemes is called *suprasegmental,* or *prosodic*. These have such characteristics as intonation, pitch, loudness, and juncture. They make up the *melody* of a language. In general, British English has far more melody than American English.

A suffix like *er* or a prefix like *un* is a morpheme or *sound cluster*. It can be *free* or *bound*. If it has meaning by itself, that is, if it can be used independently as a word, it is known as *free*. If it cannot be used alone, it is called *bound*. For example, in the word *unfortunately, un* and *ly* are bound morphemes and *fortunate* is a free morpheme.

A knowledge of the above terms, of course, will not in itself make the language teacher an authority on linguistics nor even an expert in the specialized field most pertinent to the language teacher, namely, applied linguistics. Further study of this field should be pursued in works dealing with this subject, such as those listed in the Bibliography. Needless to say, the teacher's ability to hold forth learnedly on the subject of applied linguistics will not assist his charges in speaking a language. It would merely be another instance of talking *about* a language rather than talking *in* the language.

Application. In view of the fact that language normally consists of talk between two or more persons in an everyday situation, the dialogue—not the reading selection—becomes the basis of every language lesson.

As stated before, in daily life speakers express their ideas freely, without thinking of verb forms, idioms, and grammatical structure. The classroom dialogue should be constructed on the same basis. That is, it is to be as close an approximation as possible of the everyday conversation of normal adults.

This means that the dialogue will be presented to the class at normal speed, without any concern for idiomatic expressions or subjunctives. Of course, it will have to be simple and brief in the beginning, but absolutely authentic. It will be graded but not reconstructed.

The procedure will be listening, learning, and imitating. Each dialogue will be concerned with a life or personal situation. Linguistically considered, there will be vocabulary, idioms, and grammar to deal with. Grammatical points are now referred to as *structures*. These structures, as well as the vocabulary and idioms, are learned by being practiced in pattern drills. The selection of certain utterances for practice in pattern drills is known as *dialogue adaptation*.

The Dialogue. The dialogue is the core of every lesson or unit. It may be the springboard at the beginning of the lesson or, as in the elementary school, it may be used as a summary of the structures that have been learned. In any case it furnishes the linguistic items and brings them together in a functional, lifelike situation.

All of the newer basic books contain such dialogues. In fact, the conversation piece has replaced the narrative or descriptive reading selection. Nevertheless, the teacher will find it necessary to construct dialogues occasionally, especially in the beginning stages and more particularly at the elementary level.

In constructing a dialogue, the following principles should be observed:

1. The dialogue should be short; six or eight lines are sufficient.
2. There should be only two or three roles.
3. The context should be of situational interest to the learner. This will differ with the maturity of the pupil. For younger children in

the elementary school the situations will be different, or will be treated differently, from those in high school.

4. Previously learned vocabulary and structures should be included for review.
5. There should be frequent repetition of new structures.

Procedure. The dialogue is to be memorized. The following steps are suggested:

1. The teacher gives a brief summary of the content of the dialogue. This is not to be a translation but English equivalents of key phrases should be given so that there is perfect comprehension on the part of the pupils.
2. The pupils listen attentively while the teacher reads or recites the dialogue at normal speed several times. It is suggested that this be done from different parts of the room, so that all pupils can hear clearly. Gestures and facial expression, dramatized actions, should accompany the presentation.
3. Repetition of each line by the pupils in chorus is the next step. Each sentence may be repeated a half dozen times, depending on its length and on the alertness of the pupils. If the teacher detects an error, the offending pupil is corrected and is asked to repeat the sentence. If many pupils make the same error, chorus repetition and drill will be necessary.
4. Repetition is continued with groups decreasing in size, that is, first the two halves of the class, then thirds, and then single rows—if there are six rows. Groups can assume the speakers' roles.
5. Pairs of individual pupils now go to the front of the room to act out the dialogue. By this time they should have memorized the text.

If a sentence seems to be too long, the device of "backward build-up" may be used. For example, the sentence Voy a comprar un par de calcetines en la tienda can be broken up into

en la tienda
un par de calcetines en la tienda
Voy a comprar un par de calcetines en la tienda.

If the teacher has prepared the dialogue on tape or is using a tape to accompany the textbook, the tape recorder will replace the teacher.

The various stages outlined above may be considered as listening, memorizing, practicing for fluency, and repeating for comprehension.

Dialogue Adaptation. After the dialogue has been completely mastered, pattern drills are used to provide practice in given structures and in vocabulary, so as to assure automatic response. The use of the pattern drills may be termed the *reinforcement phase;* it follows the listening and repetition phases. This additional practice helps to fix the key expressions and also makes the dialogue material more personal. The utterances of the speakers in the conversation piece are transferred to the pupils themselves, especially in the directed dialogue drill.

The various types of drills will be described later in detail. Immediately after the dialogue the most effective drill to use is that of personalized conversation. It begins with teacher and pupil; it is continued by pupil with pupil.

Step I. The teacher puts questions to individual pupils.
    A. Repetition.
        TEACHER: Voy a la tienda
            ¿Va Vd. a la tienda, Juan?   PUPIL: Voy a la tienda.
            (a la escuela, al cine, al teatro, a la casa, etc.)
        TEACHER: Voy a la iglesia.
            ¿Va Vd. a la iglesia, María?   PUPIL: Voy a la iglesia.
    B. Choice.
        TEACHER: ¿Va Vd. al cine o a la tienda?   PUPIL: Voy al cine.
            (a la escuela o a la casa, etc.)
    C. The pupil answers the question without repeating the model sentence.
        TEACHER: ¿Adónde va Vd. Roberto?   PUPIL: Voy al parque.
Step II. The teacher directs the pupil what to ask.
    A. The pupil asks the teacher a question.
        TEACHER: Pedro, pregúnteme adónde voy.   PUPIL: ¿Adónde va Vd. señor?
        TEACHER: Jorge, pregúnteme adónde voy.   PUPIL: Adónde va Vd. señor?
        (The teacher replies in each case, of course.)
    B. A pupil asks another pupil a question. (Directed dialogue)
        PUPIL: Alfredo, pregunte Vd. a María adónde va.   PUPIL: María, ¿adónde va Vd.?

(This can be followed by chain drill, each pupil asking his neighbor a question in turn.)

C. Choice is introduced.

TEACHER: Enrique, pregunte a Carlos si él va al teatro.

PUPIL: Carlos, ¿va Vd. al teatro?

TEACHER: Enrique, pregunte a Carlos si él va al teatro o al parque.

PUPIL: Carlos, ¿va Vd. al teatro o al parque?

(The other pupil is, of course, supposed to give the appropriate answer.)

Types of Pattern Drills. Pattern drills may be classified in a number of different ways, depending upon what the learner is to change or manipulate. Sometimes two or three drills are involved in the same pattern change.

1. *Repetition Drill.* This is the simplest drill; it is used at the very beginning of the course. The pupil merely repeats what he has heard the teacher say or the tape recorder produce. The repetition drill is the basic drill for the presentation of new vocabulary and verb endings. Complete sentences are used. The first and second persons are drilled before the third person is presented:

TEACHER: Me gusta el café.
PUPIL: Me gusta el café.

2. *Substitution Drill.* The pupil replaces the subject of the model sentence with a pronoun of a different person, number, or gender. He is required to make the necessary change in the verb:

Él tiene el libro. Ella tiene el libro.
Nosotros tenemos el libro. Yo tengo el libro.
Tú tienes el libro. Vosotros tenéis el libro.

A more complicated form of the substitution drill involves the so-called *tagmeme*, a *frame* with three *slots* which may be replaced. The model sentence consists of three elements: subject, verb, and predicate:

Pattern: Este muchacho se llama Juan.
Substitutions: a. Este joven, este hombre, este señor, etc.
                b. se llama, es, parece a, conoce a, etc.
                c. Juan, Roberto, Jaime, Carlos, etc.

19

The slots may be replaced alternately:

Este muchacho se llama Juan.
Este alumno es Juan.
Este joven parece a Julio.

The above is an illustration of a progressive substitution.

3. *Transformation Drill.* In this drill the model is changed from the singular to the plural, from the plural to the singular, from the affirmative to the negative, from the declarative to the interrogative, and so on:

El alumno escribe el ejercicio.	Los alumnos escriben el ejercicio.
Los niños juegan en el jardín.	El niño juega en el jardín.
Él conoce a ese señor.	Él no conoce a ese señor.
Vd. sabe la palabra.	¿Sabe Vd. la palabra?

Sometimes two changes are involved:

Yo amo a mi madre.　　Nosotros amamos a nuestras madres.

4. *Replacement Drill.* This is really the same drill as the substitution drill. Generally it involves the replacement of a noun by a pronoun:

Él ha comprado la casa.	Él la ha comprado.
Julia viene esta tarde.	Ella viene esta tarde.
Déme el libro.	Démelo.

When the replacement drill is used as a progressive substitution drill, it is not too easy for the pupils, since they must listen to the cues for the different slots.

5. *Response Drill.* In this drill the answers are patterned after the questions. They are of various types ranging from the simple Yes or No answer to a complete answer:

A. ¿Tiene Vd. un reloj de oro?　　Sí, tengo un reloj de oro.
　　　　　　　　　　　　　　　　　No, no tengo un reloj de oro.
B. ¿Tiene Vd. un lápiz o una pluma?　　Tengo un lápiz.
C. ¿Cuántos años tiene Vd.?　　Tengo quince años.
　　¿Dónde trabaja su padre?　　Trabaja en una oficina.

6. *Cued-response Drill.* In this case the teacher gives a cue before or after the question:

(los ejercicios)	¿Qué escribe Juan?	Juan escribe los ejercicios.
(en el jardín)	¿Dónde está María?	María está en el jardín.

7. *Rejoinder Drill.* This is an expansion of the cued response. The pupil is told how to respond to a given statement:

"Be polite":   Muchas gracias, señor.   No hay de qué.
"Express doubt": Él lo hizo.   No lo creo.
"Agree":   Hace buen tiempo hoy.   Sí, ya lo creo.
"Disagree": Esta película me gusta.   No me gusta a mí.
"Answer the question":   ¿Vive Vd. en una casa particular?   No, vivo en una casa de pisos.

8. *Restatement or Directed Dialogue.* (Relay Drill.) Pupils are directed to ask questions or make statements, first with the teacher and then with a classmate as dialogue partner:

Pregúnteme si tengo un perro.	¿Tiene Vd. un perro?
Dígame que Vd. no me entiende.	No le entiendo a Vd.
Pregúntele a María cuántos años tiene.	María, ¿cuántos años tiene Vd?

9. *Completion Drill.* The pupil supplies the missing word in a statement:

Él ama a sus padres y nosotros amamos a los . . .	Él ama a sus padres y nosotros amamos a los nuestros.
Ella tiene su libro y yo tengo el . . .	Ella tiene su libro y yo tengo el mío.

10. *Expansion Drill.* A simple statement is built up by adding words and phrases.

Comemos.
Comemos carne y legumbres.
Comemos carne y legumbres al mediodía.
Comemos carne y legumbres al mediodía en el restaurante.

11. *Contraction Drill.* A phrase or a clause is replaced by a single word:

Creo que Juan vendrá esta tarde.   Lo creo.
Ponga Vd. las flores en la mesa.   Ponga Vd. las flores aquí.

12. *Integration Drill.* Two separate statements are combined:

Conozco al hombre.	Conozco al hombre que vive en
Vive en la casa verde.	la casa verde.
Vi al muchacho.	Vi al muchacho a quien Vd. dió
Vd. le dió el libro.	el libro.

13. *Translation Drills.* The pupil translates English sentences involving the same structure into the foreign language:

Do you like to go to the movies?	¿Le gusta ir al cine?
Do you like to play tennis?	¿Le gusta jugar al tenis?
Do you like to drink milk?	¿Le gusta beber leche?
Do you like the film?	¿Le gusta la película?
Do you like the song?	¿Le gusta la canción?

Guiding Principles

1. Since the primary aim is the development of the ability to communicate orally, maximum use of the foreign language should be made at all times by both teacher and students.

Life situations often occur outside the scope of the lesson but lend themselves admirably for a brief oral exchange. For example, a student enters the Spanish class late. The following conversation might be carried on.

TEACHER: Vd. llega tarde esta manana. ¿Por qué?
STUDENT: My car isn't working.
TEACHER: Oh, su automóvil no marcha. Repita . . .
STUDENT: Mi automóvil no marcha.
TEACHER: ¿Por qué no?
STUDENT: The motor is out of order.
TEACHER: El motor está descompuesto. Repita . . .
STUDENT: El motor está descompuesto.
TEACHER: Muy bien. Le dispenso a Vd. Más vale tarde que nunca.
(Writes the proverb on the board and has the class repeat it.)

On all occasions in the classroom, greetings and forms of courtesy should be given in the foreign language, right from the first day.

2. In fact, the foreign language should be the language of the classroom. English should be used only when absolutely necessary.

3. During the first twenty lessons classroom activities should be entirely oral. During this prereading phase the students should receive intensive drill in pronunciation so that they master the sound system of the foreign language.

4. The sequence, as pointed out before, is listening, speaking, reading, and writing.

5. Through constant drill on basic patterns illustrating typical structures the student should be able to acquire grammar easily, naturally, and almost incidentally. Theoretical explanation cannot be eliminated entirely—the more intelligent student will ask for it—but it should be kept at a minimum.

6. As far as possible direct auditory and visual comprehension should be relied upon. This means the avoidance of translation.

7. Since listening and hearing correctly are of primary importance, the use of discs and tapes with native voices is highly recommended. In fact, these devices are now practically a *sine qua non* in the foreign language classroom. They are equally important as models for oral imitation.

8. Although stress is now placed on the audial and the lingual, the visual should not be neglected, especially in the first year. Pictures, films, models, and charts are valuable in teaching vocabulary and in building up elementary conversational ability.

Illustrative Lessons

DIALOGUE ADAPTATION

(French)

The dialogue, if it is on a tape, is run off on the tape recorder at least twice. If it has not been recorded, the teacher reads or recites the dialogue to the class, after having made a few introductory remarks in English explaining the content of the selection. The meaning should be clear to all the pupils.

The effectiveness of the reading or recitation is increased by the addition of such dramatic factors as change of voice and position for the two speakers and the use of lively gestures.

The dialogue follows:

JEAN: Bonjour, Marie. Où allez-vous?

MARIE: Je vais au magasin. Ma mère a besoin de diverses choses pour le dîner.

JEAN: Qu'est-ce que vous allez acheter?

MARIE: Je vais acheter du beurre, du pain, des oeufs, et du lait. Et vous, où allez-vous?

JEAN: Je vais à la bibliothèque me procurer un livre.

MARIE: Quel livre?

JEAN: *Tartarin de Tarascon.*

MARIE: Oh, c'est très intéressant! Au revoir!

The teacher says each line at normal speed. The class repeats it about a half dozen times. The teacher circulates about the classroom and listens intently to catch possible errors. If certain words or phrases are mispronounced, the teacher corrects them and has individuals and the class repeat.

Next, the class is divided into two groups, each one assuming the role of one of the two persons in the dialogue. Each group repeats its part chorally. The groups are reduced in size for further repetitions. At length, individual pupils take the parts and carry on the conversation. The final phase is to have two pupils play the roles before the class.

The learning of the dialogue will probably take up an entire period.

The class is now ready for the reinforcement phase. For this step the question-and-answer type of drill is suitable, followed by directed dialogue.

TEACHER: Je vais au magasin. Allez-vous au magasin?

PUPIL: Oui, je vais au magasin.

TEACHER: Je vais à la bibliothèque. Allez-vous à la bibliothèque?

PUPIL: Oui, je vais à la bibliothèque.

The drill is then expanded by introducing the names of other places to go to, for example, à l'école, au cinéma, au théâtre, à l'église, au jardin, au parc, au cirque, à la maison, and so on.

The next step is the direct dialogue, in which the pupil is instructed what to ask for or to say. This is first carried on between teacher and pupil and then between one pupil and another.

TEACHER: Robert, demandez-moi où je vais.

PUPIL: Où allez-vous, Monsieur (Madame)?

TEACHER: Je vais à la bibliothèque (etc.).

Next, the teacher tells a pupil what to ask his neighbor.

TEACHER: Charles, demandez à Jean où il va.
PUPIL: Jean, où allez-vous?

This is continued by chain drill, each pupil asking the question. The element of choice is introduced.

TEACHER: Est-ce que vous allez acheter du buerre?
PUPIL: Oui, je vais acheter du beurre.
TEACHER: Est-ce que vous allez acheter du pain ou de la viande?
PUPIL: Je vais acheter de la viande.
TEACHER: Demandez à Henri s'il va acheter des légumes ou des fruits.
PUPIL: Henri, allez-vous acheter des légumes ou des fruits?

Chain drill follows.

The third period of this unit can be devoted to extended practice on the verb *aller*. One important structure is *aller* plus the infinitive. New expressions can be introduced, such as lire un livre, faire votres devoirs, rentrer à la maison, écrire une lettre, and so on.

The conjugation of the present tense of *aller* can be taught through a repetition drill, first with liaison and then without liaison. Pupils repeat exactly what the teacher, or the tape, says:

Je vais acheter du lait.
Nous allons acheter du lait.
Tu vas acheter du lait.
Vous allez acheter du lait.

Without liaison:

Je vais lire le livre.
Nous allons lire le livre.
Tu vas lire le livre.
Vous allez lire le livre.

These structures are practiced by giving the pupil the pronoun, or a noun, and having him complete the sentence (substitution drill):

TEACHER: Je.   PUPIL: Je vais acheter du lait.
TEACHER: Vous.   PUPIL: Vous allez acheter du lait, etc.

The next step involves changes from singular to plural and plural to singular:

TEACHER: Je vais acheter du pain.   PUPIL: Nous allons acheter du pain.

TEACHER: Vous allez acheter du pain.   PUPIL: Tu vas acheter du pain.

The third person is then taken up and practiced in a repetition drill:

TEACHER: Il va acheter du lait.   PUPIL: Ils vont acheter du lait.

TEACHER: Elle va acheter du lait.   PUPIL: Elles vont acheter du lait.

If time permits, the negative may be taken up. After *pas de* has been mastered, it should be drilled with the complementary infinitive.

Problems

1. Summarize the basic assumptions of the audio-lingual approach.
2. Explain why reading is postponed.
3. Why is the dialogue so important?
4. Indicate the essential elements of the classroom dialogue.
5. Name five types of pattern drills and give an example of each.

III ʼ Audio-Lingual Activities

The first impact of any language comes from the spoken word, whether we are concerned with the baby in the cradle or the student in college. Listening is the first experience; the attempt to understand accompanies it. The acquisition of a good pronunciation depends in large measure on the learner's listening with care and discrimination.

On the teacher's part pronunciation demands clear, distinct enunciation, that is, a model in speech. It also requires the observance of a basic principle which is extremely important, but which many language teachers neglect, namely, the frequent, constant, and almost exclusive use of the foreign tongue in the classroom.

The teacher must also, consciously, plan listening activities designed to train the students in attentive listening and in careful reproduction of foreign sounds, words, and expressions. The pupils will be provided with opportunities to practice speech patterns, to construct simple sentences, and to read aloud with ease and clarity.

The Importance of Sounds

The basis of all language is sound. Words are merely combinations of sounds, and the printed page is a graphic representation of sound sequences. It is in these sound sequences that the ideas are contained. The hearing of a given word calls for the acoustic and the visual image of that word, from which meaning is obtained.

Both the eyes and the ears are aids to memory, and only through them is a linguistic memory built up. This linguistic memory consists of a stock of words, phrases, and idioms, which can easily be recalled either for use in speech and writing or for recognition purposes in reading. The larger the pupil's linguistic memory, the greater will be his ease in reading. Facility in speech is a direct asset in reading ability.

Listening. In acquiring a foreign language, listening, of course, comes first. Before one understands and attempts to speak, one has to hear the sounds, words, and speech patterns of the other language. Intelligent listening means that the hearer understands what is being said. The aim of the first step in language teaching, then, is to establish audial comprehension.

Ear-training has to be given special attention because the pupil learns his other subjects by listening to his native tongue or reading the printed page. Visual learning is stressed, whereas in the learning of a foreign language audial learning is of major importance. Much practice must be provided to increase the keenness of hearing, so that the pupil is able to automatically

1. Distinguish sounds, words, and structures
2. Associate meanings with the sounds
3. Infer meanings of words from the context.

In the beginning the model will be almost exclusively the teacher's voice. By listening carefully to what the teacher says, the pupil will acquire the habit of concentrating on sounds and meanings. Not only should the teacher enunciate clearly but he should also employ appropriate gestures and facial expressions. Dramatization is particularly effective if the utterance is accompanied by a functional situation. The pupil immediately makes direct association between the spoken language and the action; there is absolutely no difficulty of comprehension. For example, the teacher says, "J'ouvre la porte, je ferme la porte" while doing so. This simple statement can be used as a pattern in similar obvious situations such as opening and closing the window, the desk drawer, the book, the briefcase, and so on. Audial comprehension has been achieved, that is, immediate linking of sound and meaning.

Excellent practice and a test of comprehension is provided by giving the command to a pupil or to the class; for example, "Ouvrez les livres, Fermez les livres; Ouvrez les cahiers, Fermez les cahiers." Opening and closing the door, the window, and the desk drawer can be done by individual pupils.

With younger children this type of activity can be turned into a game such as "Simon says . . ." After they have learned the names of the parts of the body, they can be asked to carry out orders like, "Touchez le nez! Touchez la bouche! Touchez le bras!"

The Use of Classroom Expressions

Listening and audial comprehension will be regular features of the daily lesson if the foreign language is used for all routine class expressions and directions. These will involve greetings ("Bonjour, la classe! Au revoir, la classe!"), inquiries as to health ("Comment allez-vous?"), and comments on the weather ("Quel temps fait-il aujourd'hui?"), as well as classroom instructions ("Ouvrez vos livres! Levez-vous! Asseyez-vous! Répétez! Plus haut! Corrigez!"). Some of these expressions will be purely audial, for the pupil will have practically no occasion to say "Répétez" or "Corrigez."

The daily use of the foreign tongue will accustom the student's ear to the foreign speech pattern. Through the constant repetition of common expressions of commendation, for example, "Très bien," and the classroom instructions, for example, "Levez-vous," he will incidentally acquire a stock of useful sentences. The teacher should use such expressions from the first day, adding to them gradually.

In Spanish, for instance, the following may be used:

Buenos días, clase.
Presente. Ausente.
¿Cómo se llama Vd.? Me llamo . . .
Preste atención.
Levántese Vd.
Siéntese Vd.
Abran Vds. los libros en la página . . .

Empiece Vd. a leer.
Más alto. Más despacio.
¿Entiende Vd.?
Traduzca Vd.
Muy bien.
Lea Vd. la frase siguiente.
¿Qué significa la palabra . . . ?
Responda Vd. a la pregunta.
En una frase completa.
Cierren Vds. los libros.
Pase Vd. a la pizarra.
¿Qué faltas hay?
Corrija Vd. la falta.

Pronunciation

The teacher's own pronunciation will set the standard for the class; unconsciously the students will imitate what they hear. The teacher's speech should be clear and moderately paced. A rich, pleasing voice, of course, will make listening all the more attractive.

The foreign sound should be described in simple nontechnical language and compared with its nearest English equivalent. The use of phonetic transcription—which is of great value in French—is recommended. Also, careful instructions as to the physical production of the sound are helpful, especially where there is no English equivalent (that is, French u, oe, eu, and the nasals; German ä, ö, ü, and ch; Spanish j). Constant correction is necessary, for faulty habits once formed are difficult to break.

Foreign sounds acquire meaning and are recognized automatically only through frequent use. Only those sound combinations are spontaneously comprehended that have been learned thoroughly. Sound and meaning and meaning and sound must be identified so frequently that recognition becomes automatic.

With reference to the use of phonetic transcriptions, it must also be taken into account that to acquire facility in their use requires learning a code or shorthand in addition to the foreign language. Economy seems to dictate that the teacher be familiar with the symbols and that the pupils need only be able to recognize them. Acquaintance with their sound equivalents will enable pupils to look up the pronunciation of doubtful words by themselves.

Besides listening to and imitating the teacher's voice, the pupils should be given opportunity, whenever this is possible, to listen to native speakers on the platform, to phonograph records, tape recordings, and radio broadcasts. With the extension of foreign language programs on radio and television, a splendid opportunity is presented to the student for listening to new and interesting material every day.

The teacher's pronunciation may be excellent, but, nevertheless, taped material with the voices of natives should be used frequently. In this way the pupil will hear the foreign language at normal speed in authentic life situations, through the voices of young and old, male and female, accomplished actor and ordinary citizen. This will overcome one of the greatest weaknesses of foreign language instruction in the past, where the pupil heard only the voice of one teacher and was never prepared for contact with natives in life situations.

There is now a wide variety of audio material on the market in the form of discs and tapes. It includes anecdotes, prose selections from famous authors, recitations by actors, conversations, and descriptions. Sound films, radio programs, and taped correspondence may also be used.

Taped correspondence consists of an exchange of letters with foreign students, teachers, or schools. In exchange for English-language recordings depicting aspects of the American scene, the foreign source provides similar material in the foreign language. Topics such as family living, daily routine, school activities, shopping, outings, sports, and entertainment are particularly desirable. Such material will be too difficult in the beginning, considering the pupils' limitations in structures and vocabulary, but in the upper terms foreign correspondence should develop into a fruitful and enjoyable activity.

Testing Audial Comprehension. To make sure that comprehension is resulting, the listening experience should be followed by a check or test. This may take various forms:

1. True-false tests
2. Action response—an order or a command is carried out
3. Multiple-choice questions.

These various types of tests are described in detail under "Evaluation."

Speaking. Learning to listen purposefully and to discriminate between sounds and words is not an end in itself; reproduction must follow soon thereafter, for understanding and speaking are closely related. In fact, they are interdependent and should be developed concurrently.

On the basis of hearing and understanding, the pupil can be trained to imitate what he hears. His ability to speak fluently and intelligently depends on his skill in pronouncing correctly and smoothly the sounds and patterns of the foreign language. It is essentially habit formation, based on intensive drill. The pupil must learn to reproduce the sounds and structures of the language automatically. To do so, he must be steeped in the commonest language patterns. He must hear and imitate a considerable variety of speech patterns. These patterns should be carefully selected and drilled on the following bases:

1. The vocabulary and structures should be of high frequency.
2. There must be much opportunity for practice.
3. There must be complete comprehension on the part of the pupil.
4. The practice will be provided through a wide variety of drills.
5. In order to become automatic, the patterns must be overlearned.

The second stage of the functional situations mentioned under "Listening" is now reached; that is, the pupil not only listens but imitates. Accuracy in pronunciation is, of course, paramount.

The quality of the pupils' pronunciation will depend primarily on the standards set by the teacher. Not only should the model be good but its accurate imitation should be insisted on. In the beginning the classroom teacher's utterance is more effective than that of the disc or tape because it can be accompanied by facial expression and gesture. Also, the teacher will react to pupil errors and make immediate corrections. Through his repetition of carefully chosen drills the pupil acquires habitual control of the basic forms and structures. These he should be able to transfer automatically in new functional situations. Here, as elsewhere, the specificity of learning applies: one learns to speak by speaking.

The first stage, then, in learning to speak is purposeful listening and comprehension. The second stage follows almost immediately, that is, repeated mimicry and recall. There is much memorizing of patterns, model sentences, dialogues, and action series.

Choral recitation should be employed liberally in the beginning because it secures maximum participation and wins over the shy pupil. If inaccuracies persist despite repeated imitation, the teacher can resort to speech analysis. Ordinarily this should not be necessary; speech analysis should be confined to remedial teaching.

The pupil acquires increasing mastery of the language through practice in various types of drills. The most important drills are question-and-answer, cued-response, directed conversation, substitution, replacement, variation, and transformation.

The Dialogue

One of the basic notions of the audio-lingual approach is that language is essentially the exchange of utterances between two or more persons in an everyday-life situation. Hence, the dialogue—which is such an exchange of conversation among a number of individuals—becomes one of the major factors in language learning.

The dialogue is particularly effective at the beginning, for the learner is introduced to the foreign language in the most natural and interesting manner. He hears and imitates all of the various sounds of the target language. He talks about persons and things within his orbit of experience. He addresses people directly and speaks mainly in the first person. He speaks of matters in which he has a personal interest. He is not learning isolated words or laboriously constructing separate sentences that are grammatically correct but without the slightest personal reference.

If properly planned and directed, the dialogue may be made one of the most useful forms of exercise for teaching vocabulary, idioms, structures, and cultural material. It ought also to add considerably to the liveliness and enjoyableness of the lesson, both for the teacher and the pupil. Of course, the successful use of dialogue presupposes some imagination, ingenuity, and resourcefulness on the part of the teacher.

Two essential features of the effective dialogue are the speaking of the parts without reference to book or paper and the liberal use of gesture. It must, in other words, consist of dramatized conversation, either memorized or impromptu. Calling upon pupils to take parts and alternately to read some material from a textbook while remaining in their seats is not what is intended here.

In order for a number of pupils to experience the pleasure of understanding and speaking the foreign language, the conversation must be kept simple and brief. Not too brief, of course. Simply having pupils bob up to ask, "Comment allez-vous?" and get the unvarying reply, "Très bien, merci!" is not conversation. Of course it may be the beginning of a dialogue; it ought, however, to be extended and expanded to at least a dozen lines.

Each dialogue ought to be a little unit portraying a scene from daily life or dramatizing an anecdote or a joke. Many useful expressions and idioms may be worked in. In fact, the idiom or grammatical point may be the *raison d'être* of the dialogue.

The range of topics is practically unlimited, especially if the teacher is a little resourceful. A few suggestions follow:

The weather; meeting in the street, on the way to school, on the way home; a telephone conversation; the family, at breakfast, at lunch, at dinner, at the zoo, at the theater, at the movies; the departure, at the station, in the train, in the hotel, in the restaurant; an invitation to dinner, at the store, and so on.

Instead of taking the dialogue from the book or giving the finished dialogue to the class, the teacher can arrange an interesting and useful lesson by guiding the pupils to construct dialogue in class. Various suggestions can be elicited from the pupils. As each contribution is given, the teacher corrects it or refines it and writes it on the board. Finally, the whole dialogue is read, tried out, and copied into the notebook. Then the teacher will assign it to be memorized as homework, so that the pupils acquire fluency and so that they devote attention to the accompanying gestures.

In the beginning, rigid adherence to the wording of the dialogue will probably be imperative. This will be true, too, of the dramatized anecdote. However, as the pupil gains power and acquires vocabulary, he ought to be able to make substitutions and improvisations, especially where the topic chiefly involves vocabulary building. This would be true of the store and restaurant dialogues, where a variety of things might be ordered. The possibility of involving personal interests would add zest, surprise, and humor to the conversation. It would also test the pupil's ability to frame an adequate reply, thus developing skill in repartee.

Every effort must be made to prevent the dialogue from becoming a dull and stereotyped exercise lacking in spontaneity. Where grammatical points are involved, they must not be too forced; their recurrence should seem natural and unpremeditated.

To transform this type of oral work into something approximating actual conversation, the questions must be made coherent, interesting, personal, and lifelike. Plenty of opportunity should be provided for variant answers, for spontaneity, and for individual expression.

The usual classroom weather conversation goes about as follows:

"Good morning!"
"Good morning!"
"How is the weather today?"
"It is nice."
"Is it cold?"
"No, it is warm."
"How was the weather yesterday?"
"It was cool."
"What season do we have now?"
"It is spring."
"Name the seasons."
"The seasons are spring, summer, fall, and winter."

The above dialogue utilizes certain useful weather expressions, as well as the names of the seasons. On the other hand, it is stilted and stereotyped. The lack of vocabulary naturally limits the possibilities of expression. Therefore, as soon as the pupils have progressed far enough the dialogue should be given a greater degree of naturalness.

By the change of a few of the expressions, a far more lifelike conversation is developed:

"Good morning!"
"Good morning!"
"How are you?"
"Very well, thanks."
"Have you been outside?"
"Yes."
"How is the weather today?"
"Oh, it's fine, not too warm and not too cool."
"I'm glad; I want to go out today. But I see that you have an umbrella."
"Yes, it rained yesterday and I borrowed an umbrella. I am returning it now."
"Well, at this season of the year it often rains. But spring is nice, much nicer than the summer, the fall, or the winter."

"Yes, spring is wonderful. One could sing all the time. Let's sing a spring song!" (*The class sings.*)

The above dialogue presents the same weather expressions and the names of the seasons, but in a far more natural, likelife, and logical situation. The tone, too, is more colloquial and the language more idiomatic.

However, we are, after all, in the classroom, and we must construct our conversation so that the pupil gets practice in the words and expressions we want him to learn. Also, as pointed out above, the dialogue should provide opportunity for spontaneity, variant answers, and individual choice. This is especially possible when a shopping scene is the topic. The dialogue might be developed thus:

"Good morning, Sir (Miss, Madam)!"
"Good morning!"
"What may I offer you? (What do you wish? How can I serve you?)"
"I should like to buy a hat (tie, shirt, stockings, etc.)."
"What color?"
"Black (green, blue, yellow, etc.)."
"What size?"
"Seven (eight, fifteen, twelve and a half, etc.)."
"Here's a very nice one."
"How much is it?"
"One dollar (two, three, etc.)."
"That's a little too expensive. Haven't you anything cheaper?"
"Oh, yes. Here's something else (another one) for . . ."
"Fine. I'll take it."
"Shall I send it?"
"No, I'll take it with me."
"That will be four dollars."
"Here is a five-dollar bill."
"Your change, one dollar. Thank you, sir. Good-by!"
"Good-by!"

The above conversation permits the substitution of any variety of articles, colors, numbers, prices, and so on.

Adding a few simple properties and acting out the scene before the class transforms the conversation into dramatized dialogue. In fact, this step should be taken whenever time permits.

Auditory Comprehension. The first half of the first level is primarily devoted to audio-lingual activities in order to build up the pupil's ability to understand the foreign language when spoken at normal speed on familiar topics. Listening to the teacher and to recorded speech on discs, tapes, and sound films, the student should acquire some skill in auditory comprehension.

Almost from the start the pupil is asked to imitate what he hears, on the principle that hearing and speaking are concurrent and interdependent. If this procedure is continued, however, it will cause a considerable slowing down of audial comprehension. If the pupil is required to repeat and produce orally everything that he has heard, his progress will not be rapid. In fact, his interest will not be sustained.

It is perfectly obvious that comprehension, a passive activity, is much easier than oral production, which requires active participation. There is a great deal which the student will understand and will not be able to reproduce.

Auditory comprehension—which is, after all, quite important in life situations—is a special skill which can be trained separately. Hence, in the upper years, special lessons should be given to strengthen this ability.

Suggested activities are listening to recordings or tapes of a conversation, a short story, a dramatized dialogue, or a little play; listening to a foreign radio or television news broadcast or interview; listening to a speaker of the foreign language.

Illustrative Lessons

STEPS IN AN AUDITORY-COMPREHENSION LESSON

1. *Motivation.* An effort is made to arouse the pupil's interest in the topic or presentation.

2. *Introduction.* The situation or content is briefly described.

3. *Anticipation of difficulties.* If there are any new words or structures, these will be singled out and made clear.

4. *First listening.* The record or tape is played.

5. *Check on difficulties.* Some words and structures may still be incomprehensible to a few students. These are taken up at this point and clarified.

6. *Second listening.* Again the tape is played without interruption.

7. *Questions.* Significant expressions, key words and phrases, and structures to be learned are used in questions.

8. *Third listening.*

9. *Questions.* The teacher asks original, informal questions to test the comprehension of the pupils and to elicit reactions and appreciation of the content.

Lessons like this should be given at regular intervals, with the presentation of spoken material of increasing difficulty. The stress here is entirely on the auditory. Comprehension activities will, however, be combined continually with speaking, reading, and writing, since all of the language skills are interdependent.

Topics for Audio-Lingual Experiences

Level I. Because of the pupils' limitation in vocabulary and structures, the audio-lingual experiences will be confined to simple everyday situations. These may be part of the pupils' environment or may be set in the foreign country. They will be treated as questions and answers, brief conversational sequences, and dialogues. Suggested topics are:

1. Greetings, introductions, class routine
2. Time, days of the week, months, seasons, weather expressions
3. School day—the foreign language class, the teacher, subjects, lessons
4. The family—members, home, furniture, meals
5. Various activities—at the butcher's, baker's, grocer's; at the doctor's, dentist's; buying new clothes.

Level II. On the next higher level the pupil should have increased his linguistic competence and be able to handle the topics of Level I in greater detail. More social activities should be included in the subject matter. On the first level the present tense was chiefly used, possibly also the past and future. A new tense might be introduced. Suggested topics are:

1. In the country—uncle's farm, animals, crops, diversion
2. Vacation—at the beach, in camp, sports
3. Holiday—at the zoo, at the museum, in the park
4. Appointment on the telephone
5. Lunch at a restaurant

6. Birthday celebration
7. At the theater—a play, a film
8. A trip
9. Shopping.

Level III. The topics of Level II are developed in greater depth. Ideas, as well as situations, are introduced. Several tenses will be used, including the subjunctive. Since by this time the class is doing considerable reading, the conversational material should be correlated with it. Suggested topics are:

1. A trip—at the station, on the train, on the bus
2. Shopping in a department store
3. At the beauty parlor; the barber's
4. Meeting a friend at the airport
5. In town
6. At the library—various books, borrowing, the librarian
7. Driving a car—at the gas station
8. Music—at the concert, at the opera
9. Television—programs
10. A foreign newspaper.

The conversation can be correlated effectively with the pupils' reading—both in the textbook and outside reading—by letting individual pupils prepare oral reports. This should help in developing facility in sustained speaking. After the report has been given, the class might be encouraged to ask questions. Up to this point, the conversation has been based largely on anthropological culture, that is, everyday living. The oral reports afford an excellent opportunity to bring in refinement culture. The biographies of eminent men and women, great works of art and literature, operas, films, and interesting events may form the subject matter.

Level IV. On this level the reading material continues to assume an important place in language learning. Together with the special interests of individual pupils, it will form the basis of conversation in the classroom. Oral reports and the recitation of prose and poetry will be expanded to the presentation of dramatic scenes and possibly plays in the assembly. Conversations about life situations can be dramatized with the aid of a few props. Foreign newspapers and magazines will be read and discussed.

Since the pupil now has—we hope!—a fair hold on the foreign language, he should be able to express himself more freely on various phases of foreign culture. The oral reports will be correlated with the reading of cultural materials. As suggested above, a question-and-answer period may follow the presentation of the oral report.

Every endeavor should be made to develop an understanding of the ideals and beliefs that underlie the culture of the foreign people under study. Suggested topics are:

1. Life in the foreign country—family life, education, leisure activities, holidays, the working day
2. Geography and economic development—geography, industry, commerce, products, transportation, labor, social services
3. History and government—important historic eras, outstanding historic personages, the government
4. Cultural contributions of the foreign country to art, architecture, sculpture, music, literature, science, philosophy.

Levels V and VI. The oral work at these levels is based primarily on the reading. The latter should include some major literary selections, which may be summarized and critically evaluated. The treatment of art and music ought to develop the students' esthetic appreciation. Reproductions of art masterpieces should be shown; recordings of important musical selections should be played. A more ambitious assembly program, consisting of an entire play, may be planned.

Examples of Dialogues

IDIOMATIC EXPRESSIONS FOR A CHANCE MEETING

(French)

La Rencontre

—Bonjour, Pierre. Comment allez-vous?
—Très bien, merci. Et vous, Jean?
—Pas trop mal. Où allez-vous?
—Moi, je rentre. J'ai mes devoirs à faire. Et vous?
—Moi, je vais au cinéma avec mon cousin.
—Qu'est-ce que l'on joue?

—Aujourd'hui on joue "Crainquebille." C'est magnifique!
—Bon, amusez-vous bien. Moi, je vais écouter la radio. Lili Pons diffuse
cette après-midi. Mais voilà votre cousin.
—Et voilà votre omnibus qui arrive. Au revoir, Jean.
—Au revoir, Pierre, à demain!

From the above dialogue the verb *aller* may be singled out for
special drill. For example:

je vais, il va, nous allons, allez-vous? etc.
au cinéma, au théâtre, au magasin, au musée, au parc
à la maison, à l'église, à l'école, à la campagne
Also:
Je vais écouter la radio, la musique, l'orchestre, l'orgue
Voilà votre cousin qui arrive, votre frère, votre soeur, etc.

AGE EXPRESSIONS, THE COMPARATIVE, ETC.

(French)

L'ANNIVERSAIRE

—Ah! quelles belles fleurs!
—Oui, elles sont pour mon père.
—Votre père? Pourquoi?
—C'est aujourd'hui son anniversaire.
—Aujourd'hui?
—Oui, il est né le 24 avril.
—Quel âge a-t-il?
—Il a 43 ans.
—Mon père est plus jeune que le vôtre. Il a 37 ans.
—En quel mois est-il né?
—Lui aussi est né en avril. Mais ma mère est née en janvier.
—Quel âge avez-vous?
—J'ai 15 ans. Je suis né en juin.
—Moi aussi. Que c'est drôle!

In the restatement-relay drill and chain drill pupils ask one another's ages. ("Quel âge avez-vous?") Then the birthdays are given:
"Je suis né le 15 juin. Mon frère est né le 25 mars. Ma soeur est
née le 11 avril."

TIME EXPRESSIONS, ETC.

(German)

EIN SPAZIERGANG

MARIE: Es ist heute so schön, Elisabeth. Wollen wir nicht einen Spaziergang machen?

ELISABETH: Recht gern, Marie. Sollen wir in den Park gehen? Da ist es immer so schön.

MARIE: Jawohl. Um wieviel Uhr wollen wir uns treffen? Es ist jetzt zwölf Uhr.

ELISABETH: So früh wie du willst.

MARIE: Dan komme ich um zwei Uhr. Bist du dann bereit?

ELISABETH: Gewiss. Du kannst aber auch etwas früher kommen.

MARIE: Nun, ich komme um eins. Dann haben wir den ganzen Nachmittag für uns. Also, auf Wiedersehen!

ELISABETH: Auf Wiedersehen!

Time expressions can be practiced in a number of different types of drills. As a visual aid, a clock dial should be used. The verb *kommen* can be practiced in answer to the question, "Um wieviel Uhr kommst du, kommt er, kommt sie, . . . nach Hause?" The model with an infinitive may be drilled after the pattern: "Wir wollen einen Spaziergang machen," or, "Ich will in den Park gehen."

IDIOMS AND VOCABULARY; COLORS

(Italian)

UNA SCOMMESSA

—Vuoi scommettere un gelato che ti faccio dire "nero"?
—Accettato.
—Di che colore è il cielo?
—Il cielo è azzurro.
—Di che colore è la neve?
—La neve è bianca.
—Di che colore è il tetto di questa casa?
—Il tetto è rosso.
—Di che colore è il carbone?
—Non mi ci pigli.
—Non importa. Che colori ha la bandiera italiana?

—La bandiera italiana è rosso, bianco e verde.
—Benissimo! Ora l'hai detto!
—Va bene. Ti pagherò il gelato.

The names of colors are practiced. Pupils are shown the flags of various nations and are asked to name the colors:

I colori italiani sono rosso, bianco, e verde.
I colori americani sono rosso, bianco, ed azzurro.

Gioco

—Che caldo!
—Sì, davvero.
—Dimmi, ti piace giocare al baseball?
—Mi piace, sì; ma preferisco giocare al tennis.
—Vuoi giocare un po' con me oggi?
—Mi dispiace. Ho fatto un appuntamento quasi ogni giorno.
—Oh sì? Ma forse qualche giorno verrai a giocare con me.
—Quando, domani?
—Sì, verso le quattro.
—A domani dunque.
—Arrivederci.

The expressions: "Mi piace" and "Mi dispiace" should be practiced. For example:

Mi piace giocare, ti piace giocare . . . al baseball, al tennis, etc.

Time expressions can be reviewed by eliciting answers to the question, "Quando?"

IDIOMS AND VOCABULARY

(Spanish)

El Perro Perdido

—Buenos días, Juan.
—Buenos días, Carlos. ¿Cómo está usted?
—Bien, gracias. Y usted, ¿cómo está?
—Muy bien, muchas gracias. ¿Qué hay de nuevo?
—Pues, mire usted. Mi perro se ha perdido.

—¡Qué lástima! ¿Cómo se llama el perro?
—Se llama Toñito.
—¡Ah! ¿Es pequeño?
—Sí, bastante pequeño.
—¿Es blanco y negro?
—Sí, blanco y negro, y muy cariñoso.
—¿Corre y salta mucho?
—Sí, es muy activo.
—¿Y ladra cuando uno se le acerca?
—Sí, entonces ladra muy furiosamente.
—¿Y lleva un collar así de ancho?
—Sí, hombre, sí. Parece que usted le conoce muy bien. ¿Dónde está?
—Pues, no sé. No lo he visto. Adiós.

Individual pupils can answer, by chain drill, the question, "Que hay de nuevo?" Sizes and colors can be practiced in completion exercises:

> Mi perro es negro, blanco, pequeño, grande, etc.

If the class has had this structure already, the compound tense, negative, with an object pronoun can be practiced.

> No lo he visto, no los he visto, no las he visto, etc.
> No los hemos visto, no la hemos visto, etc.

For a first-level class this dialogue may be shortened by omitting the lines from "cariñoso" to "Sí, hombre, sí."

WEATHER EXPRESSIONS; THE SEASONS
(German)

"Guten Morgen!"
"Guten Morgen!"
"Sind Sie draussen gewesen?"
"Jawohl! Ich komme eben herein."
"Wie ist denn das Wetter heute?"
"Est ist wirklich schön—nicht zu warm, nicht zu kühl."
"Das freut mich; ich will nämlich heute ausgehen. Sie haben aber einen Regenschirm."
"Ja, es hat gestern geregnet und ich borgte mir einen Schirm, den ich jetzt zurückbringe."

44

"In dieser Jahreszeit regnet es oft. De Frühling ist aber doch schön—viel schöner als der Sommer, der Herbst und der Winter."
"Ja, der Frühling ist wunderbar. Man möchte immer singen. Singen wir ein Frühlingslied!"

(Suggested songs: "Alles neu macht der Mai," "Der Mai ist gekommen," "Leise zieht durch mein Gemüt," "Der Winter ist vergangen.")
Weather expressions can be practiced in answer to the question, "Wie ist das Wetter heute?" (kühl, schön, kalt, warm, klar, etc.)
The verb with a separable prefix can be drilled according to the model:

Ich bringe den Schirm zurück.

And, in a subordinate clause:

Ich borgte mir einen Schirm, den ich jetzt zurückbringe.
Ich borgte mir ein Buch, das ich jetzt zurückbringe.

There are, of course, different slots here that may be used; for example:

Er borgte sich einen Schirm, den er jetzt zurückbringt.
Sie holte sich ein Buch, das sie jetzt zurückbringt.

SHOPPING SCENE; VARIANT ANSWERS

(Spanish)

—Buenos días (Buenas tardes), señor.
—Buenos días.
—¿Qué desea Vd. comprar?
—Quisiera un sombrero (una corbata, una camisa, medias, una blusa, un vestido, etc.).
—¿De qué color?
—Negro (verde, azul, amarillo, rojo, blanco, etc.)
—Aquí tiene Vd. un buen sombrero de color negro.
—¿Cuánto vale?
—Un peso y medio (dos, tres, cuatro, cinco, etc.).
—¡Hombre! pero es muy caro. ¿No tiene Vd. uno más barato?
—No, señor.

—Pues le doy un peso.
—Imposible, señor, imposible.
—Un peso cuarenta.
—No, no, señor.
—Un peso sesenta.
—Bueno. ¿Lo enviaré?
—No es necesario.
—Muchas gracias. ¡Adiós!
—¡Adiós!

The conversation given above lends itself exceedingly well to dramatization with variant answers as to objects desired, colors, and prices. A student, standing at the desk, may act as shopkeeper; individual students will come up and play the part of the customer. A few props will increase the realism of the situation.

A DRAMATIZED ANECDOTE
(Spanish)

UNA RECETA CURIOSA

(Peasant with large door made of cardboard enters pharmacy)

BOTICARIO: ¿Qué es esto? ¿Por qué porta Vd. una puerta en la botica? No soy carpintero, soy boticario.

PAISANO: Lo sé. Esto es una receta.

BOTICARIO: ¿Una receta?

PAISANO: Sí, una receta.

BOTICARIO: Hombre, es Vd. loco. ¿Cómo puede ser una puerta una receta?

PAISANO: ¡Muy fácil!

BOTICARIO: ¡Muy fácil! ¡Muy fácil! Es estúpido.

PAISANO: No es estúpido, de ninguna manera.

BOTICARIO: Pues, explíquemelo.

PAISANO: Con placer. Mi mujer está enferma.

BOTICARIO: ¿Su mujer?

PAISANO: Sí, mi mujer. Entonces viene el médico. Toma el pulso. Quiere escribir una receta. Pero yo no tengo ni papel ni pluma. No tengo que un pedazo de tiza. ¿Y sabe Vd. que el médico usa de papel?

BOTICARIO: ¡Ninguna idea!

PAISANO: ¡La puerta! Escribe la receta en ella. Mírela. De este modo una puerta puede ser una receta.

BOTICARIO: ¡Magnífico!

The above dialogue can be dramatized by having the pupil playing the peasant carrying a door—not too large!—made of paper or cardboard. Structures that can be practiced are the following:

¿Es Vd. carpintero?   No, soy boticario (médico, panadero, abogado, etc.)

Un carpintero hace (puertas)

Un boticario hace (medicina)

Un panadero hace (pan)

No tengo . . . ni papel, ni pluma, ni tinta, ni tiza, ni pan, ni mantequilla, ni agua, ni leche, etc.

Mírelo, Mírelos, Mírela, Mírelas.

Tómelo, Pórtelo, Escríbalo, etc.

Problems

1. Indicate what skills the pupil is to acquire through purposeful listening.

2. What are the special advantages of using taped materials?

3. In what ways should auditory comprehension in the upper years go beyond audio-lingual activities of the first two years?

4. Make a list of conversational topics for the third level.

5. Construct a dialogue and indicate three structures that it illustrates.

IV ' Reading

Importance of Reading

Listening and speaking are the primary activities in learning a foreign language; close thereafter comes reading. Modern means of communication, like the telephone, radio, and television, have given added importance to the spoken word. Since, however, the major part of communication is still carried on by means of the printed page, reading remains a basic linguistic skill.

As pointed out in an earlier chapter, language is essentially a vehicle for ideas. In teaching a foreign language we equip the student with an additional tool of communication. Fundamentally, our ultimate aim is to acquaint him with the foreign people and its civilization. Since the student cannot be transferred bodily to another country, one of the best ways of attaining this aim is through teaching him to read in the foreign language.

Since strong motives and permanent interests that will inspire the student are to be developed, reading in the foreign language must be made an enjoyable activity. To find joy and satisfaction in any activity, the student must be able to pursue it with a certain amount of ease. Facility, then, developed to the point of enjoyment in comprehending the printed page is the immediate objective.

Reading should begin as soon as the pupil has had sufficient practice in hearing and speaking. It may constitute the basis of a lesson or can be added as supplementary work. In either case, it should be a satisfying activity and not a disagreeable chore. To assure facility in comprehension right from the start, the material should be graded. All difficulties should be anticipated and eliminated.

Types of Reading. Reading may be intensive or extensive; it may be a classroom activity or a supplementary exercise; it may be done aloud or silently.

Intensive reading, whether silent or oral, is a controlled activity, carried on under the guidance of the teacher. It involves focusing upon new words and expressions, so that comprehension of the content may be facilitated. Extensive reading, on the other hand, is not concerned with the detailed study of words and structures. Its aim is to have the learner secure a rapid comprehension of the content.

Supplementary reading, which is largely done independently by the student, should be started on Level II. In the beginning only selections related to the textbook, or plateau readers, should be used, in order not to confront the learner with unnecessary difficulties.

Silent reading can be employed for both intensive and extensive practice.

Pleasurable Reading. A student's pleasure in learning to read a foreign book depends upon a number of factors. These include the type of book selected and the teacher's ability to make the reading attractive. A well-edited volume with clear print and ample illustrations will attract the learner. The reading material should appeal to the student's interests and be on his level of maturity. It will be up to the teacher to hold the student's interest and to make the reading an enriching experience.

What Is Reading? Reading may be defined as the rapid fusion of word symbols into consecutive units of thought. Through reading the experiences of the reader are extended, his power of thinking is stimulated, and he is enabled to interpret life more intelligently and accurately.

The ability to read quickly and accurately is usually an excellent index of intelligence. During the last few years there has been much concern over the fact that a large proportion of our school children are several grades below their norm in reading. Some reasons for this retardation are based upon physical factors; others are psychological. We may mention, for instance, defective vision, irregular eye movements, lack of interest, immature language habits, and a narrow span of recognition. The subject of reading difficulties has received considerable attention in recent years. It is certain that by means of improved methods, through reading clinics and remedial teaching by specialists, a change for the better will be brought about.

Reading a Foreign Language. Learning to read a foreign language is not, however, identical with learning to read one's native language. The student approaches the second language with certain reading and learning habits that are already well established. Some of these habits are directly related, in this case, to the nature of the English language.

The problem of the foreign language teacher is to build upon the already acquired reading habits of the pupils and to improve them, if possible. In addition, the teacher must help the pupil develop those new habits which the spelling or structure of the foreign language demands.

Fundamental Considerations. The following guiding principles should be kept in mind by the teacher in planning the reading lesson:

1. The reading selection should be properly motivated.
2. Difficulties in vocabulary and structure should be anticipated and eliminated.
3. There should be different types of reading: (a) model reading by the teacher; (b) reading aloud by pupils; (c) silent reading; and (d) reading in parts, if there is dialogue.
4. Comprehension of the content should be tested.
5. Visual and aural aids should be employed.
6. Cultural references should be elaborated on.
7. New words and expressions should be studied and practiced.
8. The selection should be reviewed through oral (or written) activities.
9. All considerations of grammar, vocabulary, and structure should lead to clarification of the content, so that the reading may be a pleasurable experience.

The primary aim in beginning reading is to lead the student to associate the spoken word with the printed symbol. This is facilitated by reading aloud, individually and in chorus. The latter

50

should help to improve pronunciation, intonation and fluency. At the earliest stage, only material that has been practiced audiolingually should be presented for reading. Later on this material will be expanded, so that the student also learns new structures and adds to his vocabulary.

Introduction to Reading. A beginning may be made with a dialogue that has been memorized by the class. This is to observe the principle that the learner is to see graphically only what he has already heard and said.

Before looking at the printed page, the class repeats the dialogue several times orally. Then the text is looked at, followed by two or three oral readings. The choral reading is followed by oral reading.

Another approach is to have the teacher or a voice on tape read the text while the pupils listen. The oral reading by the teacher is repeated while the pupils silently follow the printed text. Next, the teacher reads phrases aloud, which the class repeats in chorus. Finally, teacher and class together read the entire selection aloud.

These procedures are, of course, to be used only in the beginning. The oral presentation by the teacher will be eliminated gradually. During the second stage the pupil will read aloud what he has heard only once, and at a later stage what he has read silently. Finally, the pupil will be confronted with entirely new material. This is the beginning of independent reading.

Reading Should Be Properly Motivated. By a few apposite remarks and deft comments, the teacher can easily arouse the interest of the pupils in the selection to be read. *Motivation is,* after all, but *the assigning of a worthy or useful purpose to a task.* The pupil ought to be convinced of the need of what he is to do.

The teacher may secure motivation by telling or reading part of the selection and remarking, "Now, how many of you would like to find out what finally happened to . . . ?" Or, he may indicate the topic of the selection by saying, "Today we are going to read a very interesting story about. . . ." Very effective at all times is the personal touch. "When I was a child of ten, I had a very exciting experience which I shall never forget. One day. . . ." Or, "When I was in Heidelberg last summer, an amusing incident. . . ."

In more advanced classes correlation with other subjects can be employed effectively. "When you studied the causes of the French

Revolution in history you certainly came upon the name of that interesting character and stimulating writer Voltaire. Today we are going to read a selection from one of his works which . . ."

Sometimes questioning can be employed to lead up to the topic of the selection: "How many of you would not walk under a ladder or would refuse to be the thirteenth at a table? . . . Is there any scientific basis for such beliefs? . . . Are people in general superstitious? . . . Well, today we shall read an incident in the life of . . . which shows how much his course of action was determined by superstition."

Not only should the main topic of the reading selection be motivated; *each step or change in activity deserves a brief introductory comment to enlist and maintain interest.* The pupils will certainly follow more readily and intelligently if they know what the purpose is of the activity they have been asked to pursue.

"Now that we have learned the meanings of the new words, we can turn to our story and . . .

"I shall ask you questions on what you have read. Use as much as you can of the question in your reply. That will make it easier for you and give you practice in using the new words. . . .

"Let's sing the *Lorelei,* since that is also concerned with the beautiful Rhine about which we have just read. . . .

"In order that we may be clear on what went before, let's have a brief summary of the preceding page."

Such unintroduced, unmotivated, and abrupt commands as "Look at the board!" "Study these words!" "Turn to page 38!" have no place in the progressive language teacher's methods.

Difficulties Should Be Anticipated. Before asking the pupils to read the selection, the teacher should select those words and expressions that are new and write them neatly on the board. The teacher may select a definite number of words and place them on the board before the period begins, or he may choose them as the reading progresses. Or, the pupils may be asked to indicate, as they go along, what words they are unfamiliar with. Selection by the teacher in advance is probably the best way, for it makes the choice of new words definite and permits smooth, uninterrupted reading.

The meanings should be elicited from the pupils; only as a final resort should the teacher give them. If done skillfully, this will not consume much time. Meanings can be elicited by circumlocution, gesture, pantomime, the employment of synonyms, antonyms, or cognates, and so on. A few examples follow (italicized words stressed in speaking):

CIRCUMLOCUTION

"Cuando quiero comprar algo, entro en una tienda. El *dependiente* pregunta: ¿Qué quiere usted? Digo al *dependiente:* Una camisa.

"El *dependiente* trabaja en la tienda. ¿Qué es un *dependiente?*"

"Le *rouge-gorge* est un oiseau. Il vient au printemps et il a la *gorge* [pointing] *rouge*. Nous disons en anglais *poitrine rouge* [pointing]. Qu'est-ce que c'est, un *rouge-gorge?*"

GESTURE

"J'ai faim." [Rubs stomach and looks hungry.]

"J'ai froid." [Holds arms and shivers.]

"C'est un grand *étendu.*" [Moves extended hand, palm down, to indicate level surface.]

"Es schmeckt gut!" [Smacking lips.]

"Ho male di testa." [Rubs forehead, wrinkles brow.]

USE OF SYNONYM, ANTONYM, AND COGNATE

"Heute morgen bin ich *heiter*. Ich habe gut gefrühstückt, die Sonne scheint, ich bin *froh*. Ich lächle, ich bin *lustig*.

"Heute bin ich nicht *heiter,* ich bin *traurig*. Ich habe Kopfweh, das Wetter ist schlecht, ich bin nicht *heiter,* ich bin *melancholisch, trübsinnig, besorgt.*"

"Il est *laid,* il n'est pas *beau.*"

"C'est *réjouissant*. C'est *drôle, joyeux, gai.*"

"Il *court*. Que fait un 'courier' en anglais?"

"*Dormire*. Che fanno gli studenti nel 'dormitory?' "

After the meanings have been elicited, these and the words should be repeated, either by individual pupils or in concert. The same should be done with idioms and new expressions. If there are any peculiarities of syntax or structure, these should be mentioned and briefly explained.

Reading Aloud

The ability to recognize and pronounce words in print is another facet of language mastery. The passages to be read aloud should be short, complete, and timely. As the student learns to grasp meaning from the auditory forms of familiar words and phrases, he is ready to increase his recognitional span to include the reading of new words through an analysis of syllables, suffixes, prefixes, and stems. Drill should proceed from the sound to the word, to the phrase, and to the breath group. This fundamental training stimulates the rapid association of sound-word concepts and affords practice in pronunciation and expression.

Choral Reading. A unique and rather recent method for the improvement of pronunciation and oral expression is choral reading. Contrary to accepted opinion, it has been found that pupils are sometimes more careful in group participation than in individual work. The consciousness that the success of the whole depends upon the excellence of the contribution of each calls for the best in many pupils. Working as a group also overcomes the inherent timidity of many pupils, who are embarrassed when called upon to use the foreign language orally.

After some use of choral reading, a marked improvement will be noted in articulation. Greater precision and distinctness are secured, which carry over into the speech of the individual. Furthermore, through choral speaking the pupil has impressed on him the beat, the rhythm, and the pattern of the foreign language. The individual pupil is frequently hesitant about imitating the teacher's inflections. In the group, however, even the most timid will imitate with a certain amount of pleasure.

In French, choral reading has been found particularly effective. For beginners children's songs are recommended, since they are full of sound combinations, alliterations, and assonances. For advanced students selections can be found in the fables of La Fontaine, which are excellent because they combine dialogue with narration. For instance, in the fable of the wolf and the lamb the class is divided into three groups, the high voices representing the lamb, the low voices the wolf, and the average voices the narrative passages. Also, individual pupils of special ability can be trained to interpret the two roles.

Ballads, too, lend themselves nicely to group treatment. Especially recommended are Paul Fort's *Ballades Françaises* and adaptations of the ballad form, as in Alphonse Daudet's *Lettres de Mon Moulin*. Lyric poetry, such as that of Victor Hugo, de Lisle, and Verlaine, is also suitable.

When learning choral reading, the class is divided into three groups, according to voice quality: light, medium, and heavy. After reading and discussing the selection, the class takes up the pronunciation. Difficult words and difficult combinations are analyzed and repeated slowly. After the technical difficulties have been overcome, the poem as a whole is taken up. The interpretation is planned, the intonation and the rhythm are indicated. After the class has practiced as a whole, the parts are assigned to the several groups and to individuals.

Choral reading has been found an effective aid in teaching oral French and improving pronunciation. It is heartily recommended to the teachers of other foreign languages.

Intensive Reading. As has often been pointed out, the fast reader, not the slow reader, is the one who is the more intelligent. Fluency in reading depends essentially on the quick recognition of words and expressions. Physiological as well as psychological factors are involved. The rapid comprehension of thought groups and structural patterns strengthens the rhythmic progression of eye movements, which is the basis of quick reading. The stops and pauses caused by failure of immediate recognition produce regressive eye movements.

It is therefore of the utmost importance at the start to remove all difficulties in pronunciation and comprehension. This will be done by the teacher during the first reading. Direct translation should be avoided; as far as possible the foreign language should be employed. This can be accomplished by resorting to synonyms, antonyms, simple definitions, circumlocution, gesture, restatement, and so on. (Helpful devices are given under "Word-Study Techniques" on page 89.) The words and expressions selected for special study should be written on the board, explained and pronounced, used in sentences by the teacher, and repeated by the class and by individual pupils.

The intensive reading lesson may proceed as follows:

1. While the books are closed, the students listen to the teacher while he recites, paraphrases, or reads the new selection. Oc-

casionally he will ask a question to make sure that everything is clear.

2. The new words, phrases, and idioms are written on the board. They are pronounced and used in original sentences.

3. The pupils open their books and the teacher reads the first part of the selection aloud. Gestures and dramatic devices are used to heighten the effect and to aid in comprehension. Reference is made to words on the board.

4. The selection is now read by the class, alternating silent and oral reading. It is suggested that narrative or expository passages be read silently, whereas conversation or dialogue be done orally. Pupils may be assigned parts.

5. The selection may now be summarized in various ways. Selected pupils may be asked to give a brief summary in English or in the foreign language. The teacher may ask a series of sequential questions. As each answer is given, it is written on the board. Finally, all of the answers, comprising a résumé of the selection, are read aloud. Or, question slips are given to a number of pupils, the answers to which are written on the board. Or again, a number of brief completion or comprehension exercises may be done at the board.

At one time, oral reading was frowned upon and silent reading was stressed. Oral presentation is, however, very important. Reading aloud helps the pupil to associate the spoken word with the graphic symbol. It also aids in improving pronunciation, speech pattern, and fluency.

However, in the beginning stages of instruction, only material that has been predigested and comprehended through silent reading should be assigned for oral reading. In addition, the study of new words and expressions will add to the pupil's stock of vocabulary and idioms.

Silent Reading. After the new words and expressions have been learned, the actual reading can begin. Some teachers prefer to tell the whole story first, especially if it is brief, or read it to the class. This has its advantages and disadvantages; the pronunciation of all words in the text is given to the pupils, but interest in the story is somewhat destroyed when the content is revealed to them in advance.

In fact, the reading can be given greater motivation if the teacher reads or tells only the beginning of the story and challenges the pupils to find out what happens in the end.

Perhaps the greatest amount of interest is secured by a happy combination of reading aloud by individual pupils, reading aloud by the teacher, and silent reading by the class. When a pupil reads aloud, the audience situation should prevail: he should rise and face the class. Preferably, he should stand in the front of the room. Since in oral reading expression and accurate pronunciation are important elements, the reader's classmates should be called upon to offer suggestions and corrections in this regard. The teacher's own reading should, of course, set a model in accuracy and expressiveness. He ought to simulate the deepest interest and greatest enthusiasm and endeavor to arouse similar feelings in the class.

As pointed out above, motivation should be skillfully employed to introduce the lesson; it should also be used to introduce the various paragraphs or sections of the selection. Some of this may be in the nature of direction or guidance by the teacher and may be done orally or in writing.

The teacher may have read the first paragraph aloud. Then he remarks, "Now read the next two paragraphs silently and find out why the man did not want to. . . ." This will give purpose and direction to the silent reading. Meanwhile, the teacher can write three to five questions on the board about the next paragraph.

Or, he can read silently with the class and make a helpful comment every time an unfamiliar word or an unusual expression is encountered. In any case, a dead silence need by no means prevail.

For every paragraph or section a goal is set; the teacher's next step is to discover whether or not the goal has been attained. Has comprehension taken place on the part of the pupils?

Comprehension Should Be Tested. Whether or not the pupils understand what they have read can be tested by questions based on the text, by translation, or by summarizing.

Translation has been the traditional method for centuries. Although it has now fallen into disrepute because of its invariable and unskillful employment, translation has a function. In the final analysis, the ability to translate thought accurately and smoothly from one language to another does indicate comprehension. The trouble is that much translation done in the traditional classroom was neither accurate nor smooth, and it often turned out to be an exercise in the mutilation of the mother tongue. This was particularly true of the Latin classroom. Translation is an art requiring a good hold on the two languages involved and a keen sense of the niceties of expression.

We are not, however, trying to train skilled translators. Furthermore, we are trying to break away, as soon as possible, from the intermediate step of translating mentally. It is, therefore, wise to resort to translation only when the meaning of the text may not be quite clear or when an idiom occurs that is expressed differently in the vernacular. Occasionally, too, for the gifted pupil, translation may be called for as an exercise in good English. *The old-fashioned method, however, of "read-and-translate" is definitely to be discarded.*

The approved method of testing comprehension is by questions on the text. These may be asked in a number of different ways. If the text is fairly simple, the pupils should be able to answer without reference to the book. If, however, the text is new and rather difficult, they may be permitted to look in the book and get their answers directly from the text.

As to the language used, three variations are possible: questions and answers in English, questions in the foreign tongue and answers in English, and both questions and answers in the foreign tongue. Sometimes, if the selection is not too long, all three methods can be employed successively. This does not mean, of course, that the same questions are asked each time.

Questioning is probably the favorite device in classrooms all over the world, even though a good deal of it is purposeless and uninteresting.[1] In the foreign language classroom the question has a double purpose, for we want the student not only to communicate a thought but also to express it correctly in a foreign language. In fact, in many cases the accuracy of expression is more important than the thought involved. Also, we attempt through the answer to provide practice in using the foreign tongue. It is, therefore, reasonable to frame the question so that the language difficulties are at a minimum. In the beginning grades, questions should be so worded that they contain most of the answer. For the sake of the practice involved, the pupil should be required to answer in a complete sentence each time.

Questions should follow in logical sequence and exploit the text. *Color and life can be added by the employment of humor and the introduction of the personal element.* "What was the man's occupation? What did he do? What do *you* do? Do you enjoy it?"

[1] See Supplement, Ch. XIV, "The Question-and-Answer Method."

The question form ought to be replaced occasionally by a command or request. "Tell us what the girl did in the garden." "Describe the soldier's arrival in his native village."

This type of exercise can also be employed for the résumé. When a whole story is to be summarized, it is probably more reasonable to require a summary only in English, unless it has been prepared at home, or unless a native student who has a rather good command of the spoken tongue can be called on.

Visual and Aural Aids Should Be Employed. If properly used, pictures, charts, maps, slides, and records will certainly make the reading lesson more interesting, more colorful, and more effective. Everyone likes to look at pictures. By careful guidance on the teacher's part, the picture (whether a drawing on the board, a mounted illustration, a slide, or a photograph) can be employed to enrich the text, stimulate the pupil's thinking, and build up his vocabulary.

Place names mentioned in the text should be located on the map; cultural references should be illustrated with pictures or photographs; musical references should be enriched with the playing of records. This should not be done haphazardly, but after careful planning, so that its effectiveness can be increased.

Every foreign language room ought to be provided with a good map of the foreign country. If there is no map or the one available is not up to date, one can be drawn with colored chalk on the board. A very satisfactory map can be made by drawing and lettering with colored ink on a window shade.

The teacher who has some ability in drawing can make effective use of the blackboard for illustrative purposes in connection with the reading lesson.

As for pictures and illustrations, the teacher ought to have a complete file of these to refer to at any time. The displays on the walls ought also to be of such a character that they can be referred to in connection with the reading.[2]

The most practical aural aids are the phonograph and the radio.[3] If an important composer is mentioned in the text, one of his compositions can be played as an illustration of his works.

Cultural References. Words and expressions in the foreign language become meaningful to the student to the degree that his con-

[2] See Ch. IX, "Audio-Visual Material and Techniques."
[3] Radio is discussed in Ch. IX.

cepts are enriched. This is true not only of proper names but also of the common nouns. The skillful teacher will give the necessary information, or elicit it, in connection with word study and reading. For example, *vendredi* might lead to the following: "What verb does this remind you of? *Vendre?* 'Why to sell'? What has Friday to do with it?" And then a brief description is given of market day in a French town.

The occurrence of *château* in the text should lead to the showing of a picture of a typical French château. The expression "Renaissance style" would elicit *naissance, naître, renaître, renaissance.* A comment on the châteaux of the Loire and on Francis I would also be in order.

If this is done regularly, the student will gather a great deal of interesting information incidentally and at the same time enlarge and enrich his vocabulary.

In order not to go too far afield, however, the teacher should carefully note in advance the words or expressions he plans to elaborate. Particularly interesting and important items may be given as special assignments to individual pupils for brief written reports. If this is done, the teacher should also indicate the name of a book or two in the library in which the student may look up the reference.

New Words Should Be Studied. The reading lesson lends itself particularly well to the expansion of the pupil's vocabulary. New words should be presented in context and drilled through conversation based upon the selection. The words to be explained and studied should not, however, be left to chance or to the inspiration of the moment. There may otherwise be too many words or a disproportionate emphasis on unimportant items.

In planning the lesson the teacher should determine upon teaching a fixed number of words, let us say, ten, fifteen, or twenty. (It is impractical to take a greater number.) The number will depend upon the time available, the intelligence of the class, the difficulty of the vocabulary and of the text, and so on. The teacher may underline the selected words in his own book and put them on the board as the class proceeds with the lesson. Of course, if a word comes up with which a number of pupils are unfamiliar, it should certainly be included.

On the other hand, the teacher may begin the lesson with word study. The attention of the class is directed to the words that appear neatly written on the board. Each word is pronounced carefully by the teacher and repeated in concert by the class and by individual pupils. The meanings, as far as possible, are elicited from the pupils by means of synonyms, antonyms, definitions, use in sentences, circumlocutions, cognates, and so on. After the meanings have been made clear to the class, the words are again pronounced and the meanings given.

After vocabulary difficulties have been eliminated, the class is ready to proceed with the reading. The selection is read and reviewed. Attention is again devoted to the words. They are used in questions and answers and in original sentences. They are copied by the pupils into their notebooks for study and future reference. They should be used as the basis of a permanent, active vocabulary for the term. The vocabulary list should not consist solely of isolated words but should include phrases, expressions, and idioms.

Review Through Oral Activities

The favorite method of testing comprehension and using the new words of a reading selection is through question and answer. There are, however, a number of other methods that can be employed advantageously. There is the oral summary based on key words that have been written on the blackboard; the summary of each paragraph, or of the entire selection, in English; a reproduction of the selection by a number of pupils; conversation on the basis of an illustration in the book; and dramatization of appropriate passages, for example, those with dialogue or conversation.

Every effort should be made by the teacher to keep the oral work as natural and informal as possible, even though he has carefully selected the words he wants to present and the questions he intends to ask. Humor, pathos, and personal comment should be freely introduced. Part of the oral discussion can be in English, especially if ideas are presented for which the pupil lacks the foreign vocabulary.

The reading lesson should be an enjoyable experience, not a stereotyped classroom exercise.

Intensive Reading. The type of reading done in the classroom is, on the whole, chiefly intensive. The following is suggested as a procedure for the treatment of a reading selection that may be covered in one period:

1. After motivating the reading, the teacher presents the story, in whole or in part, by
   a. giving an almost exact reproduction from memory (this will be done in the case of a beginner's selection, where every word counts)
   b. retelling the story, more or less freely (this can be done later, when the students already have a pretty good vocabulary)
   c. reading the selection aloud and asking questions about new words and expressions as they occur.
2. The new words and expressions are listed on the board. The words are pronounced, the meanings are discussed, and the words are used in original sentences by the students.
3. Pupils may then be called on successively to read aloud.
4. The teacher asks questions on what has been read, in English or in the foreign language. Answers may be written on the board by the pupils. The questions may be so framed that the answers will form a sequential written review of the reading selection.
5. The paragraphs or sections that follow may be read silently by the class. While the students are reading, the teacher writes two or three questions on the board for each paragraph. These are answered orally when the reading has been completed. This is a test of the pupils' comprehension.
6. After the entire selection has been read, it may be summarized in English or in the foreign language. To guide the student, the teacher may write key words on the board.

Extensive Reading. Extensive reading is generally done outside of class, for it is essentially silent reading. It should be prepared for as follows:

1. The reading is motivated by the teacher.
2. Difficult passages and new words are explained.
3. A number of questions are assigned; the answers are to be written.
4. Students are to prepare various types of summaries: written, oral report, and so on.
5. After the reading has been completed (it may be a longer selection requiring several days), it should be discussed in class.

Supplementary Reading. One of our ultimate objectives in teaching a foreign language is to develop the interest of the student to the point where he will be eager to read books and articles in the foreign language outside of school. Such reading is bound to increase his skill in the language and his command of words. Moreover, it enriches his knowledge of the culture of the foreign people and introduces him to more mature and more timely material than that found in school textbooks. It also provides an excellent opportunity for correlation with any special field in which the student is interested—science, sports, history, travel, art, music, and so on.

For the beginning student supplementary reading will, of course, have to be done in English. As soon as possible, however, reading in the foreign language should be attempted, especially by the brighter and more ambitious student.

Available material consists of the following:

1. Newspapers and magazines, in the foreign language, intended for the learner. This type of publication is very helpful, since the articles are graded and a vocabulary is provided. Appearing periodically, they are able to present up-to-the-minute news items.

2. School editions of the classics are also valuable, because they are usually graded and supplemented by notes and vocabulary. In addition, they generally contain a preface, discussing the literary significance of the work, and a short biographical sketch of the author. This is the best sort of introduction to literature.

3. Newspapers, bulletins, travel folders, and magazines in the foreign language. The student will be fascinated to find he is able to read in the foreign language what he has already seen in the daily press. Sports terms and advertising slogans will amuse him. In our larger metropolitan areas, both dailies and weeklies are published in French, German, Italian, and Spanish. Although the language is not always the best, the editorials and the magazine feature articles are usually written in good style. The airlines and the tourist bureaus issue gratis a wealth of beautifully illustrated material, in English and in the foreign language.

Supplementary reading should be part of the term's work; every student should be required to read at least one book. It will be helpful if the teacher maintains a small library in the classroom or if the department provides books. The school library should, of course, have a special section for the use of students in foreign language classes. Students should be encouraged to keep a record of new words and expressions. A summary, oral or written, should be presented as evidence of the reading.

Illustrative Lessons

A READING LESSON WITH MUCH SPEAKING

(French)

The lesson is based on the story entitled "La Ruse de Martin," from *Pas à Pas*. The teacher introduced the selection by saying, "Today we will read a story about a donkey named Martin who is tired of working so hard and decides to play a trick on his master. Let's see whether his trick was successful!"

The teacher proceeded to tell the story in simple French but employed the key words, which she wrote on the board. *La ruse* was compared with its English cognate; *un âne* was described as "un animal très stupide" (the pronunciation was contrasted with that of English *an*); *gaiment* was compared with the English, and the significance of *-ment* was commented on. Other words that the teacher used and wrote on the board were *conduit, marché, chargé, ramener, glisser, légère, lourde, éponge*.

After all the key words had been commented on, the class was asked to read the story silently. Meanwhile the teacher wrote a series of guiding questions on the board.

After completing the reading, various pupils were called upon to answer the questions on the board. For additional exercise, the teacher wrote out ten true-false statements which were answered orally.

At the end of the period, the whole story was summarized in English by a pupil standing before the class. For homework assignment, the pupils were asked to prepare a brief summary in French.

The next day the story was read aloud by various pupils and selected portions of it were translated. The teacher called for certain expressions, sentences, and idioms; she varied this by asking, "What word tells you that Martin was lazy? . . . How do you know that his master was angry?"

Being familiar with the story and the key words, the pupils were now ready to answer questions in French, without reference to the text. The teacher asked:

"Pourquoi Martin est-il triste d'être un âne?"
"Que porte-t-il sur le dos?"

"Où est-il conduit chaque jour?"
"Qu'est qu'il fait quand il arrive à la rivière?"
"Que trouve-t-il quand il continue son chemin?"
"Que fait-il le lendemain?"
"Le maître comprend-il la ruse de son âne?"
"Quelle leçon donne-t-il au paresseux animal?"

Some of the brighter pupils were then called upon to reproduce the story in the foreign language.

Comments. With special emphasis on the key words, orally and in writing, with silent and oral reading, and with a home assignment, the pupils should readily become so familiar with the story that they can reproduce it with little effort. Learning the key words and memorizing entire phrases and sentences of the text makes possible a fluent and accurate oral rendition.

AN INTENSIVE READING LESSON

(Spanish)

This lesson is based on "Don Juan Bolondrón," in Castillo and Sparkman's *Graded Spanish Readers*, Book II. The story is that of the poor shoemaker whose fame for having killed seven flies in one blow reaches the ears of the king, who summons him to kill a fierce tiger. The beast is killed by the soldiers but Juan gets the credit for it and marries the king's daughter.

The teacher elicits a brief oral summary in Spanish of the first three paragraphs, which have been read previously. He remarks, "Vamos a ver lo que pasa a este hombre valiente llamado Juan Bolondrón Mata-Siete." (Motivation.)

Before asking the class to proceed with the silent reading of the next few paragraphs, a number of new words and expressions are taken up. (Removal of difficulties.)

"Bosque . . . ¿Qué es un bosque? . . . ¿Un gran número de árboles? . . . Muy bien . . . ¿Y un tigre? . . . Nombre unos otros animales salvajes. . . . ¿Se comió? . . . Sí, comer 'to eat' . . . comerse 'to eat up' . . . llegó a oídos del rey . . . ¿Cómo se puede expresarlo con una palabra? . . . Mandaré que venga . . . ¿Por qué el subjuntivo? . . . etc.

After the class has read silently to the bottom of the page, the teacher asks questions on this portion of the text. After each question has been answered correctly, a student is sent to the board to write the answer:

1. ¿Qué había cerca de la ciudad?
2. ¿Qué hacía el tigre?
3. ¿Por qué se llevaba parte de los cuerpos al bosque?
4. ¿Qué hacían los hombres fuertes al ver al tigre?
5. ¿Qué llegó a oídos del rey?

While the class was reading silently, the teacher wrote on the board:

1. Dé lo contrario de "hacía mucho mal."
2. Dé lo contrario de "valiente."
3. ¿Qué es un palacio?
4. Dé un sinónimo de "enorme."
5. Dé un sinónimo de "tenían miedo del tigre."

The teacher points to these items on the board and elicits answers from individual students: "Pero, vamos a ver lo que el rey ofrece al zapatero . . . ¿Qué significa: 'Me traerás'? . . . ¿'cortarte la cabeza'? . . . ¿'llevar armas'? . . . ¡Muy bien, escuchen!"

The teacher reads the next paragraph or two aloud while the students follow in the book. Then the teacher makes a number of true-false statements. Individual pupils are called upon to repeat the sentence and to say "Sí" or "No."

1. El rey dará su hija al zapatero si matará al tigre.
2. El zapatero dice que traerá el cuerpo del tigre a la iglesia.
3. Si no mata al tigre, perderá la cabeza.
4. La hija del rey es fea y tonta.
5. El zapatero no tiene miedo.

Now the answers that were written previously on the board are corrected and read in chorus by the class. The story is completed with the same procedures, that is, difficulties are removed, questions are asked, there is silent and oral reading.

Directed dialogue can now be carried on. The teacher suggests various questions that students may ask their classmates: "Pregunte . . . si él puede matar siete moscas de un solo golpe . . . ¿qué es un tigre? . . . ¿dónde se puede ver un tigre? . . . ¿qué otros animals se pueden ver allí? . . ." etc.

A bright student may be called upon to give a brief oral summary of the story in Spanish.

AN INTENSIVE READING LESSON

(French)

This lesson is based on an adaptation of Alphonse Daudet's *La Mort d'un Prince*. The text follows:

LA MORT D'UN PETIT PRINCE

Le petit prince est malade, le petit prince va mourir. Dans toutes les églises du royaume, on prie pour la guérison de l'enfant royal. Toutes les rues de la vieille ville sont tristes et silencieuses, les cloches ne sonnent plus, les voitures vont au pas.

Tout le château est en émoi. Il y a une nombreuse assemblée de médecins. Les corridors sont pleins de gens qui vont d'un groupe à l'autre demander des nouvelles à voix basse. Le roi est allé dans une salle au bout du château, il veut être seul. La reine est assise au pied du lit du petit malade qui repose, les yeux fermés. On croit qu'il dort. Non, il ne dort pas. Il se tourne vers sa mère. Il lui dit:

"Madame la reine, pourquoi pleurez-vous? Vous oubliez que je suis un prince et que les princes ne peuvent pas mourir; ainsi . . ."

A ce moment, un prêtre s'approche de l'enfant. Il se penche vers lui. Il lui parle longtemps à voix basse. Le petit l'écoute d'un air de plus en plus étonné. Puis, tout à coup l'enfant royal l'interrompt avec colère:

". . . Mais alors," crie-t-il, "d'être prince, ce n'est rien du tout."

Et sans vouloir plus rien entendre, le petit prince se tourne vers le mur, et il pleure amèrement.

The teacher introduced the selection by saying, "Today we are going to read the story of a little prince who is very, very sick. The best physicians in the country have been consulted; his case is hopeless. The entire country, with the exception of the little prince, is plunged in despair. Why is he so optimistic?

"In the story we will find many familiar expressions. There are, however, a few new ones. Let us study them, so that we may be able to read our story more easily.

"A country ruled by a king, *un roi,* is called a kingdom, *un royaume.* He and the queen, *la reine,* live in the castle, *le château.* What are some English words related to *roi, reine, royaume?"*

"Royal, regent, regency, regime . . ."

"What is the English translation of *château?* Let us spend a few minutes on the history of this word. In olden days when bands of lawless robbers marauded the countryside, the village folk would seek shelter in the nearby castle. The castle was a fortress and offered them protection. In fact, in Latin, the language from which French is derived, a fort is called *castellum.* The French word *château* developed from the Latin *castellum.* This is an interesting word. Note how the *c* before the *a* became *ch.* Other examples of this are *catta–chat, canis–chien, caballus–cheval.* What happened to the *s* in *castellum?"*

"It dropped out."

"Yes, and to indicate that it was once there a circumflex accent mark is placed over the *a.* The same is true of *fenêtre, blâmer,* and *ôter."*

"But *castellum* has two *l's."*

"That's right. The *l's* were not pronounced very clearly and were gradually dropped entirely. Note how few changes were made in English: *castellum–castle."*

The following words and phrases were also given some attention, though not in such detail: *la mort, mourir, église, le prêtre, sonner les cloches, la ville, la rue, pleins de gens, demander des nouvelles, être en émoi, tout à coup, rien du tout, d'un air étonné, la colère, guérir, la guérison.* These words and expressions had been written on the board by the teacher.

The text was now read by the teacher while the class followed, books open. Here and there the teacher asked a question to see whether the pupils were following the thread of the narrative. At the conclusion the teacher asked, "Why was the little prince so optimistic about his ill health? Who disillusioned him? What does 'disillusion' mean? . . .

"Now read the story by yourselves and see if you can find the answers to the questions I am going to put on the board."

The questions the teacher wrote were:

1. Qui va mourir?
2. Pourquoi les rues de la vieille ville sont-elles tristes et silencieuses?
3. Qui demande des nouvelles?
4. Où est le roi? la reine?
5. Que dit le petit prince à sa mère?
6. Qui s'approche de l'enfant à ce moment?
7. Pourquoi le petit prince pleure-t-il?

Individual pupils answered these questions. Then, by using the key words on the board, various pupils retold the story in simple French.

Comments. In this lesson a good deal was made of cognates, related words, and derivations. This phase of the French lesson has been somewhat neglected in our schools; in European schools, where practically all secondary pupils take Latin, it is emphasized.

If in the present instance it is felt that the word study interferes with the narrative, especially if many of the new words are to be treated in such detail as *château*, the lesson can easily be given in two sessions. Word study will then form the major part of one lesson and a consideration of the narrative the major part of the other. In any case, the detailed treatment of a word, such as that given for *château*, should provide the pupils with some simple and fundamental etymological principles which will help them in deciphering the meaning of new words in the future.

Cognates are important and useful; care must be taken, however, to point out continually how the meanings of words change and to guard against the uncritical acceptance of words that look alike in both languages. Examples of this are such words as *demander* and *crier*.

READING WITH THE USE OF PANTOMIME AND GESTURE

(French)

While five pupils went to the board with index cards, the teacher took up the story entitled "La Vieille Femme et le Corbeau" on page 21 of *Colette et Ses Frères*. The teacher asked individual pupils original questions on the text, while the class read silently, line-by-line, section-by-section in their books. Much resourcefulness was displayed by the teacher: she not only brought out the meaning of the content but stopped here and there to clarify points in etymology and vocabulary. For example, the significance of the circumflex accent in the word *forêt* was brought out. The French word was compared with the English word. Also, the Italian pupils in the class were asked to contribute examples from the Italian. This led to a comparison of the words *maître* and *maestro*, *fenêtre* and *finestra*. The teacher checked the pronunciation of the pupils carefully.

On the board she listed, as she went along, *la forêt, le corbeau, demeure, perché, fromage, drôle, le bec, goute, le bol*, and *pleure*.

The story was made more effective and interesting by having certain actions illustrated by pupils. For instance, pupils were called upon to illustrate "Il ferme les yeux l'un après l'autre" and "Il est très drôle." Other words and expressions illustrated in gesture and pantomime were "Elle a faim. Elle met le bol devant la fenêtre. Elle laisse la porte ouverte. Il mange. C'est bon. Où est mon fromage?"

Then a girl was sent to the front of the room with a library card on which appeared instructions in French. The girl acted these out and individual pupils were called upon to tell what she did. The girl ran, looked for her bowl of cheese, opened the door, wept, and cried "Coac! Coac!" The teacher asked in each case, "Que fait-elle?"

A second girl was given another index card prepared by the teacher and followed the same procedure. She ran quickly, she fell, she jumped, and she pretended she was eating. The vocabulary was based on this selection and those previously read in *Colette et Ses Frères*.

Finally the whole story was done several times in pantomime by pairs of pupils.

Comments. This lesson contained a variety of interesting activities, with the stress on gesture and mimicry. The latter added considerably to the effectiveness and enjoyment of the lesson, especially with younger pupils. The making of connections between the pupils' past experience and their present learning (that is, in the comparison of certain French words with their English and Italian equivalents) was also commendable. Questioning, which usually predominates as a classroom activity, was here reduced to a minimum. The pupils, on the other hand, were given ample opportunity to express themselves in French orally and by gesture or dramatization.

TREATMENT OF AN ANECDOTE
(French)

The teacher tells the class that they are about to hear a very amusing and instructive anecdote about Molière and the servant. Who was Molière? Molière's life is discussed briefly. The teacher names some of his works in English and urges the pupils to read them.

A few new words and difficult expressions are studied. They are written on the board, and the meanings are elicited. The words include the following: *écrivain, siècle, pièce, par conséquent, il avait des distractions, la clef, reviendrai.* Cognates are mentioned. The words are used in original sentences by the pupils.

Then the teacher reads the anecdote aloud with appropriate gestures.

> Molière était un grand écrivain du dix-septième siècle. Il pensait toujours à ses pièces et par conséquent il avait des distractions.
>
> Un soir, il retourne chez lui à minuit. Il cherche la clef dans sa poche. Il ne la trouve pas. La porte est fermée. Il frappe. Son domestique le regarde par la fenêtre. Il demande:
>
> —Qui est-ce? Qui cherchez-vous?
>
> —Monsieur Molière, répond l'écrivain.
>
> —Il n'est pas à la maison. Revenez demain, dit le domestique.
>
> —Bien, répond Molière, je reviendrai demain. Et il part.

After the teacher has completed the reading, he asks five questions in French to test comprehension.

The mimeographed sheets containing the anecdote and the exercises are then handed out. Individual pupils are called upon to read parts of the selection. A group of boys act the part of Molière and a group of girls take the role of the servant. Finally, one boy and one girl act out the two parts.

Some of the exercises are done orally, others are written on the board.

Exercises

I. Answer the following questions in complete sentences in French:
1. Qui était Molière?

2. À quelle heure retourne-t-il à la maison?
3. Pourquoi Molière frappe-t-il à la porte?
4. Que dit le domestique au grand écrivain?
5. Qu'est-ce que Molière lui répond?

II. Tell whether the following statements are true or false. If false, give the correct statement in French.

1. Molière était un ècrivain du dix-huitème siècle.
2. Il retourne à la maison à sept heures.
3. L'écrivain ne trouve pas la clef.
4. La porte est ouverte.
5. Molière frappe à la porte.
6. Le domestique ouvre la porte.
7. L'écrivain entre dans la maison.
8. Molière dit qu'il reviendra demain.

III. Select the phrase which most suitably completes the incomplete sentence.

1. Un écrivain fait   *a.* des statues *b.* des pièces *c.* de la musique *d.* des tableaux *e.* du vin.
2. Molière était   *a.* écrivain *b.* sculpteur *c.* homme de science *d.* général *e.* peintre.
3. L'heure de minuit est à   *a.* onze *b.* trois *c.* neuf *d.* douze *e.* sept heures.
4. Le domestique regarde par   *a.* le livre *b.* le journal *c.* la fenêtre *d.* la clef *e.* l'écrivain.
5. Quand on perd une clef on la   *a.* regarde *b.* montre *c.* cherche *d.* frappe *e.* gronde.

IV. Find in the text a cognate for each of the following words:

1. pensive
2. perdition (loss)
3. pouch
4. portals
5. responsive
6. departure
7. demand
8. mansion
9. grandeur
10. return
11. distracted
12. dictum (saying)

V. Select from Column B the French equivalents of the English sentences in Column A.

A	B
a. It is said that many famous authors were absent-minded.	1. Ils étudient toujours leurs leçons; par conséquent, ils les savent.
b. What does he see when he looks out of that window?	2. Vous êtes chez lui presque tous les jours.
c. You are at his house nearly every day.	3. On dit que beaucoup d'auteurs

d. They always study their lessons; consequently, they know them.

e. Please don't think of your examinations now.

célèbres avaient des distractions.

4. Ne pensez pas à vos examens maintenant s'il vous plaît.

5. Que voit-il quand il regarde par cette fenêtre-là?

VI. Learn the following series:
1. Je retourne à la maison.
2. La porte est fermée.
3. Je cherche la clef dans la poche.
4. Je ne la trouve pas.
5. Je frappe à la porte.

VII. Dictation. Two or three sentences summarizing the anecdote.

READING COMBINED WITH BOARD WORK

(French)

The text used in this lesson was "Jeanne Redon" in Greenberg's *French for Beginners.* The teacher introduced the selection as follows:

"Yesterday we were speaking of Jeanne d'Arc. Who recalls why the French cherish her name? . . . Today we are going to read about another Jeanne who may not be as famous as Jeanne d'Arc, but who nevertheless displayed as much courage."

A sufficient portion of the story was then told by the teacher to arouse the pupils' interest and to provide opportunity for putting the new words on the board. The words were copied by the pupils into their notebooks.

"Let us read and find out what her particular kind of bravery was."

The teacher read the opening paragraphs, questioning the pupils only when she believed them to have missed the point. When the conversation occurred, the teacher exclaimed, "Que dit Jeanne? Que dit son père?" This lent variety to the reading.

After the first reading, the class was asked to reread the passage silently. Index cards, containing two questions each, were handed to five pupils for work at the board. The questions were as follows:

1. Qui est Jeanne Redon?
2. A-t-elle des frères?
3. Pourquoi va-t-elle à la pêche avec son père?
4. Que dit Jeanne à son père?
5. Que fait son père? etc.

While the answers were being written on the board, the teacher asked questions on the text. The customs and occupations of the Bretons were discussed with the class.

As soon as the pupils at the board were finished, their work was examined and corrected. Since the questions had been asked in logical sequence, the answers formed a summary of the story.

Comments. As shown above, board work can be successfully combined with the reading. The pupils can write the answers to questions on index cards, or each pupil answering orally can put his answer on the board. This is a double check, for it provides an opportunity not only for speaking but also for writing. The final reading of all of the sentences is a splendid review and summary of the story.

Problems

1. Take a given passage of about a half a page and tell how you would use it for testing the pupils' reading comprehension.

2. Make a list of books that could serve as a collection for supplementary reading on the fourth level.

3. Plan an intensive reading lesson for a class on the third level.

4. Plan an intensive reading lesson for a class on the fourth level.

5. Tell how the tape recorder can be used to strengthen the ability to read silently.

V ' Writing

Values. Many a pupil gets a deep satisfaction out of being able to say "Bonjour," or to sign his friend's autograph album with "Bonne chance." Psychologically, receptive or recognitional phases of learning precede active or reproductive phases. It is not possible to determine with any degree of reliability just what foreign language skill may prove of practical use to the student later on. Certainly, in an age in which literacy is emphasized, the ability to read and write is one of the stepping-stones in every human activity.

Furthermore, a strong urge exists to use the skill one has acquired in speaking and in writing. In fact, effective learning is the result of habit formation through frequent usage, for there is "no impression without expression." Expression fixes a fact far more firmly in memory, on the principle of multiple-sense appeal. If a word, or expression, that has been heard, read, and pronounced is also written, its retention is tenfold as strong.

No matter how limited the material may be, the pupil derives a definite satisfaction from writing the simplest sentence that he himself has conceived in relation to a situation. It thereby becomes a creative and original experience for him. Hence, written work, which has its function in translation, dictation, vocabulary-building, and grammar instruction, may in itself be made a distinctly pleasurable and interesting experience for the pupil.

Introducing Writing

In view of the disparities between the written and spoken forms of any language—notably English—it is advisable to postpone systematic writing until a firm audio-lingual foundation has been laid. Written work will be based largely on what the pupils can say. Aural comprehension and reading comprehension are reinforced by writing. Even skill in speaking is strengthened by the pupils' writing correctly what they can pronounce. In fact, this fourth skill introduces desirable standards of accuracy, especially in the case of the more visual-minded learner.

Writing in the foreign language can be introduced shortly after the pupil has begun reading. However, as stated under "Homework," even at the very start, in the prereading phase, there will be writing—largely in English, to a very limited extent in the foreign language. Pupils will label pictures of common objects, flowers, animals, members of the family, rooms of the house, pieces of furniture, and so on. Such activities are useful in building up vocabulary. They may be considered as a sort of preparation for "writing readiness." From the beginning, absolute accuracy should be insisted upon.

Imitative Writing. The first written work of the pupil will consist of copying material he has already mastered by hearing, speaking, and reading. It will be material he has memorized or with which he is familiar. This "imitative writing," as it is called, should be practiced frequently. Word groups, sentences, and phrases, rather than single words, should be written. Copying sentences in the foreign language reinforces the pupil's speaking and reading skill and fixes the correct written form in his mind. Sentences may be taken from the dialogue that has been memorized. Complete sentences in coherent context are particularly desirable to avoid having the writing become merely a mechanical exercise.

Dictation. After there has been sufficient practice in imitative writing, the next step is writing from dictation. A very easy transition is made by letting the pupil have before him a sentence with one or two words missing. The teacher reads the entire sentence and the pupil fills in the missing word or words. This is followed by straight dictation, based on familiar material.

The chief value of dictation is that it reveals the degree of the student's aural comprehension and his ability to spell correctly. As an exercise it affords opportunity for training in auditory acuity, understanding of the oral word, correct spelling, and grammatical accuracy.

In fact, dictation involves a number of important aspects of language learning. Briefly these are:

1. Listening purposefully
2. Distinguishing sounds, words, and thought groups
3. Comprehending the meaning of a selection
4. Recognizing grammatical forms
5. Spelling correctly
6. Observing correct punctuation.

Dictation should be given at frequent intervals. The selection used should be related to what is being taught at the moment. The same passage may be used a number of times, that is, for reteaching or for testing. In fact, in the beginning, only material that has already been studied and mastered should be used for dictation.

At first brief classroom expressions may be used. Gradually these are expanded to a short paragraph, then to two paragraphs. The material may be chosen from a dialogue that has been learned, an item in the news, or a passage in the textbook.

The text selected should always be fairly brief and either familiar material or something not beyond the pupils' range of comprehension. If the text is an entirely new one, a few words of explanation, indicating the nature of the material, should precede the reading. This introductory explanation, of course, will be given in English.

A suggested procedure for giving dictation is as follows:

The selection is read three times. During the first reading, the pupils listen and make no attempt to write. The teacher's reading should be normally paced, clear, and expressive. The second reading is given more slowly and in breath groups while the pupils write. The teacher does not repeat. The third reading is at normal speed; the pupils listen and make whatever corrections they believe necessary. Punctuation should be dictated in the foreign language. While the class has been writing, one pupil has been taking down the dictation on a rear blackboard. The class now faces about and looks at the work on the board. Errors are pointed out. The pupils correct either their own work or exchange papers.

In making the corrections, the following procedures are suggested:

1. Each pupil may correct his own work or exchange his paper with a neighbor.
2. The class faces about to look at the work of the student who wrote the dictation on the rear board.
3. The exercise is read sentence-by-sentence.
4. Errors are pointed out and corrections are made by pupils.
5. The mistakes are erased, by the teacher or by a board monitor.
6. The correct forms are inserted.
7. The teacher summarizes the most common errors made and offers suggestions for avoiding them in the future.

It is recommended that pupils keep their dictation exercises in a special section of their notebooks, so that they have a record of their errors and corrections for reference.

Guided Writing. After imitative writing and dictation, a third step is reached, that is, guided writing. It is called guided writing because the short written responses of the pupils are guided by the teacher. The responses may take various forms:

1. The teacher, after reading a brief passage twice, makes incomplete statements based on the selection. Pupils complete the statements in the foreign language.
2. The teacher, after reading a selection twice, asks a number of questions based on the passage. Pupils write the answer to each question. The passage and the questions are reread by the teacher, so that the pupils may check their work for errors.
3. The teacher reads a given passage twice at normal speed. Pupils are asked to (a) rephrase the passage in their own words; (b) put the sentences into another person; (c) change the tense of the verbs; (d) change the sentences to the plural.
4. Pupils are asked to complete pattern drills. Examples:
   a. Pattern
      Me lavo la cara.
      Me lavo _____.
      Me lavo _____, etc.
   b. Pattern
      El libro está debajo de la mesa.
      El libro está _____ la mesa.
      El libro está _____ la mesa, etc.
   c. Pattern
      Nosotros tenemos hambre.
      Él _____ hambre.
      Vd. _____ hambre, etc.

5. Pupils write the answers to a series of questions based on a given topic. Example:

¿A qué hora se levanta Vd.?
¿A qué hora se desayuna Vd.?
¿A qué hora va Vd. a la escuela? etc.

All material is, of course, based on what the pupils have already mastered audio-lingually. The phrases and sentences should be carefully graded, so that no unexpected difficulties are encountered.

As in the case of dictation, one pupil may be asked to write on the rear blackboard. This will help in making corrections. The corrected exercise will serve as a model to the class.

Controlled Writing. After sufficient practice has been given in guided writing, the next step may be taken. This is controlled writing, phases of which have already appeared in guided writing. The transition is, therefore, an easy one. The student merely expands the skills he has acquired through transformation and substitution drills. The activity consists basically of rewriting a given selection, that is, changing a narrative passage into dialogue or vice versa. The pupil has already been prepared for this by the rewriting of dictated material in different tenses and persons.

A more difficult exercise is rewriting a narrative or a dialogue in the form of a letter. After considerable practice in rewriting, the student should be able to write a summary of the passage in the foreign language. It will help him if the summary is first done orally. Key words and expressions may be offered by the teacher. As the student expresses himself more and more freely, the summary really becomes a form of composition.

Composition

"Composition" is derived, of course, from "compose" and means the original, independent, and free manipulation of language, primarily in written form. It requires imagination, resourcefulness, and skill; it requires knowledge of the language. In other words, it demands ideas and a stock of words and expressions.

The chief difficulty with composition work in any foreign language class, particularly in the lower grades, is that the pupil is unaware of his own limitations in linguistic expression. He is apt to attempt to express ideas he cannot formulate correctly, not realizing that the foreign mode of expression is quite different from the English. The more intelligent the pupil, the more elaborate the ideas he wishes to express are likely to be and the worse the resulting composition.

The problem in teaching composition, then, is to devise a situation where material learned may be reproduced freely, but not too freely. It should be a situation requiring the pupil to evolve from his consciousness previously acquired language patterns which, by the pupil's application of them to the situation, become for him an original piece of work. The pupil must be taught to restrict himself to constructions he has previously learned without too greatly hampering his powers of expression.

Various devices may be used. The teacher may give a series of suggestive words and phrases outlining the theme. "Write a composition telling about your day, using as a guide the following series of expressions (in the foreign language): to get up, to dress, to breakfast, to go to school, to study, to answer questions, to go home, to play in the street."

Composition may follow a model sequence given in the textbook or constructed by the teacher.

A model textual summary for French would be:

> Pierre is a French boy.
> He lives in Paris.
> He is fifteen years old.
> He goes to school.
> He studies English.
> He likes sports.

Such a composition sounds choppy, of course. With a little skill, by rearranging words and introducing connections, one can give it a little more variety:

> Here's a picture of Pierre.
> He is a French boy and lives in Paris.
> His father is not rich, but they live well.
> As he is fifteen years old, he goes to a lycée.
> Pierre likes to study but he also likes to play.

An outline for a "guided" composition may be based on one of the following procedures:

1. A model chart or pattern description is prepared for the student to copy and to alter to fit his personal situation.
2. A list of expressions and key words is arranged in a sequence.
3. A series of questions is posed, the answers to which, written in paragraph form, will constitute a composition.
4. A passage is taken from a text describing an action, a happening, or a situation, which the student uses as a basis for describing a personal experience.

An interesting procedure to employ in beginning classes is the use of a picture. The picture may be one that the individual pupil has, or it may be a larger one shown to the class by the teacher. By pointing out given objects and persons, by making appropriate comments, by supplying key words, and by asking pertinent questions, the teacher can elicit a series of statements that will form a composition.

Controlled Composition. With a lessening of the controls, the student's writing becomes controlled composition. In addition to summarizing passages in their own words, students may be asked to write a composition based on a model. They can be guided and helped by being given a topic sentence for each paragraph or for key words and expressions. The composition may assume the form of a letter. Brighter students may be asked to write an article in the foreign language for the school magazine or newspaper.

Directed Composition. When the student receives detailed directions from the teacher concerning the form and content of the composition or letter, the activity is referred to as directed composition. Directions may be given in English or in the foreign language, orally or in writing. Example: "Write a letter to your cousin Robert inviting him to spend the summer with you on your uncle's farm. Mention the fields and the forest. Tell him that there is a stream where you can go swimming and fishing. The scenery is beautiful; the air is cool. Your aunt is an excellent cook."

Free Composition. When the student is able to express himself without difficulty in brief narratives, descriptions, reports, dialogues, and letters, he has reached the highest level of writing, namely, free composition. This stage involves independent manipulation of the foreign language, with originality of thought and freedom from common errors. To be successful the student will have to possess imagination as well as a considerable stock of words and mastery of grammar. Since this is so, free composition will have to be postponed until the later years. Only after much practice in guided and controlled writing will the student be able to express himself freely and independently.

Composition is one of the most effective forms of language learning, for it fixes the words, idioms, and structures that have been acquired through oral practice. With reference to form and spelling, composition demands absolute accuracy. In his efforts to express himself freely, the student will unconsciously enlarge and enrich his vocabulary. He will thereby gain in fluency of expression and will acquire a finer feeling for the nuances of the foreign language.

Illustrative Lessons

COMPOSITION BASED ON PICTURES

(French)

The students are asked to select from a newspaper or magazine a picture of some kind, for example, a news photograph, advertisement, cartoon. They are instructed to write as many statements in French about the picture as they can, without looking up new words in the dictionary. The purpose of the composition is primarily to provide an opportunity for self-expression.

Of course, the pupils are not left entirely to their own devices. The teacher gives them some guidance by saying, "Dans cette image on voit . . ." or "Voici . . ." or "Il y a dans la photographie . . . ," followed by an enumeration of persons or objects. Suitable adjectives are added. The pupils are asked to invent possible reasons for the actions represented or to imagine facts pertaining to the picture. The teacher may outline sample compositions.

"Voici deux hommes et une femme. Voici une maison. La maison est blanche. La maison a trois fenêtres et une porte. La femme et les hommes sont devant la maison. Il fait beau."

The teacher has ready a number of interesting pictures clipped from magazines. (Colored ones are preferable.) He uses these for oral-composition activities. By question and comment, suggestion and criticism, he is able to elicit a more or less connected discourse.

He endeavors gradually to expand the ideas and raise the activity to a higher level.

A photograph of several prominent statesmen yields the following result:

"Il y a trois hommes dans l'image. Ils sont assis. Ils portent des chapeaux. Ils parlent. Un des hommes s'appelle Charles de Gaulle."

An advertisement for a breakfast food brings forth:

"Le père et l'enfant sont assis à la table. L'enfant a faim. La mère apporte le déjeuner. Elle place le déjeuner sur la table. Le déjeuner est bon. Tout le monde est content."

More pretentious becomes a paragraph on an illustration showing a man and woman placing luggage in a car while two children watch.

"Dans cette image il y a un homme, une femme, et deux enfants. Le père et la mère sont les parents des deux enfants. Les enfants portent quelque chose à la main. La mère aide le père. Ils demeurent peut-être près de New York. Ils vont peut-être dans une autre ville. Ils vont rendre visite à leurs amis. La femme porte un manteau parce qu'il fait froid. C'est l'hiver. La neige est sur la terre."

Meanwhile, three pupils have written brief compositions on the board, based on pictures on the walls.

As a homework assignment each pupil is instructed to affix the picture he has selected to a sheet of paper and to write his composition on it. The compositions are read and criticized in class the next day.

Comments. Writing compositions in this manner is not merely a novel device; it possesses genuine pedagogic values. It is adaptable to different levels of ability. Even the weakest pupil can find something to say, and the best pupil has here the opportunity of using his knowledge to its full extent. It is the type of assignment that encourages maximum effort at any level.

The pupil is made aware of his study of the foreign language at other times and in other connections than in the classroom. Furthermore, the activity is initiated within the pupil. He finds his own material, applies his own knowledge, expresses himself on the basis of a stimulus he finds for himself; the lesson is, for that reason, more interesting than a teacher-given assignment. Still, it is concrete and not too difficult. Finally, it is a creative effort, through which the pupil applies what he has learned and which affords him considerable pleasure and satisfaction.

DIRECTED COMPOSITION

(French)

(From the *Foreign Language Revision Program for Secondary Schools, French*, Level III, Board of Education, City of New York)

The class is given the following instructions:

Imaginez que c'est le jour de votre examen de Regents en mathématiques, et la veille de votre examen de français. Écrivez un paragraphe en français où vous racontez ce que vous avez fait ce matin et ce que vous comptez faire pendant le reste de la journée. Dites:

1. À quelle heure vous vous êtes levé ce matin
2. Ce que vous avez pris au petit déjeuner
3. Comment vous avez passé la matinée à la maison
4. À quelle heure vous êtes parti pour l'école
5. Comment vous avez voyagé à l'école
6. Comment vous avez trouvé l'examen
7. Avec qui vous comptez jouer au tennis après l'examen
8. Ce que vous avez l'intention de faire après le dîner
9. Ce qu'il vous faut repasser pour votre examen de français
10. Quelle note vous espérez recevoir dans votre examen de français.

DIRECTED COMPOSITION (A LETTER)

(Spanish)

The class is given the following instructions:

Escriba Vd. una carta a sus padres, diciéndoles que Vd. ha llegado a Madrid, donde Vd. pasará un mes con su tío y su tía. La carta debe consistir de diez frases completas, mencionando los puntos indicados. Escríbales a sus padres que:

1. El viaje en el avión fué muy interesante, el almuerzo excelente
2. Vd. charló con el viajero a su derecha
3. El tío y su primo estuvieron al aeropuerto a su llegada
4. Vd. no tenía dificultad con su español; todo el mundo lo alabó
5. Los tíos viven en una casa magnífica
6. Madrid es una ciudad hermosa
7. El domingo Vd. irá a una corrida de toros
8. Más tarde, en automóvil, visitará Segovia
9. Le gustan los españoles y España.

Problems

1. Make a list of twenty words in any foreign language that are likely to be mispronounced by an English-speaking person because of the spelling.

2. Make a list of fifteen items in connection with the home or family, pictures of which can be labeled by pupils during the pre-reading period.

3. Prepare a guided writing lesson for the second half of Level III.

4. Describe how you would prepare pupils for a lesson in controlled writing.

5. Plan a lesson in directed composition for the fourth level.

V I ' Vocabulary

Subject Matter

We have been discussing the various phases of language learning, that is, the skills involved and their development. But there is also a body of knowledge, a set of rules, which must be learned so that the linguistic skills may function properly.

The subject matter of language consists essentially of a stock of words and expressions and of the rules that govern the syntax of its speech patterns, that is, vocabulary and grammar.

What Words Should Be Taught?

That question is easy to answer for Latin, in which field all the words occurring in the basic texts have been counted and classified. In modern languages, word counts have also been made and word lists have been prepared. They have not always been satisfactory, because of the differences of opinion as to what types of text material should be the basis for establishing word frequency. The earliest lists, like many of our foreign language dictionaries, were predominantly literary in tone. Modern, practical material, such as "battery," "radio tube," "dial the telephone," were entirely missing. The tendency in the newest textbooks is not to be guided too strictly by word lists. Useful, everyday words, especially if they have English cognates, are introduced right at the start (for example, "television").

On the other hand, it is not much of a task to construct a practical first-year vocabulary. The great difficulty is to keep the number of words down. By actual experience it has been found that for even the most elementary conversation a minimum of 750 words is required. It should be possible for the normal pupil to acquire that many active words during the year of language study.

Word lists have been compiled in various ways—alphabetically, according to parts of speech, in order of frequency. Experience has shown, however, that the most sensible arrangement is according to categories, because words with related meanings make associational learning possible. A selection of from 750–800 words for the first year may be grouped under some forty or fifty headings. Starting with the more immediate situations these may be school, the lesson, languages, the family, relatives, professions, descriptions of persons, descriptions of objects, animals, nature, men's garments, women's garments, colors, time, months, the days, the body, health, the house, daily actions, etc.

To make the various categories useful for conversation, they should not consist exclusively of nouns but include various parts of speech. For example, *la leçon* would list

le cahier	lire	la page
les devoirs	écrire	l'exercise
facile	apprendre	n'est pas
difficile	étudier	parce que

It is obvious that with such an arrangement it is possible to construct many sentences—even long ones. (For example, "J'apprends la leçon difficile, parce que j'étudie beaucoup.")

Word lists for the second, third, and fourth years are more difficult to construct. The choice of words depends largely upon the grammar and reading texts used in the course.

Vocabulary Range. In the first and second years minimum vocabulary lists can be set up, but after that, with the students' greater reading facility, that is not possible. As the pupil strengthens his reading power he relies more and more on passive or recognitional vocabulary. There are many words whose meaning he can infer immediately from the context or recognize by analogy or analysis.

Although the recognition of these many words will facilitate his reading comprehension, he will not be able to use them in speaking and writing with equal ease and correctness. It would, therefore, not make sense to limit the student's vocabulary to the words he has thoroughly mastered audio-lingually. The range of vocabulary would be so great that a list would be entirely unwieldy. Furthermore, it would be unlikely that it would be satisfactory, for, in analysis, vocabulary depends essentially on the character of the reading matter. A list might be confined to literary subjects; on the other hand, it could stress scientific, commercial, or cultural topics.

Topics That Determine a Vocabulary. Pedagogically, a vocabulary is also determined by its linguistic aspect. There is bound to be some overlapping between topics, although not complete identity. The vocabulary used in audio-lingual exercises will be entirely active words; the words required for extensive reading will be far greater in number and largely passive. During the first three years vocabulary may be determined by the following topics:

A. Audio-lingual activities
   1. Classroom expressions
   2. Everyday activities—school, home
   3. Going somewhere—appointment, transportation
   4. Games and sports
   5. Introductions; social amenities
B. Conversation
   1. Everyday activities—shopping, using transit facilities, etc.; the daily routine
   2. Situations with cultural implications—at the library, bookshop, museum, concert; TV, radio
C. Intensive reading. This will depend entirely on the character of what has been read—whether narrative, novel, drama, short story, history, poetry, and so on.
D. Extensive reading. This, too, will depend on the nature of the reading. An attempt should be made, however, to cover art, music, science, history, biography, travel.

In other words, the vocabulary of the upper years is largely determined by the students' areas of interest.

Learning Vocabulary. The learning of vocabulary is based on the formation of specific habits. Since this involves the association of symbols and their meanings, it is clear that an enrichment of the meaning of the word is as important as its frequent repetition. The more numerous the associations, the longer the retention will be and the easier the recall will function. Since the size of one's vocabulary is basic to all facility in speaking and reading, the aim should be to secure permanent retention and automatic response. This is best attained through drill.

If rightly used, drill is the most economical method of learning, for through it can be secured speed, accuracy, ease, and precision. Good motivation should be provided and the laws of learning should be carefully observed.

Drill, of course, should not be used exclusively; its function is limited. Also, drill does not necessarily mean learning by rote. Drill, or better, practice, may be given in such interesting forms as games, dialogues, dramatization, and songs. The printed or written list of items need be used only as a check or a guide.

Effective Practice. The important features of a drill exercise are its proper introduction (motivation), the maintenance of the pleasurable and satisfying elements of the activity (effective practice), and the checking of results (measurement of learning).

Hence it is quite inadequate for the teacher to announce, "For tomorrow learn the vocabulary on page 62." It is the teacher's primary role to arouse the pupil's interest in the activity and to make his learning as pleasant and efficient as possible. He should at least be given instructions as to how to go about it. Preferably, the actual teaching and learning should be done in class, so that the homework assignment may consist largely of review, application, and further practice.

Habit Formation. Learning is largely habit formation. In this connection we may recall the three excellent maxims of William James, namely:

1. In the acquisition of a new habit or the leaving off of an old one, we must take care to launch ourselves with as strong and decided initiative as possible.
2. Never suffer an exception to occur till the new habit is securely rooted.
3. Give the habit exercise.

Word-Study Techniques. Every new word should be pronounced carefully by the teacher and repeated in concert by the class and by individual pupils. The pronunciation must be accurate, for, as Wundt says, "The words which an individual is unable to pronounce correctly he is also unable to hear correctly, because of the deficient sense of articulation." Multiple-sense appeal is very important. Thus, to give the pupil a visual image of the word, the teacher should write it on the board, unless it appears in the printed lesson vocabulary.

For each word the English equivalent should be elicited or a definition given in the foreign language. It should also be used in a brief original sentence.

Inferring Meanings. The important factor, of course, is the meaning of the word. The simplest way would be simply to give the English equivalent to the pupil, but this would certainly not be the most effective way of teaching. As far as possible, the meaning should be elicited from the pupil under the skillful guidance of the teacher. The method employed will depend entirely upon the type of word.

If the foreign word is related to an English word, the meaning can be derived readily by asking, "What English word does this resemble?" (For example, *soldado, Lokomotive, beauté, educazione.*)

It is equally important to warn the pupil if the foreign word resembles an English word in appearance but not in meaning (for example, *Feind, fumer, alumno, tempo, cura*).

The pupil may also be led to infer the meaning of the word by noting the context.

> Il regarde dans la boîte et voit un petit oiseau.
> —Est-ce un rouge-gorge? demande Jean.
> —Non, dit son père. C'est un petit corbeau.

The class has just learned that *rouge-gorge* means "robin"; they infer that *corbeau* is also a bird. The teacher leads to the meaning by referring to the picture in the book and asking, "De quelle couleur est le corbeau?" "Noir." "Correct. Et quel oiseau est noir?"

Adjectives and adverbs may be readily inferred from synonyms and antonyms. "La vieille femme est *laide;* elle n'est pas *jolie.*" "Er war *traurig.* Gestern war ich *traurig,* weil es regnete; heute bin ich *fröhlich,* weil die Sonne scheint." "El caballo marcha *lentamente;* no corre *rápidamente.*" "Con *accelerazione*—con *rapidità.*"

Another way of eliciting the meaning of a word is to ask the pupil to give a definition in the foreign language of the word. "*Panadero*

—un panadero es un hombre que hace pan en una panadería."
"*Schreibmaschine*—eine Schreibmaschine ist eine Maschine, mit der man schreibt." "Il est très *faible* veut dire qu'il n'est pas *fort.*"
"*Tedesco*—tedesco è una lingua straniera; i tedeschi parlano tedesco."

It is also very effective, especially if an action is involved, to have the pupil illustrate the word by gesture or pantomime. The following sentences would readily permit such an interpretation:

Je ferme la fenêtre lentement.
La vieille femme pleure.
Er war sehr müde.
Der arme Bettler bat um ein Almosen.
Me miro al espejo y me peino.
Se quita la chaqueta.
Pescavamo.

The teacher can give drill on the new word by using it in a command to be carried out by the class in concert and by individual pupils.

The pupil can also infer the meaning by guessing a habitual action or common characteristic of the object mentioned. "Der Löwe brüllte laut. Was tat der Löwe? Well, what would a lion do?" "El perro ladraba. What was the dog doing?"

If the word is the name of an object that can be pointed out, as something in the classroom or a part of the body, the teacher should point to it and name it. The same applies to any bodily action. "Er zwinkerte mit den Augen." "Elle pleurait." "Él dejó caer la carta."

In a carefully prepared reading lesson the teacher may even bring in the object, especially if it is of cultural value, to show it to the class. Examples are a *mantilla,* a *triangle,* a *Tropfenfänger.* Where the object is not available, a picture or photograph is useful.

The above are a few ways of eliciting the meaning of the new word. The pupil's attention has been focused on it; a reaction has been stimulated, but the word has not yet been learned. Application and drill are necessary.

If the new words are being learned as part of a reading exercise, the drill may be given after the reading has been completed. Before the lesson the teacher writes the new words on the board, elicits the meanings, uses the word in a sentence, but reserves the practice for later.

Practice. Before making provision for practice, the teacher may add to the associations of the word (more cognates or related English words, an interesting anecdote or the story of its derivation, other interesting members of the same word family, and so on). The associations should be as numerous as possible so that the pupil has little difficulty in remembering the word.

The drill may take any one of a variety of forms or a combination of them. Suggested procedures are:

1. The class and individual pupils repeat each word three times.
2. For each word several original sentences are composed.
3. The new words are used in questions and answers.
4. The words on the board are key words selected in sequence. By using them various pupils give a résumé of the reading selection.
5. The teacher goes through the class rapidly, getting each pupil to give the foreign word for the English, and vice versa.
6. Competing teams answer the teacher's question involving the word or give the foreign word for the English.
7. At the close of the period a brief written test is given to determine what words have not been thoroughly learned. Each pupil writes his failing words five times for homework.

Illustrative Lessons

TEACHING PARTS OF THE BODY

(French)

After "Alouette" had been recited a number of times by individual pupils, it was sung by the entire class. In the singing, stress was placed on the different parts of the bird which are plucked, for example, "Je te plumerai *la tête . . . le bec . . . les pattes . . . le cou . . . le dos.*"

The following conversation then took place:

"Hélène a-t-elle une tête?"
"Oui, mademoiselle, Hélène a une tête."
"Marie a-t-elle un bec?"
"Non, mademoiselle, Marie n'a pas de bec."

"What does Mary have instead of a *bec*?"

"A nose . . . *un nez*."

"What do we have instead of claws?"

"Hands and feet . . . *les mains, les pieds*."

"What English words are related to these two words?"

"Manual, manuscript, manufacturer; pedal, pedestrian, pedestal."

"The hand is at the end of the arm . . . *le bras*. The foot is at the end of the leg . . . *la jambe*. Combien de bras avez-vous, mademoiselle? . . . Combien de jambes avez-vous, mademoiselle? . . . Montrez-moi vos deux mains. . . . Levez la main droite. . . . Baissez la main droite. . . . Levez la main gauche. . . . Baissez la main gauche. . . . *Le bras* is bent as the elbow, *le coude*. What part of the leg corresponds to the elbow?"

"The knee . . . *le genou*."

"What do we find at the end of our hands?"

"The fingers . . . *les doigts*."

"What is a 'digit'? . . . A 'prestidigitator'? . . . Combien de doigts avez-vous, mademoiselle? . . . What brittle substance do we have at the end of our fingers? . . . Nails . . . *les ongles*. . . . Combien d'ongles avez-vous? . . . Qui n'a pas dix ongles? . . . Levez la main."

The names of the parts of the body that had been learned were now reviewed and summarized. As the teacher pointed to the words on the board, the class pronounced them in concert and gave the English meaning of each. Then a pupil was called to the front of the room and as the teacher pointed to the part of the body, the class named it in French. The teacher asked in each case, "Qu'est-ce que c'est?"

The following were the words that appeared on the board and were thus reviewed:

la tête	le coude	le pied
le bras	le genou	le dos
la jambe	le cou	le doigt
le nez	la main	l'ongle

The above words also appeared on flash cards which a pupil held up while his classmates recited. For each word the pupil reciting gave a sentence and pointed to the part mentioned. For example, "J'ai un nez. Le voici."

Next, a number of pupils were called successively to the front of the room to ask their classmates questions in French, similar to the following, about parts of the body:

> Montrez-moi votre tête.
> Combien de doigts avez-vous?
> Qu'est-ce que c'est?

Finally, the teacher gave a brief written test in which the pupils wrote the French equivalent for each English word.

Comments. Any lesson is made more effective by the teacher's increasing the number of associations and bonds with familiar material. This was accomplished rather happily in the lesson just described. A poem and song, which the class already knew, was used as the motivation and the point of departure. What a far more interesting and colorful lesson this was than the mere listing and memorizing of the names of a dozen parts of the body! Activity and action were introduced, the object was connected directly with the foreign word, and relationships between French and English were pointed out. Four different exercises were employed for review and drill; three of these were conducted by the pupils themselves. As a final checkup, a written test was given on the twelve words learned. Through this the teacher made sure that the pupils also knew how to write correctly the words they had been using orally. It is worth noting that in the flash-card drill, an equivalent word was not just given; the foreign word was used in an original sentence while the object was pointed out.

UNLOCKING THE MEANINGS OF WORDS

(French)

After briefly reviewing the selection previously read in *Colette et ses Frères,* the teacher inquired, "Would you like to read another story about Colette?" The class enthusiastically replied, "Yes."

The teacher introduced the selection on page 19, entitled "Le Petit Oiseau," with a few pertinent remarks in French. "First, I'll give you a few new words so that you can understand the story."

The meanings of the new words were elicited by circumlocution, cognates, gesture, use in sentences, and so on. For example, for *voit* the teacher said, looking closely at a girl, "Je vous vois"; looking at a book, "Je vois le livre"; looking at the window, "Je vois la fenêtre"; pointing to a pupil looking at a picture, "Jean voit l'image." *Il voit* was written on the board after a pupil had given its English meaning.

For *s'approcher de* the teacher walked toward the desk and said, "Je m'approche de la table," and approaching a girl, "Je m'approche de la fille," and so on. To enforce the expression the teacher asked various pupils to use it in the third person and also as a command.

In the case of "Fermez les yeux!" the teacher pointed to her eyes and then gave commands to individual pupils and to the class, "Fermez les yeux! Ouvrez les yeux!" The speed of these orders was gradually increased, much to the delight of the class.

Rouge-gorge was unlocked by pointing to a red disc and to the throat and remarking, "Le rouge-gorge est un oiseau. Comment s'appelle-t-il en anglais?"

As the meaning of each word was elicited, the teacher wrote it on the board. Finally the following appeared: *il voit, s'approcher de, la surprise, fermez les yeux, le rouge-gorge, le corbeau, le nid, la cage, il pose.*

Then, as the teacher pointed to them, individual pupils gave the meanings of the French words in English.

While the pupils had their books closed, the teacher read the selection expressively, pausing after every sentence or two to ask a question in French.

Next, the books were opened and the pupils were asked to read the story silently. The teacher meanwhile put five guiding questions on the board. These were in French. At length the books were closed and individual pupils were called upon to answer the questions.

Finally volunteers were called for to retell the story in French. Each pupil contributed three or four sentences. The teacher did not interrupt, but made judicious comments or helpful suggestions after each pupil had recited.

Comments. A good deal of skillful word unlocking can be done by means of gesture, use in sentences, and questions. Direct connection can thus be made between the foreign word and the concept, without the English word as an intermediary. Translation should be resorted to only in the case of abstract ideas, the meaning of which would be difficult to convey in any other way. The use of English is thus reduced to a minimum and the language of the classroom is French.

A SECOND LESSON WITH CLASSROOM OBJECTS

(Italian)

The pupils are now familiar with the names of certain classroom objects, for example, *la sedia, il muro, il quaderno, il gesso, la penna, la carta*. To these the teacher adds *la finestra, la scrivania, la matita, la cartella,* and *la lavagna,* together with *qui* and *là*.

The teacher points to the location of the object and then puts the question as follows:

> "La matita è qui. Dov'è la matita?"
> Class in concert, then individuals, "La matita è qui."
> "La finestra è là. Dov'è la finestra?"
> "La finestra è là," or "Ecco la finestra."

The same procedure is followed with all the nouns. They are then practiced by means of a game. One pupil steps into the hall and another one meanwhile conceals an object somewhere. The pupil who has stepped out is called back into the room. He is given three chances to guess where the object is. Various pupils ask him the same question, "Dov'è la matita?" He answers, pointing, "La matita è qui," or "La matita è là." If the pupil who stepped out guesses correctly, he has the privilege of going out again.

Next, the teacher reviews the nouns learned by asking pupils to point to the object. "Mi mostri . . ." "Dov'è il . . . ?"

Comments. By means of the procedure employed in the two lessons described above, the pupil learns the names of a dozen classroom objects, the use of *ecco,* and the distinction between *qui* and *là*. The teacher can easily expand the range of the oral work by introducing other nouns and a few adjectives.

Problems and Questions for Discussion

1. Plan a lesson in word study (fifteen to twenty words) based on a given reading selection. Suggest cognates, cautions in pronunciation and spelling, antonyms, and illustrative sentences.

2. Tell what instructions you would give a class of beginners for learning new words at home.

3. Plan a lesson in which you would teach the meaning and use

of eight words related to a given product, the place where it is made or sold, and the maker or vendor (examples: *pan, panadería, panadero*).

4. Prepare five series of twenty words each under specific themes that would be useful in a first-term class (for example, the family, the house, at school).

5. Name six different devices or exercises by which vocabulary may be reviewed.

VII ′ Grammar

Need for Grammar. Grammar is the syntactical structure of a language. Like the skeleton of the body or the steel framework of a building, it supports and gives form to the organism or edifice, although it is not apparent to the observer. Just as the framework is not visible to the eye, the native speaker is entirely oblivious of grammatical relationships and forms while he is talking.

For centuries the traditional method of acquiring a foreign language was to learn the rules and principles of grammar and then to apply them in the construction and translation of original sentences. The procedure was based primarily on the written language, on the textbook. Practice in speaking was incidental.

The new concept of language teaching reverses this procedure completely. Grammar is not thought of as a logical arrangement of forms, paradigms, and rules extracted from the written language but a succession of structural patterns that occur constantly in the spoken language.

After listening carefully, the learner familiarizes himself with given structures through constant practice in pattern drills, chosen on the basis of their importance and frequency. Instead of identifying parts of speech, parsing sentences, memorizing rules, acquiring a grammatical nomenclature, and constructing or translating sentences, he learns the foreign language through speaking, more or less as a child does.

Language Learning of the Child. For the student in school the learning of a foreign language is a definite and separate activity; the little child's learning of his mother tongue is part and parcel of his mental development within his cultural environment. Furthermore, it is quite unconscious, unplanned, and incidental; the child can tell us nothing of the process involved. He has plenty of time; he gets constant practice, day after day. He is intensely motivated, for on his ability to express himself depends his success in getting food and drink, in playing with his fellows, in securing relief from pain. He learns primarily by imitation, by association, and by trial and error. Much time and effort are wasted. Compare this process with the planned procedures of school instruction which are based on limited time schedules, on economy of effort, and to a large extent on group learning.

Audio-Lingual Approach to Grammar. The learning of grammar, like the acquisition of the four fundamental language skills, is based on audio-lingual procedures. The pupil first listens to utterances purposefully and is trained to recognize similarities and differences in sounds, in forms, and in structures. Then he tries to imitate what he has heard, practicing pattern drills containing specific structures. After a while the latter become automatic in given situations; the student is able to use them habitually. A great variety of pattern drills will be provided, for they are to cover all of the important areas of structural variations that are to be learned at a given stage.

Change of Emphasis. Later, on the second level, the audio-lingual activities will be somewhat reduced and a considerable portion of the time will be devoted to reading and writing. This means that most of the new structures will be learned from reading passages. Specific grammatical items will be illustrated in the selections, although these should be chosen primarily for their intrinsic value.

The change in emphasis will be about as follows: listening, 20 per cent; speaking, 20 per cent; reading, 50 per cent; and writing, 10 per cent. To make it easier for the student to retain the grammar that he has learned, he should be provided with a set of model sentences illustrating the most common structural forms. The basic book will contain grammar reviews; to handle them effectively the student will have to be familiar with grammatical terms.

Analysis and Explanation. In the beginning stages the pupil will not be required to explain why he is using a given form. All he need do is recognize it and use it correctly—an example of "functional" grammar.

Since, however, the acquisition of skills and knowledge must be systematic and cumulative, grammatical forms must sometimes be explained. The pupil, especially if he is bright, may even ask for it. He should certainly be aware at all times of what is being said.

However, the grammatical form should be first used in a drill and then explained. The procedure to be followed would be (1) a pattern drill involving the new structure is given; (2) attention is called to the new point; an explanation is elicited from a pupil or given by the teacher; and (3) the drill is resumed.

Explanations should be kept to a minimum, for language is learned by analogy and practice rather than by analysis and description. The aim should be to teach each item functionally before explaining it grammatically. The memorization of meaningful structural patterns in functional situations is the essence of language learning.

The following principles should be observed:

1. In order to become part of the pupils' habits of expression, the function of the structure must be made clear through its usage.
2. A grammatical point—that is, a structure—is learned by applying it, not by listening to an explanation.
3. If the drill is well constructed, analysis and explanation will usually not be necessary, or will be reduced to a minimum.

Structures should be selected on the basis of their relative simplicity, their importance in the spoken language, their relationship to other structures that have already been learned.

Terminology. The ability to use grammatical terminology bears little relation to oral competence. Hence the learning of technical terms is not an aim in the study of a foreign language. The more common grammatical terms should be part of the general knowledge of the pupils. In teaching certain forms and structures the teacher may find it advantageous to use them.

Conventional Approach to Grammar. Since many beginners' books are so constructed that specific instruction in grammar and the doing of exercises are assumed, and since examinations require active ability, it may be well to suggest effective means of the more conventional grammar teaching. The following principles will prove useful:

1. A grammatical point should be introduced by means of illustrative sentences which should be analyzed by both teacher and pupils. The principle involved should be derived from these examples. Since the whole purpose is to secure clearness of comprehension, the vernacular may be used in the beginning stages.
2. Intensive study should follow, consisting of (1) connected text, and (2) suitable exercises, such as question-and-answer, completion, series, transposition, substitution, true-and-false, matching, multiple-choice, memorization, vocabulary, best answer, original sentences, and the like, with some translation of short English sentences into the foreign language. Such translation is a means, not an end, and should be limited in quantity and complexity.
3. Familiar vocabulary should be employed in introducing a new principle of grammar. Likewise, new grammatical phenomena should be related to those previously learned, whenever feasible.
4. Oral grammatical exercises should precede written exercises. In this way, mistakes in writing will be reduced to a minimum.
5. Learning of paradigms and rules should be subordinated to functional, living grammar exercises. It is the function of the teacher to create situations in which the form to be learned becomes a language activity on the part of the pupil.

Too many opportunities for use of the newly learned construction cannot be provided, since an abundance of natural situations is required in which to establish a language habit. The memorizing of the rule and the understanding of the grammatical point are not sufficient. *Fixation comes only through practice in the appropriate situation.*

The paradigm, for instance, is a concentration of forms in schematic arrangement. It is easily memorized but does not carry over readily to connected discourse. A more natural situation is approximated if the conjugation or declension is given in an entire sentence.

As pointed out previously, the naturalness or verisimilitude of the situation has a great deal to do with pleasant and effective learning. In using the textbook, the teacher should not feel compelled to have the pupils run through all the exercises in a given lesson or all the sentences in an exercise. The good teacher shows his skill by choosing only those sentences which best serve the purpose of the lesson. Stilted and artificial exercises should be avoided.

Whenever possible *the personal element should be introduced.* Where this is not possible because of the character of the topic or the limited vocabulary, the drill can be based on the reading material. This will permit the pupil to devote his entire attention to the form and will save him the additional struggle with the thought.

Everything should be done to make the use of the language perfectly natural and to simplify the procedure. New vocabulary should not be introduced together with a new point in grammar; explanations and instructions should usually be given in the vernacular. It is always well to accompany the rule with a model sentence. Often a clever mnemonic device is very helpful.

Structures To Be Taught During the First Two Years: French

The following list of grammatical points to be taught during the first two years of French is taken from *Foreign Language Revision Program for Secondary Schools: French,* Levels I and II, Curriculum Bulletin No. 2a, and is reprinted by permission of the Board of Education, City of New York.

Level I: Scope and Sequence. The structures listed in Levels I and II are to be taught for mastery within the limits indicated. The model sentences and phrases are illustrations of the applications intended. This does not preclude the occurrence in a particular level of structures other than those listed here. Such other structures, however, are not to be drilled for mastery but are to be treated as vocabulary items. Following this principle, the teacher may make use of whatever vocabulary and patterns are natural in a particular dialogue, limiting intensive drill only to the items that appear in this list.

Grammar Topics (Structures)

Level I: First Half
1. Articles
    a. Definite
    b. Indefinite
    c. Contraction with *à*
    d. Contraction with *de*
    e. Use of *de* to show possession
2. Nouns
    a. Gender and number
    b. Formation of regular plural

3. Pronouns
   Subject pronouns including *ce*
4. Adjectives
   a. Agreement and position; formation of regular feminine
   b. Possessive
5. Negatives
   Ne . . . pas
6. Verb structures
   a. Present tense of first conjugation; affirmative, negative, interrogative; use of *est-ce que*
   b. Present tense of the following irregular verbs: *avoir, être, aller, faire, dire*
   c. Use of *voici, voilà, il y a*
   d. Common idioms with *avoir, être, faire*
   e. Reflexive verbs in present tense: *s'asseoir, s'appeler, se lever,* and in affirmative commands as needed
   f. Imperative forms as needed
7. Numerals
   a. Cardinals: 1 to 100
   b. Simple arithmetical expressions
8. Time expressions
   a. Telling time
   b. Days, months, and seasons
   c. Dates; ages

Level I: Second Half
1. Articles
   a. Partitive: simple affirmative, simple negative
   b. With parts of body; clothing
   c. With parts of the day
   d. Ommission with *cent, mille*
2. Nouns
   a. Irregular plurals, including nouns ending in *-al, -eau, -s, -x, -z,* as they occur
3. Pronouns
   a. Single direct and indirect objects, including *en*
   b. Interrogative: *qui, que, qu'est-ce que*
   c. Demonstrative: *ceci, cela, ça*
   d. Disjunctive: with possessive adjective (mon livre à moi), with être (ce livre est à moi), with objects of prepositions, with compound subjects, as they occur
4. Adjectives
   a. Irregular feminines, including adjectives ending in *-e, -f, -x, -en, -on, -er, -el, -et,* and others as they occur; isolated irreg-

ular forms to be presented first as vocabulary items, for example, the feminine of *blanc, long, gros, sec, frais*
   b. Interrogative: *quel,* and so on
   c. Demonstrative: *ce, cet, cette, ces,* with and without *-ci* and *-là*
   d. Comparison: regular, some irregular (*bon, mauvais*)
5. Adverbs
   a. Those frequently used as vocabulary, for example, *bien, mal, seulement, vite*
   b. Regular comparisons
   c. Use of *donc* with imperatives
6. Negatives
   Ne . . . jamais
7. Verb structures
   a. Present tense of the three regular conjugations (all four forms—affirmative, negative, interrogative, interrogative-negative)
   b. Present tense (all four forms) of the following irregular verbs: *lire, écrire, voir, mettre, vouloir, venir (revenir, devenir), prendre (comprendre, apprendre), sortir, partir, boire, ouvrir*
   c. Compound past (passé composé) of the three regular conjugations and of the irregular verbs studied in Level I, first and second half
   d. Agreement of the past particple with *être* verbs: *aller, arriver, entrer, partir, sortir, rester, tomber, venir, monter, descendre*
   e. Orthographical changing verbs as needed
   f. *Pour* plus infinitive; *aller* (present) plus infinitive; *vouloir* (present and conditional of courtesy) plus infinitive

Level II: Scope and Sequence. The following outline of grammar topics for Level II is predicated on the assumption that all the topics and skills included in "Grammar Topics" (Structures) in Level I have been covered and tested for mastery. A thoroughgoing and well-planned review of Level I is essential as a foundation for further learning.

Grammar Topics (Structures)

Level II: First Half
   1. Adjectives
      a. Ending in *eux, ien, er, if*

    b. Agreement and position

2. Pronouns
    a. Personal
        1) two object pronouns
        2) simple use of *y*
        3) *y* or *en* in combination with other object pronouns
        4) disjunctive
    b. Interrogative
      qui, que, quoi, qu'est-ce qui, qu'est-ce que
    c. Relative
      qui, que

3. Adverbs
    a. Formation (regular)
    b. Position
    c. Irregular comparison

4. Negatives
    ne . . . plus; ne . . . rien; ne . . . personne; ne . . . que

5. Verbs
    a. Irregular: *tenir, dormir, connaître, falloir*
    b. Review present tense and compound past of all verbs previously taught.
    c. Imperfect and future tense of regular and irregular verbs listed for Level I and Level III, first half
    d. Reflexive verbs in all tenses listed above for the following: *se lever, se laver, s'habiller, se coucher, se reposer, s'endormir, se trouver, se dépêcher, s'approcher, se brosser*
    e. Formation and translation of the three forms of the imperative
    f. Idiomatic expressions with *faire* and *penser*

Level II: Second Half

1. Pronouns
    a. Demonstrative: *celui, celle,* etc.; with and without *-ci* and *-là*
    b. Possessive
    c. Relative: *ce qui, ce que, lequel, dont, où*
    d. Indefinite: *quelqu'un, personne, rien, quelque chose, on*
    e. Interrogative: *lequel* and its combinations

2. Prepositions
    Use of *à, en, dans, de* with commonplace names

3. Verbs
    a. Irregular: *croire, devoir, rire, courir, mourir, se souvenir*
    b. Verbs requiring spelling changes in certain tenses: *manger, commencer, envoyer, appeler, jeter, lever, mener, espérer*
    c. Tenses

1) for active use: present, imperfect, future, compound past
2) for limited use (as needed in conversation or in reading comprehension—without intensive or exhaustive drill): simple past, pluperfect, conditional and conditional past

d. Conditional sentences: the use of the future and conditional tense
e. The implied future after *quand, lorsque, dès que* and *aussitôt que*
f. Tenses required with *depuis* and *depuis quand*
g. Idiomatic expressions with *avoir* and *venir*

Structures To Be Taught During the First Two Years: Spanish

The structures listed in Levels I and II are to be taught for mastery within the limits indicated. The model sentences and phrases are illustrations of the applications intended. This does not preclude the occurrence in a particular level of structures other than those listed here. Such other structures, however, are not to be drilled for mastery but they are to be treated as vocabulary items. Following this principle, the teacher may make use of whatever vocabulary and patterns are natural in a particular dialogue, limiting intensive drill only to the items that appear in this list.

Grammar Topics (Structures)

Level I: First Half
1. Articles
   a. Definite
   b. Indefinite
   c. Contractions with *a* and *de*
   d. Use with titles and classifying nouns (limited to constructions such as *el señor, la señora, la señorita, la avenida, la calle*
   e. Use with languages (include omission after *hablar*)
   f. Omission with nouns of nationality and profession
2. Numbers
   a. Cardinals: 1 to 100; ordinals: as needed
   b. Common arithmetical expressions

3. Nouns
   a. Number
   b. Gender
   c. Use of *de* for possession
   d. Use of personal *a*
4. Pronouns
   a. Subject. For "you" in the plural, use *Vds*. Delay the use of *vosotros* until it is needed in reading
   b. Interrogative: *quién (es), qué, a quién (es), de quién (es), cuál (es)* with *ser, cuánto*
5. Adjectives
   a. Number and gender
   b. Simple agreement
   c. Position
   d. Common limiting adjectives such as *otro, mucho, poco, mismo, todo, bastante, demasiado*
   e. Common descriptive adjectives
   f. Exclamatory and interrogative *que* (¡Qué bonito! ¡Qué día hermoso! ¿Qué hora es?)
   g. Interrogative: *¿cuánto?*
6. Adverbs
   a. Common adverbs as vocabulary
   b. Interrogatives such as *cómo, cuándo, dónde, por qué, para qué*
7. Negatives
   Placement of *no*
8. Verb structures
   a. Present tense of regular verbs of the three conjugations and of the following irregular verbs: *decir, estar, ir, ser, tener, ver*
   b. Formation of questions (including negative-interrogative)
   c. Tag questions: *¿verdad? ¿no es verdad? ¿no?*
   d. Polite commands: familiar command, singular, as needed
   e. Idioms with *tener* and *hacer*, such as *tener . . . años (hambre, sed, frío, calor, sueño); hace frío (calor, viento, sol, buen tiempo, mal tiempo)*
   f. *Hay*
9. Time expressions
   a. Telling time
   b. Days, months, seasons
   c. Age; dates
Level I: Second Half

1. Numbers
    Cardinals: 101 to 1000; ordinals: 1st to 10th
2. Pronouns
    a. Single direct object (the use of *lo* as direct object for "him" instead of *le* is recommended for beginning students)
    b. Single indirect object
    c. Position of object pronoun with verb forms studied
    d. Prepositional (with *con, para, de*)
3. Adjectives
    a. Possessives
    b. Demonstratives
    c. Short forms of *bueno, malo, primero, tercero, ciento, uno*
4. Negatives
    Nada, nadie, nunca
5. Verb structures
    a. Present tense of the following irregular verbs: *caer, conocer, dar, hacer, oír, poder, poner, querer, saber, salir, traer, venir*
    b. Preterite of regular verbs, and of the following irregular verbs: *dar, decir, estar, hacer, ir, oír, poner, ser, tener, traer, venir*
    c. Principal uses of *ser* and *estar: ser* with predicate noun and possession; *estar* with location and health; both with predicate adjective
    d. Complementary infinitive (with *poder, desear, querer, necesitar, deber, saber, gustar*)
    e. *Ir a* to express near future (Voy a comer a las dos.)
    f. *Tener que* plus infinitive
    g. *Para* plus infinitive (Trabaja para ganar dinero.)
    h. *Gustar*
    i. *Había* (past of *hay*)

Level II: Scope and Sequence

Grammar Topics (Structures)

Level II: First Half
1. Articles
    a. Plural of indefinites *(unos, unas)*
    b. Masculine article with nouns ending in *-ma, -pa, -ta* (el programa, el mapa, el artista)
    c. Omission with languages after *en* and *de*
    d. Omission after *ser* with days (Es lunes)

e. Use with time expressions (el año pasado, la semana próxima)

f. Use with common geographical terms as needed (el Perú, la Argentina, los Estado Unidos)

g. Use with nouns of weight and measure (dos pesos la libra, or la docena)

2. Pronouns

a. Possessive: *el mío, el nuestro, el tuyo, el suyo,* and so on; *el de Vd.,* and so on; *el de mi hermano,* and so on; omit *el suyo de Vd.,* and so on

b. Prepositional: after common prepositions; with object pronouns for clarification and emphasis (le escriben a él, me habló a mí)

3. Adjectives

a. Possessives *(mío, tuyo, suyo,* and so on) after *ser* and in expressions like un amigo mío

b. Short forms of *grande, alguno, ninguno, santo*

4. Comparisons

a. Comparisons of inequality and equality: *más rico que; más libros que Vd.; más que Vd.; más de tres;* also with *menos, mejor, peor, mayor, menor, más grande, más pequeño; tan bueno como; tanto dinero como; tanto como*

b. Superlative: María es la muchacha mas bonita de la clase. María es la más bonita de la clase. María es la más bonita. María es la más bonita de las dos.

5. Adverbs

Formation with *-mente;* comparison (más despacio que, tan fácilmente como)

6. Negatives

no . . . tampoco; ni (yo) tampoco

7. Verb structures

a. Present progressive of verbs studied

b. Imperfect, including irregulars *(ser, ir, ver)*

c. Preterite of *poder, querer, saber; caer, creer, leer*

d. Imperfect vs. preterite

e. Direct commands *(Vd., Vds., tú),* and indirect command (first plural)

f. Reflexive verbs in tenses studied *(levantarse, desayunarse, llamarse, quedarse,* and so on); also, *quitarse (el abrigo), lavarse (las manos), ponerse (el sombrero);* and *deseo levantarme, podemos levantarnos, debes lavarte las manos, para sentarme necesito una silla*

g. Reflexive used for passive: *se habla (español), se venden (zapatos);* and *se dice, se sabe, se cree;* also, *Se cree que es rico. No se dice esto*

h. Idiomatic use of *hace* plus present tense (Hace una hora que estoy aquí); and *hace* plus preterite for "ago" (Vino hace una semana.)

i. Radical-changing verbs in tenses studied: *cerrar, pensar, almorzar, recordar, jugar, perder, volver, entender, sentir, dormir, pedir, servir, vestirse*

j. Idioms with *tener* and *hacer*

Level II: Second Half

1. Pronouns
   a. Demonstratives
   b. Double objects; position with verbs learned
   c. Redundant use of indirect object (Pregúntele a Juan)
   d. Relatives: *que* for that, which, who, whom; *quien(es)* after a preposition

2. Prepositions

   Distinctive uses of *por* and *para: para* for purpose, destination and time (Estudian para aprender. Salieron para Méjico. Este libro es para mí. Prepárelo para el lunes.); *por* for through, by (agent), for the sake of, exchange, and with simple time expressions (Caminaba por las calles. Es un libro escrito por Cervantes. Lo hago por mi mamá. Pagó dos pesos por el libro. Estudian por la tarde.)

3. Verb structures
   a. Present perfect tense and future tense, but not an exhaustive treatment
   b. Present with future meaning (Te lo doy mañana. Lo hago la semana que viene.)
   c. Orthographical-changing verbs in *-car, -gar, -zar* in tenses studied: *buscar, sacar, tocar; pagar, llegar, jugar; comenzar, empezar, almorzar*
   d. *al* plus infinitive
   e. *hay que* plus infinitive
   f. Infinitive after prepositions *(después de comer, sin hablar,* etc.)
   g. Common verbs requiring *a* and *de* before infinitive *(empezar, tratar,* etc.)
   h. Common uses of *saber* and *conocer:* Saben la lección. Saben que el trabaja. Yo sé bailar, Conozco a este señor. ¿Conoce Vd. a Madrid?

Structures To Be Taught During the First Two Years: Italian

Level I: First Half
1. Articles
    a. Definite
    b. Indefinite
    c. Articles used before nouns beginning with *s* impure or *z* such as *lo studente, lo sbaglio, lo zio, lo zucchero,* etc.
    d. Use of *di* to show possession
2. Nouns
    a. Gender of nouns: ending in *o, a, e* (for those ending in *e* both masculine and feminine, such as *il padre, la madre, il pane, la classe, la lezione*)
    b. Plural of nouns
3. Adjectives
    a. Classes: ending in *o* and *e*
    b. Agreement and position
4. Pronouns
    a. Subject: uses of *tu, Lei, voi, Loro*
    b. Object: *lo, li, la, le*
5. Verbs
    a. Present of *avere* and *essere*
    b. Infinitive and present tense of the three regular conjugations; affirmative, negative, interrogative, negative-interrogative
    c. Required verbs: *trovare, perdere, finire* (isco verbs), *sentire* (non-isco verbs)
6. Numerals
    a. Cardinal: 1 to 100
    b. Simple arithmetical expressions
7. Time
    a. Telling time
    b. Days; months; seasons
    c. Age and dates
Level I: Second Half
1. Articles
    Contractions of the definite article with the prepositions *a, con, da, di, in, per,* and *su*
2. Nouns
    These common irregular plurals: *l'uovo–le uova; il dito–le dita; la mano–le mani*

3. Adjectives
   a. Agreement of adjectives with nouns of mixed genders
   b. Possessive
4. Numerals
   a. Cardinal: 101 to a million
   b. Ordinal: 1 to 20
5. Verbs
   a. Future of *avere* and *essere*
   b. Present perfect *(passato prossimo)* of the three regular conjugations with *avere* and the following with *essere: andare, arrivare, entrare, essere, partire, uscire, venire*
   c. Present of the following verbs: *dare, fare, sapere, dire (chiamarsi, alzarsi, sedersi,* as needed)

Level II: First Half
1. Adjectives
   a. Possessive: distinction among *il tuo, il Suo, il vostro,* and *il Loro;* distinction between *il suo* and *il Suo; il loro* and *il Loro*
   b. Interrogative: forms and uses of *quale, quanto*
   c. Forms of *poco* and *molto*
2. Pronouns
   a. Possessive
   b. Interrogative: *chi, che (cosa)*
   c. Direct and indirect object
   d. Demonstrative: *questo, quello*
3. Verbs
   a. Present perfect *(passato remoto)* of the verbs: *aprire, chiudere, dare, dire, fare, leggere, mettere, rispondere, prendere, scendere, escrivere*
   b. Imperfect of *essere, avere,* and the three regular conjugations
   c. Future of irregular verbs: *essere, avere, andare, venire*
   d. Future of verbs ending in *-care, -gare, -ciare, -giare; dimenticare, pagare, incominciare, mangiare*
   e. Verbs forming compound tenses with *essere*
   f. Preterite *(passato remoto)* of regular verbs and *andare, venire, salire, scendere*

Level II: Second Half
1. Nouns
   a. Plurals of nouns ending in *-co, -go, -cia, -gia,* and *-ista*
   b. Masculine nouns ending in *-o* having feminine plural ending in *a: il braccio, le braccia; il labbro, le labbra; il muro, le mura; il lenzuolo, le lenzuola.*

112

2. Adjectives
   a. Plural of adjectives ending in -co and -go; bianco, bianchi; lungo, lunghi; ricco, ricchi
   b. Demonstrative: questo, quello
   c. Comparison of regular adjectives
3. Pronouns
   a. Relative: che, il quale, cui, il cui, colui che, colei che, quello che
   b. Interrogative
   c. Demonstrative
   d. Pronoun objects with imperative: Mi dia il libro! Datemi la penna!
4. Verbs
   a. Passato remoto of irregular verbs: essere, avere, fare, chiudere, dare, dire, leggere, mettere, sapere, scrivere
   b. Imperative mood
      1) The regular conjugations
      2) Affirmative and negative forms of irregular verbs: essere, avere, andare, dare, dire, fare, stare
      3) Reflexive verbs: lavarsi, vestiri, sedersi, alzarsi, chiamarsi

Structures To Be Taught During the First Two Years: German

Level I: First Half
1. Article-noun combinations
   a. Definite article, all cases, genitive and plurals as they occur
   b. Indefinite article, all cases
2. Pronoun-verb combinations
   a. Singular and plural
   b. Polite forms of address (to be emphasized)
   c. Familiar forms
   d. Nonpersonal uses in the third person: er, sie, es, for masculine, feminine, and neuter nouns respectively
3. Adjectives
   a. Uninflected adjectives: positives and a few simple comparatives such as schlecht–schlechter, klein–kleiner, gut–besser, gross–grösser
   b. Possessive adjectives in noun combinations: Ich habe mein Buch. Er hat sein Buch. Sie hat ihr Buch.

113

4. Verbs
   a. Weak verbs, present tense. Verbs with connecting *e*. All verbs with omitted *s*-sound, as listed in the vocabulary list
   b. Imperatives; polite forms to be used at all times
   c. Reflexives, such as *sich setzen, sich waschen, sich kämmen, sich anziehen;* present tense only
   d. Verbs of high frequency, such as *geben–nehmen, kommen–gehen, stehen–sitzen, sprechen–lesen, schreiben, sein*
5. Word order
   a. Normal; initially and after coordinating conjunctions
   b. Inverted; interrogative, and when words other than subject begin the sentence
   c. Position of the negative
6. Prepositions
   a. Governing the dative case
   b. Governing the accusative case
   c. Governing either dative or accusative
   d. Contracted forms: *am, aufs, beim, im, ins, zum, zur,* etc.

Level I: Second Half
1. Article-noun combinations
   a. Definite and indefinite
   b. Plural, all cases
   c. Weak nouns: *Knabe, Junge, Herr, Mensch, Student*
2. Adjectives
   a. Possessive; plural, all cases; genitive plural as it occurs
   b. Demonstrative: *dieser; jener* as it occurs
   c. *Der*-words: *jeder, welcher; manche, solche,* in plurals
   d. Uninflected adjectives
   e. Inflected adjectives as they occur in fixed phrases such as *Guten Morgen, Guten Tag, Schönen Gruss, Guten Appetit*
   f. Equal and unequal comparisons to be used with adjectives in the vocabulary list according to the following pattern: *(nicht) so . . . wie; (nicht) . . . -er als*
3. Pronouns
   a. Personal pronouns, except genitives
   b. *Der*-words used as pronouns: *dieser, welcher, jeder, jener*
4. Verbs
   a. Tenses: present, simple past, compound past, and future
   b. Compound past with *sein*
   c. Modal auxiliaries, present tense; basic meanings only
   d. Other modal forms as they occur; for example, *ich möchte (essen)*
   e. Imperatives; polite forms to be used at all times

f. Reflexives, such as *sich anziehen, sich kämmen, sich setzen, sich waschen*

g. Strong verbs of high frequency, such as *bleiben, brechen, essen, fallen, finden, gehen, halten, helfen, kommen, laufen, lesen, liegen, nehmen, schlafen, schlagen, schliessen, schreiben, schreien, sein, singen, sitzen, sprechen, stehen, tragen, treffen, treten, trinken, tun, ziehen, werden*

5. Prepositions

Da- and *wo-* compounds

6. Word order

  a. Sequence of adverbs: time, manner, place

  b. Review of normal and inverted word order, initially and after coordinating conjunctions

Level II: First Half

1. Article-noun combinations

  a. Genitive plural

  b. Genitive of weak nouns

  c. Nouns formed from adjectives, such as *jung–der Junge; alt–der Alte, die Alte; warm–die Wärme; kalt–die Kälte*

  d. Nouns formed from infinitives, such as *das Essen, das Trinken*

  e. Neuter collectives, such as *das Gebirge, das Geschrei*

  f. Gender determined by affixes, such as *-ei, -ie, -heit, -in, -keit, -schaft, -ung*

  g. Omission of articles: (1) before names of substances; (2) before unmodified nouns of nationality and profession after the auxiliary *sein*

2. Verbs

  a. All tenses except the future perfect

  b. Verbs with inseparable prefixes, such as *bekommen, empfangen, erhalten, gefallen, hören, vergessen, verlieren, versprechen, zerbrechen*

  c. Verbs with separable prefixes, such as *aufstehen, sich hinlegen, einschlafen, sich niedersetzen, hingehen, herkommen, hineingehen, herauskommen*

  d. Mixed verbs, such as *brennen, kennen, bringen, denken, nennen, rennen, wissen, wenden*

  e. Verbs governing the dative, such as *antworten, danken, dienen, helfen, gefallen*

  f. Verbs used in impersonal expressions, such as *es regnet, es schneit, es hagelt, es blitzt, es donnert, es klingelt*

  g. Modal auxiliaries in the present and simple past tenses in their most common meanings

h. Strong verbs of high frequency, such as *befehlen, beginnen, bekommen, binden, bitten, fangen, fliegen, fliehen, fliessen, geschehen, gewinnen, greifen, heissen, leiden, reissen, reiten, rufen, scheinen, schiessen, schneiden, schreien, schreiten, springen, steigen, sterben, stossen, vergessen, verlieren, wachsen, waschen, werfen*

3. Adjective-noun combinations
   a. Strong declension of adjectives
   b. Weak declension of adjectives, nominative and accusative only

4. Word order
   a. After subordinating conjunctions, such as *bevor (ehe), dass, weil (da), nachdem, obgleich*

5. Numerals
   a. Cardinal: 1 to 1000
   b. Fractions, such as *ein halb, anderthalb, zweieinhalb, dreieinhalb, die Hälfte, ein Drittel, ein Viertel*
   c. Multiplication and division
   d. Ordinal: 1 to 100, nominative and accusative only

Level II: Second Half

1. Article-noun combinations
   a. Plurals of high-frequency nouns, such as *Buch, Kind, Haus, Tür, Vater, Mutter, Tochter, Sohn, Hand, Fuss, Freund, Freundin, Bleistift, Feder, Schule*
   b. Gender of compound nouns

2. Pronoun-verb combinations
   a. Present perfect tense, strong and weak verbs
   b. Past participles of strong and weak verbs
   c. Past tenses of *sein, haben, werden, können, müssen, wollen*
   d. Strong verbs of high frequency such as *beissen, biegen, bieten, blasen, dringen, gelingen, gelten, geniessen, giessen, graben, klingen, kriechen, laden, leihen, messen, schelten, schieben, schweigen, sinken, spinnen, stechen, stehen, streiten, treiben, verbergen, verderben, verzeihen, werfen, wissen, zwingen*
   e. High-frequency reflexive verbs, such as *sich erkälten, sich kämmen, sich schämen, sich befinden, sich waschen*

3. Pronouns
   a. Relative pronouns, *der, welcher*
   b. *Wo-* compounds as relative pronouns
   c. Review of personal pronouns as objects

4. Prepositions

a. Review of "doubtful" prepositions: *an, auf, hinter, hin, neben, über, unter, vor, zwischen*

b. Prepositional compounds with *da-* and *wo-*

c. Prepositions as separable prefixes, including colloquial forms, *'rein, 'raus, 'rauf, 'runter*

5. Word order

a. After *als, bis, damit, indem, ob, wenn, während*

b. Use of *als, wenn, wann*

c. Interrogatives as subordinating conjunctions: *wann, wo wie, warum, was*

6. Numerals

a. Cardinals: after 1000

b. Review of the four arithmetical operations

Problems

1. In two parallel columns compare the learning of a child acquiring his mother tongue with a student learning a foreign language in school.

2. Plan a lesson with drills to teach a given structure.

3. Make a list of grammatical terms that might be considered part of the common learnings during the first year of language study.

4. Show how a given structure can be taught by analogy with a grammatical point previously learned.

5. Prepare a list of twenty-five sentences to illustrate structures of the first half of the first level.

VIII ' The Lesson

Essential Elements. The basic elements in any formal learning situation are the teacher, the pupil, and the lesson. The latter is the unit of learning through which specific skills and knowledges are practiced and acquired. The success of the lesson depends upon the teacher's skill in the selection of the material, in the methods employed, in providing suitable activities, and in getting the pupils to put forth their greatest effort. To attain maximum effectiveness, the lesson must be planned.

Importance of the Plan. The importance of the lesson plan cannot be overstated. It is as essential for the teacher as the blueprint is for the builder. Briefly, it is a statement of the objectives to be realized and the means by which they are to be attained, as the result of activities engaged in by the pupils. Lesson planning is really anticipatory teaching, for the learning situation is lived through, mentally, in advance.

Unless the teacher is teaching a lesson that he has taught repeatedly and has practically memorized, he should write out his plan. Even then, a brief outline is advisable. The comprehensiveness of the written plan will depend upon the nature of the lesson, the teacher's familiarity with the subject, and the length and breadth of his experience. It is best for the beginner to make a rather detailed outline. The effectiveness of even the experienced teacher is strengthened if he makes at least a few brief notations of the general scheme to be followed.

Advantages of the Lesson Plan. As stated above, when the teacher is rather inexperienced, his plan should be comprehensive. He should even write out the questions he is going to ask and list precisely what new words and verb forms he plans to practice. The written plan prevents overloading as well as omissions.

The advantages of the plan, then, are almost obvious. A good lesson plan

1. Sets up specific aims to be attained
2. Delimits the material to be taught
3. Indicates the most economical procedures
4. Relates each lesson to what precedes and what follows
5. Makes for orderly progress.

Characteristics of a Good Plan. As stated above, a given lesson may require a detailed plan; for another lesson a brief outline will suffice. In any case, the plan should state the aim (immediate and ultimate), specify the means used (questions, board work, textbook, oral activities, and so on), indicate the various steps of the lesson, and provide for an assignment for the next lesson.

The plan itself should

1. Be brief but with sufficient detail to be precise
2. Assign a definite number of minutes for each activity
3. Indicate exactly what words, facts, items are to be learned
4. Provide for all four phases of language learning
5. Make use of a variety of classroom activities.

The Scheme of the Plan. Every subject can be taught in a number of different ways; there is no one best procedure. The skillful teacher, however, will plan the lesson with due consideration of the intelligence level of the class, the ethnic and cultural background of the pupils, the type of textbook used, and the illustrative materials available. Most important of all is the nature of the topic itself.

For instance, a Spanish lesson on shopping for articles of clothing which takes place in a metropolitan high school class composed mainly of Puerto Rican children whose English is not quite up to par will be quite different from a lesson on the same topic presented to a high school class in a better residential area, where the children are stock Americans, living in comfortable homes and planning to go to college.

Despite the fact that it goes back to the last century, the Herbartian scheme of five steps is still an extremely useful pattern for planning a lesson. It can be applied to any subject in the curriculum and to any type of lesson.

It consists basically of the five following categories: (I) Motivation, (II) Presentation, (III) Explanation, (IV) Application, and (V) Summarization (or Evaluation). The extent and importance of these groupings will vary according to the type of lesson taught. In a grammar lesson Explanation will assume major importance; in a reading lesson Application will be stressed.

Aim. The aim should always be stated at the beginning of the lesson; it may even be written on the blackboard. Usually, there are a number of objectives. For example, the reading selection is to be read, a new grammar point is to be taught, some previous items may be reviewed. Also, every lesson should have a cultural reference or two.

Outlining the Lesson Plan. The first consideration is the amount of subject matter to be taught. It should fit in the allotted time. Next, some thought should be given to motivation. With a little skill this can be done through the introductory conversation. The body of the lesson consists, of course, of the presentation, explanation, and application. Provision should be made for a variety of exercises; many otherwise good lessons are weak in that they do not provide for sufficient practice. The summary, or evaluation, can be made by means of oral questions or a brief written quiz. Occasionally, the lesson should end with a song.

Questioning

The importance of the question in learning, formally and incidentally, cannot be overestimated. The question is among the very first stimuli that touch the mental life of the child. In fact, it is that which starts mental activity on his part.

The effectiveness of instruction is measured largely by the nature of the questions that the teacher asks and the care with which he frames them. The question serves a number of functions. It may be employed to test pupil achievement, stimulate interest, provide drill, develop the habit of evaluation, stimulate thought, or interpret an experience correctly. Or, from the disciplinary point of view, it may be used by the teacher to secure individual or class attention.

Questions may be classified as to function or mental process. The former category includes drill, analysis, and comparison; the latter stresses memory, imagination, and thinking.

A good question should

1. Be clearly and concisely stated
2. Require thought
3. Be adapted to the ability of the learner
4. Require an extended response
5. Involve single ideas
6. Reflect a definite purpose on the part of the teacher.

Among the general techniques of questioning it is stated that the form of the question should not suggest the answer. This, however, does not apply to foreign languages, where the teacher, in the earlier stages, frames the question so that the student does repeat most of it in his answer.

Teacher Technique in Questioning

The teacher should always address a question to the class before designating a given pupil to respond. The reasons for this are:

1. General attention is secured.
2. All are given an opportunity to formulate a tentative answer.
3. The critical attention of the entire class is focused on the answer given.

Questions should be distributed as evenly as possible. It is unfair to call on the bright and eager student continually.

Sufficient time should be allowed the student for the formulation of his answer.

A general rule that is given all beginning teachers is: Do not repeat the question and do not repeat the pupil's answer. In the teaching of foreign languages this does not apply. In comprehension and dictation exercises there is always repetition; in fact, in dictation, the custom is to read the selection three times. It is, therefore, not wrong to ask the same question twice.

The same may be said about repeating the pupil's answer. The pupil's answer should not be repeated by the teacher mechanically, habitually, but only for emphasis, for better pronunciation.

Devices

A method of teaching is a well-defined procedure for an entire subject, with specific aims based on given psychological and philosophical principles. One may name the "direct" method, the "phonetic" method, the "natural" method, the "reading" method, and so on.

A device, on the other hand, is a trick of method that contains certain elements of surprise and variety. The skillful teacher will use devices generously, for they are bound to maintain interest, increase enjoyment, and provide pleasurable practice.

Devices may be classified in various ways:

A. According to general purpose
   1. Practice and drill
   2. To teach a given point (colors, numbers, classroom objects)
   3. To arouse interest
   4. To afford enjoyment
   5. For administrative and routine purposes, etc.
B. According to the different phases of language teaching
   1. Vocabulary building
   2. Grammar
   3. Reading, etc.
C. According to type of classroom activity
   1. Oral activities
   2. Written activities
   3. Board work
   4. Reading, etc.
D. According to type of device
   1. Illustrative
   2. Games, etc.

Useful Devices. Among the many devices that may be used in the classroom are the following:

A. For oral activities
 1. Calling on pupils in unexpected order
 2. Calling upon them in regular sequence
 3. Asking questions
 4. Asking questions with a personal reference
 5. The "chain method" (each pupil asks his neighbor a question in succession)
 6. Matches: half the class against the other half, or boys vs. girls, to test vocabulary, idioms, verbs
 7. Flash cards
 8. Pronunciation charts (particularly important in French)
 9. Reciting memorized proverbs
 10. Concert or chorus recitation (should not be overdone)
 11. Carrying out orders: individual pupil or entire class (commands given by teacher or by a pupil)
 12. Gouin series (pupil describes the action while performing it)
 13. Dramatization
 14. Dialogue
 15. Pupil acts as teacher
 16. Use of objects, pictures, clock dial
 17. Oral composition
B. Administrative and routine
 1. Calling on pupils in order
 2. Use of flash cards
 3. Board slips
 4. Facing class, coming to front, etc.
C. Devices in learning
 1. Repeating answer
 2. Writing a word five times
 3. Covering a column with a slip of paper
 4. Not looking at the board
 5. Erasing portions of an exercise, etc.
D. Illustrative devices
 1. Clock dial
 2. Drawing on the blackboard
 3. Pictures, charts, and maps
 4. Pointing out pupils (for differences in size, height, etc.)
 5. Using objects and articles
 6. Motions and actions (by teacher, by pupils)
E. In connection with board work

1. Board monitor
2. Changing tense or pronoun in sentence
3. Unscrambling a sentence (words given in wrong sequence)
4. Building up a sentence (by adding modifiers, relatives, etc.)
5. Writing answers to questions in sequence
6. An original sentence for each new word in the vocabulary
7. Cards or slips for board assignments
8. Drawing on board; labeling
9. Writing date on board at beginning of each lesson
10. Requiring given form for heading ("Je m'appelle _____.")

F. For written activities
1. Short test at beginning of period
2. Student keeps notebook: for vocabulary, for idioms
3. Word missed to be written five times by the pupil
4. New-type exercises: completion, multiple choice, insertion, matching
5. Translation: into the foreign language, into English

G. In reading
1. Reading aloud
2. Silent reading
3. Model reading by the teacher
4. Assigning parts to pupils
5. Writing questions on the board on given paragraph
6. Asking for synonyms, antonyms, related words, cognates
7. "Find the word that _____"
8. Filling in missing word on the board
9. Résumé in English; in the foreign language

H. Games
1. Guessing an object or person decided on
2. Buzz
3. Vocabulary, idiom, verb matches
4. Carrying out commands ("Simple Simon says _____")

Conduct of the Recitation

In the organization and conduct of a foreign language lesson there is always a wide range of possibilities. No two teachers will treat the same topic in the same way. There are, however, certain basic principles of pedagogy and laws of learning that should be observed if the lesson is to approach a maximum degree of effectiveness. For instance,

1. Every lesson should begin with a greeting in the foreign language and a brief conversation between teacher and pupils. Through this conversation the lesson may be motivated.
2. The foreign language should be used for all common classroom orders and for commendation or reproval.
3. Precision should characterize the individual pupil recitation.
4. Pupils should face the class when reciting.
5. There should be a variety of activities in every lesson, including board work, textbook reading, written work, oral activities, questions and answers, and some spontaneous, original conversation.
6. The assignment should grow out of the lesson.
7. Every activity, every exercise should be motivated.
8. The lesson should close with a summary or brief test.
9. If a few minutes are left, an appropriate song should be sung.
10. Current events and anniversaries should be brought into the lesson.

The Assignment. For the average teacher or pupil, "assignment" is simply a fancier term for "homework." Unfortunately the whole idea of outside preparation was frowned upon for a number of years, with some educational reformers demanding a complete abolition of homework. However, the pendulum has again swung in the opposite direction and it is generally recognized that home preparation on the part of the pupil is an essential part of the learning process. It is absolutely indispensable in the case of skill subjects. A pupil meets his piano teacher only once a week, but he has to practice the instrument five days in preparation for each lesson.

The assignment applies to that part of the lesson devoted to the clear recognition and acceptance by the pupil of the next unit of learning to take place and of the ways in which this learning may be achieved most effectively. In simpler language this means: (1) a given task is planned; (2) appropriate and effective means for accomplishing it are indicated; (3) the teacher assigns, the pupil freely accepts, the assignment; and (4) the pupil, we hope, will learn willingly through a self-imposed activity.

Actually, the homework assignment means studying. It is therefore of the utmost importance for the teacher to show the pupil how to attack the assignment and how to accomplish it successfully.

Characteristics of a Good Assignment. A homework assignment completely vitiates its purpose if it is merely busy work or a task imposed for no good reason. The pupils must be impressed with the need for it; they should have a feeling of satisfaction in doing it.

Among the characteristics of a good assignment the following stand out:

1. The task to be done is defined clearly and concisely. It will require a given amount of time.
2. The teacher checks to see that each pupil knows exactly what is required.
3. Special difficulties are anticipated and explained.
4. The assignment is carefully motivated so that the pupil's interest is aroused and he is eager to do it.
5. The new work is related to what has been learned.
6. Some provision is made for individual differences.

Differentiation of Assignments. A homework assignment may be differentiated in a number of ways: for the bright and for the slow, or for the gifted, the average, and the slow.

Another very interesting way of handling the assignment is on the basis of effort. The following distinctions are made:

1. The assignment for tomorrow will be exercises A and B on page 167.
2. Those who want extra credit may also do exercise C.
3. Those who think they need extra practice will do exercise D.
4. Those who are deeply interested will also do exercise E for the sheer joy of it, without credit.

Making the Assignment. The assignment may be given at the beginning or at the end of the period. If it grows out of the day's lesson, it may come in the middle of the period. If it is given at the end, it should be announced before the bell rings and not hastily while the students are dashing from the room. Common practice is to give the assignment at the beginning of the lesson.

A good way of doing it is as follows: While the class is entering the room, the teacher hands the assignment to a student who writes it neatly on the front board. It will be in the foreign language; the date is given. As soon as the class is seated, and has been greeted, the teacher will ask a student to read the assignment aloud. If there are any difficulties, a translation may be asked for. The teacher asks, "Are there any questions?" If there is something quite new or difficult in the assignment, the teacher will say, "Let us turn to page

_____ and try the first two sentences." The teacher should comment on the importance of the assignment and its value for the next lesson.

Homework During Prereading Phase

During the prereading phase no written assignments can be given; habits of listening attentively and pronouncing correctly are to be enforced. How is this to be done? The problem has not yet been solved satisfactorily.

In the ideal situation the pupils would be supplied with discs or tapes containing the material they have been practicing in the classroom. The use of tapes involves a certain amount of expense, and they may be lost or damaged. Furthermore, not all children have tape recorders at home. Perhaps in the future the tape recorder will be as common in the home as the phonograph or the television set.

If the school has a language laboratory, pupils can be assigned to practice outside class. The period should be limited to twenty minutes. Furthermore, at the beginning, careful supervision is highly advisable.

For practice in listening there are foreign language programs on radio and television. These will not link up directly with the lesson, but they will provide pupils with an opportunity to hear foreign voices, at normal speed, in typical situations.

Finally, if the members of the student's family know the foreign language taught in school, pupils can practice on their relatives.

If none of the above-mentioned opportunities exist, students can be asked to look up and bring in reports on such topics as the following:

1. Foreign language communities in the city
2. The importance and value of studying the foreign language
3. Foreign relations of the United States
4. Contributions of foreigners to the civilization of the United States
5. Foreign actors and actresses
6. Famous works of art, music, and literature
7. The relationship of the foreign language to English
8. Foreign expressions that have gone over into English.

The above topics will also be useful when the reading and writing stages have been reached.

There is absolutely no objection to the pupils' reading widely in English about the foreign country and the foreign people. In fact, it is recommended, since it will build up interest in the study of the language as well as provide a pleasurable activity.

As soon as the students are ready for it, reading in the foreign language should be assigned. In the beginning it will be confined to material already practiced orally in class. When the pupils have acquired a sufficient mastery of structures and they have a fair stock of vocabulary, new material can be assigned. The home reading will be largely extensive reading. The student should get accustomed to finding meanings by inference.

Written work should not be assigned until the audio-lingual basis has been firmly established. In the beginning, writing will be limited to copying what has been practiced orally. This involves reinforcing the structure patterns, and such copying may be considered "imitative" writing.

The pupil copies patterns and dialogues, labels pictures of objects and persons, and does substitution and transformation drills. This is a beginning; later more difficult forms are dealt with. Various types of exercises are done, for example, answering comprehension questions, using sentences as well as single words, based on reading selections. The written work gradually advances on the higher levels to composition and letter writing. Free composition comes on Levels V and VI.

The basic principles to be observed with reference to assignments are:

1. Homework should be based on what has been learned in class.
2. The home assignment should be an integral part of each lesson.
3. Homework should be checked and corrected.

Correction of Homework. Various practices are used in correcting homework. The commonest ones are:

1. The written homework is passed in at the beginning of the period. It may be collected by a monitor, who notes the names of the pupils who have not turned in any paper.
2. The teacher goes over and marks each paper. This is laborious, especially if he teaches five classes a day.

3. The teacher gives the sets of papers to a bright and reliable student who corrects them.
4. The teacher makes a spot check of a number of papers.
5. All of the corrected papers are returned to the pupils.

More economical and effective is the following procedure: Five or six pupils are asked to go to the blackboard and write out a portion of the homework. The rest of the class have their homework papers spread on their desks. The teacher circulates and inspects the work rapidly. As soon as the pupils at the board are finished, their exercises are inspected and checked for errors. (Since brighter pupils have been sent to the board, there are few or no mistakes.) The pupils at the seats compare their work with that on the board and make the necessary corrections. The teacher circulates and makes comments, noting the types of errors made. This procedure relieves the teacher of the great burden of personally correcting each paper and places the responsibility on the individual pupil.

Illustrative Lesson Plans

LESSON IN DIRECT OBJECT PRONOUNS
(Spanish)
(Normal class, eighth or ninth year; shortly before Christmas; 9:15–10:00 A.M.)

Aim
1. To teach Christmas vocabulary
2. To review articles of clothing
3. To teach direct object pronouns *lo, la, los, las*
4. To sing Christmas carol: "Noche de Paz."

I. Motivation 9:15–9:20
Greetings. Conversation: weather. *Nieva, la nieve.*
What season? What holiday? Christmas—*La Navidad* (*nacer*, nativity).
"Feliz Navidad" (on board).

II. Presentation 9:20–9:30
Mention shopping. Show articles of clothing (review). "¿Qué es esto?"
On board: *Camisa, blusa, corbota, medias, sombrero, pañuelo,* etc.
Pupil points and asks: "¿Qué es esto?" "Ahora, vamos a hacer compras.

129

Unas nuevas palabras: *comprar, vender, tienda, el precio, ¿Cuánto es? caro, barato, quisiera, tomo.*" (Oral practice on these.)

III. Explanation 9:30–9:40

Object pronouns on board: *lo, la, los, las*
Practice in sentences such as Lo tomo. Lo compro. Las vendo.

IV. Application 9:40–9:50

Oral exercises on object pronouns: (a) answering questions, (b) translation, (c) substitution. Meanwhile six pupils to board. (d) Dramatization: shopping scene, pupils enact at teacher's desk. "¿Qué quiere Vd.?" "Quisiera un . . . ." "Aquí tiene Vd. un . . . ." "¿Cuánto es?" ". . . pesos." "Es caro." ". . . más barato." "Lo tomo." "Bueno." "Gracias." "Adiós."

(If time permits) *Regalo.* "¿Qué regalo tiene Vd. para su madre, su padre, etc.?" On board: *pipa, juguetes, muñeca.*

V. Summarization 9:50–9:55

Oral practice. Brief sentences E–S, S–E. What have we learned?
Assignment: make Spanish Christmas card.

Song 9:55–10:00

Have words of "Noche de Paz" on blackboard. Read in breath groups.
Class sings, softly.
Dismiss with "Feliz Navidad."

LESSON IN DEMONSTRATIVE ADJECTIVES

(Spanish)

(Normal class, ninth year. Text: *El Camino Real*)

Aim

1. To teach singular of demonstrative adjectives
2. To present fourteen new words
3. To develop concept of the *plaza*.

I. Motivation

Greetings. Conversation: "¿Cómo está Vd.?" "¿Qué tiempo hace . . . aquí, en Méjico, en Sevilla, en Lima?" "Calor." "La plaza es el centro de la vida de la ciudad." "We will read about the plaza tomorrow." (Have pupil put new words on board.)

II. Presentation

1. The Plaza. Describe briefly; show pictures: (a) Lima—cathedral,

statue of Pizarro, his mummy, palace; (b) Cuzco—Indian statue, Compañía church, students.

2. New words: pronounce, discuss; seek cognates; use in sentences.

el agua	cada	la fuente
el árbol	aquí	la vida
el banco	la banda	cerca de
el joven	la música	entre
el criado	la criada	

III. *Explanation*

Demonstrative adjectives. Point to pupils. Get class to deduce forms and use. Have rule formulated. Put on board.

IV. *Application*

Do exercises in book (Ex. I, pp. 141–42) and on board. Assign Ex. II and III, p. 142. (Check.)

V. *Summarization*

1. Written quiz on vocabulary (10 items)
2. Oral: rule with reference to demonstrative adjectives
3. Song (words on board): "Me gustan todas." (Vary words: *esa, aquella rubia, ese, aquel rubio.*)

Problems and Questions for Discussion

1. Write out a plan for a lesson on indirect object pronouns. The class is of average ability; the textbook used is good. Thanksgiving is a few days off.

2. Prepare a plan for a lesson in which the parts of the body are taught. Bring in a dramatized dialogue in a doctor's office. Try to find a song that can be used for drill ("Alouette").

3. Plan a composition lesson in which each pupil uses a different picture as the basis of his exercise.

4. Prepare the plan of a lesson about a famous composer. Introduce pictures. Play a selection or two on the phonograph. Indicate how you would build up the appreciation of the music.

5. Write a set of plans for an entire week, indicating how each lesson is linked to the next one.

6. Prepare an assignment for a class, making four differentiations.

I X ʹ Audio-Visual Materials and Techniques[1]

The Scope. In the widest sense of the term, audio-visual techniques include everything used in teaching except the textbook. There is, first, the real experience of the child, which may appeal to all five senses. Then there is the contrived experience—models, objects, exhibits, pictures, charts, etc.—which is largely used in school. In this category might be included demonstrations in the classroom and trips outside of school.

In a more limited sense, however, we think of "audio-visual" as designating those devices, techniques, and materials which appeal directly to the ear and eye of the learner. The simpler ones, in every-day use in the classroom, consist of pictures, charts, diagrams, and maps. The more elaborate ones are the phonograph record, radio, the tape recorder, the motion picture, various types of films, and tele-

---

[1] This topic is treated in greater detail in the author's *Audio-Visual Techniques in Teaching Foreign Languages* (New York: New York University Press, 1960).

vision. Different combinations of the mechanical devices in one unit constitute the laboratory.

The Effectiveness of Audio-Visual Materials. Audio-visual methods and materials are, of course, used in every area of learning. A rather comprehensive discussion of the whole field is found in Edgar Dale's *Audio-Visual Methods of Teaching*, Revised Edition (New York: Holt, Rinehart and Winston, 1954).

Audio-visual techniques are effective in teaching because

1. They contribute to the efficiency, depth, and variety of learning.
2. They offer a close verisimilitude of experience which is stimulating.
3. They tend to hold the interest and attention of the learner.
4. By appealing to several senses they make learning more permanent.
5. Their esthetic character makes learning pleasant and enjoyable.

Flash Cards. One of the simplest visual devices that may be made up by any teacher is the flash card. It is particularly used in beginning classes, where it may be used for the teaching of pronunciation, of vocabulary, and of verb forms. Flash cards lend themselves well to rapid and lively reviews.

The cards should be clean pieces of cardboard or oaktag of uniform size. The legends should be neatly and plainly lettered in black ink, sufficiently large so that they may be read with ease from any part of the room.

Flash cards may be used to drill the following types of material:

1. Vocabulary. The English word appears on one side of the card, the foreign word on the other.
2. Articles and demonstratives. The noun appears with a blank to be filled in. (_____ craie; _____ pupitre, etc.)
3. Idioms. The noun, verb, or other key word is given. Or, the phrase is to be completed. (Weather expressions: frío, calor, sol, fresco, etc.; or yo _____ frío, el _____ calor, etc.)
4. Verbs. The infinitive is given.

Flash cards may also contain pictures or rather simple outline sketches. These may be used to drill case forms, as in German or Russian, or to test knowledge of idioms or proverbs.

The cards may be used in different ways. The usual procedure is for the teacher to stand in the front of the room and have the class recite, row-by-row. This may be varied by the teacher's calling on pupils at random and also by letting a pupil hold the cards. In drilling vocabulary the practice of giving the English word for the foreign word or vice versa should be varied by

1. Using the foreign word in a sentence
2. Using the foreign word in a question
3. Giving a synonym for the foreign word
4. Giving an antonym for the foreign word
5. Pronouncing the foreign word, using it in a sentence, and pointing out the object, if possible (*veste:* "Porto una veste di seta"; *oreja:* "Tengo dos orejas")
6. Giving two other words belonging to the same word family (*Bäcker:* "Der Bäcker bäckt in der Bäckerei"; *carnicero:* "El carnicero vende carne en la carnicería")
7. Giving a definition of the word (*professeur:* "Un professeur est un homme qui enseigne dans l'école"; *Kuh:* "Die Kuh ist ein Haustier; sie gibt uns Milch").

The teacher can add an element of fun and friendly rivalry to the flash-card drill by dividing the class into two competing teams. The remedial phase of the drill should consist of the teacher's having the pupil who misses study his word so that he can give the correct answer after the others have recited. The drill may also be given for speed and a time record kept for comparison with previous performances.

It is good practice to have sets of cards covering various subjects such as adjectives, weather expressions, time, parts of the body.

Charts. These may include tabular arrangements of words for pronunciation, verb paradigms, classroom expressions, and the vowel triangle. The latter and the pronunciation charts (which can be purchased) are eminently useful in beginners' classes in French. The difference between charts and flash cards is that charts present material in tabular or systematic arrangement, that they are permanently on display in the classroom, and that they are usually referred to with a pointer.

For greater effectiveness, the same format suggestions as for flash cards apply: the charts should be on clean, stiff, light cardboard, and all the lettering should be clear and simple, uniform, and in black ink. White on black is also striking.

For vocabulary drill and conversation there are also several neatly printed charts with pictures. Best known, probably, are *Heath's*

Modern Language Wall Charts,[1] which cover the commonest subjects treated in beginning classes. These are in black and white. Extremely attractive are the colored wall charts of French and German manufacture.

The picture chart may be used in various ways. The teacher or a pupil may point out, and individual pupils may name persons or objects represented. "El padre," "La madre," "El abuelo," "La criada," and so on. Or, a statement may be made about each. "El padre lee el periódico," "La madre hace una falda," "El abuelo está sentado y fuma," and so on. As a summary a pupil may be called upon to describe the entire scene.

Care should be taken that the charts on permanent display, such as pronunciation charts which may be used for daily reference, do not become torn and soiled.

Pictures. This is a field very rich in possibilities: pictures of all types are easy to procure, the supply is inexhaustible, they may be used in many different ways, and they make a strong appeal to everyone. There are available reproductions of paintings, engravings, magazine and rotogravure illustrations, photographs, snapshots, and drawings. As for use, they fall into three classes: those on permanent exhibition, those on temporary display, and those presented for illustrative purposes.

The first category constitutes part of the room decoration and are put up largely for the purpose of creating a foreign language atmosphere. They ought to be fairly good modern representations of foreign scenes or eminent men or reproductions of famous paintings. They ought to show good taste and give the pupils who gaze at them every day a favorable impression of the foreign country. If possible, they ought to be framed.

The pictures on temporary display include illustrations and photographs that are put up on the bulletin board. Every foreign language room should have one of the latter, with the appropriate heading, "Actualités," "Neuigkeiten," etc. Contributions should come from both teacher and pupils; they may consist in the main of clippings and pictures from current newspapers and magazines pertaining to foreign events. On the other hand, if the class is studying a special topic, the bulletin board may be used for a systematic display of

---

[1] *Modern Language Charts* (Boston: D. C. Heath). Set of 14. Word lists available in French, German, Italian, and Spanish.

pictures concerned with the topic, for a week or two. Possibilities would be Paris, Normandy, the French peasant, famous cathedrals, Rome, Naples, Venice, Columbus, and so on.

The bulletin board may also be used to feature reproductions of the works of a famous artist each week. In fact, a special frame may be constructed in which each week a different picture is displayed with a brief explanatory caption.

The pictures that are used for illustrative purposes and as a basis for conversation should form a fairly extensive collection. They may include collections of foreign postcards, snapshots made by the teacher in the foreign country, clippings from the *National Geographic* and foreign magazines, illustrations from domestic publications, and so on. How are these pictures to be used?

1. In the teaching of culture, pictures are indispensable. Nothing can vivify the text or the teacher's verbal description better than a few excellent pictures. Not too many should be shown, of course, and in each instance the teacher should point out what is to be looked for. Pupils must be trained in accurate habits of observation. Snapshots taken by the teacher himself and shown accompanied by personal comments are particularly interesting. Postcards may be passed around the class. In the teaching of culture authentic and modern pictures of foreign street scenes, buildings, costumes, and so on, are desirable. It makes a poor impression on the pupil if he is shown a photograph of the Place de la Concorde with taxicabs of 1907 chugging about.

Many foreign language departments take pride in maintaining a carefully indexed file of pictures of foreign countries for the use of their staff. The teacher then simply borrows a dozen pictures or so for the lesson he is giving.

2. Frequently some cultural item is mentioned in the reading. Nothing enlivens such a mention better than the display of a good picture.

3. As described in Chapter III, pictures can be used very effectively as a basis for conversation and oral work. For this type of work a different kind of picture is necessary from that used for cultural purposes. The picture should be fairly large, so that all details can be seen from every part of the room; if possible, it should be colored. Advertisements, covers, and full-page illustrations in the larger popular magazines furnish an excellent source for such pic-

tures. It is best to mount them and to provide them with clips or hooks so that they can be suspended in the front of the room.

The picture may be used to review vocabulary or to expand it. In the latter case, the teacher must provide the pupils with the new words that they need. The oral work may be descriptive or narrative. The latter requires more imagination, a good command of verb forms, and considerable vocabulary.

A colored magazine advertisement of canned fruit might result in the following:

> Auf dem Tisch stehen sechs Büchsen. In den Büchsen ist Obst. In der ersten sind Birnen, in der zweiten Pfirsiche, in der dritten Pflaumen, in der vierten Kirschen, in der fünften Ananas, und in der sechsten Trauben. Die Birnen und die Pfirsiche sind gelb, die Pflaumen sind blau, und die Kirschen sind rot. Ich esse Obst gern.

A cover design showing a boy deeply engrossed in a copy of *Treasure Island* might elicit:

> Vemos aquí a Juan, un muchacho típico americano. Ha leído con gran interés cinco capítulos de la famosa novela *La Isla del Tesoro*. Es un libro interesante y lleno de muchas aventuras vivas. Él está tan absorbido que no percibe la mosca en su oreja izquierda. Cuando niño yo también he leído este libro con mucho gusto.

4. Pictures may also be used to test the pupil's knowledge. A good way to review proverbs or idioms is to present a picture to illustrate each and let the pupil supply the appropriate caption. Important buildings, distinguished men, and famous paintings can also be treated this way. Besides naming it correctly, the pupil may also be asked to make a statement about it in the foreign language or in English.

If the teacher can draw well, he may make use of his ability frequently on the board to illustrate vocabulary or scenes from the textbook. If he is not a good artist, he can call upon pupils to do the drawing.

Room Decorations. Room decorations, especially in the case of the foreign language classroom, are not a trifling matter. The creation of a foreign atmosphere will demand some thought, time, and expense on the part of the teacher, but he will be amply repaid for his efforts if he devotes genuine interest and a little skill to the matter. The French, German, Italian, or Spanish room cannot be made by putting up a few nondescript items. It requires the display of beautiful and useful material, which will arouse and maintain the pupils' interest in the foreign country.

Among the wall displays of the foreign language room nothing is more attractive than travel posters. Most of them are veritable works of art worth framing. They may be obtained—in some cases free of charge—from the foreign railroad, steamship, or airline agencies (see Appendix B). Since they are large, they ought to be hung high on the walls.

The space below them can be reserved for framed pictures or series of photographs. These ought to represent characteristic features and well-known buildings of foreign cities (in the French room: Mont St. Michel, the Eiffel Tower, Versailles, the Arch of Triumph, Notre-Dame, for example). Also, historical and artistic subjects should be represented (Napoleon, Joan of Arc, Pasteur, Victor Hugo; the Horse Fair, the Angelus). If a series of pictures about a certain subject is mounted, it ought to be labeled in neat, legible lettering. In the larger wall decorations beauty should be the determining factor; in the smaller ones it should be usefulness in connection with the reading, the exercises, and the work in civilization.

The bulletin board has already been mentioned; it ought to be a definite part of every language room. The same may be said of verb and pronunciation charts, especially in the French room. Among other printed or lettered material may be included proverbs, idioms, classroom expressions, the names of the months and the days of the week, and the names of famous men and women. These can be lettered by a gifted pupil on strips of cardboard about five inches wide and may be attached to the upper blackboard sill and the top of the wardrobe.

Additional space is often provided by wardrobe panels. This is an excellent place for the display of smaller illustrations which must be seen close at hand or for pupil contributions such as maps, charts, drawings, scrapbooks, calendars, book reports.

Besides the pictures and illustrations there are a few other materials that may be put on display, such as flags, costumed dolls, models made by the pupils, and souvenirs brought from the foreign country. The following sections suggest what may be done:

138

French Room. Colored pictures illustrating the fables of La Fontaine; a French flag; a small rack containing dolls dressed in provincial costumes and labeled; models in wood and pasteboard of the Eiffel Tower, a Norman peasant house, the Arch of Triumph, the *Normandie,* a Louis XIV room; a chart of Paris; menus from French restaurants; French coins; a French calendar; posters.

German Room. German railroad posters; sets of photographs of Nuremberg, Berlin, the Rhine, the Bavarian Alps, Vienna, Oberammergau; shelving over blackboards on which stand beer steins and plates; a cuckoo clock; *Wandsprüche;* German dolls.

Italian Room. Photographs taken from Italian travel magazines; models of the Tower of Pisa, the Colosseum, a gondola, the Ponte Vecchio; peasant dolls in costume; several Chianti bottles; scrapbooks on Italian cities; pictures of Dante, Michelangelo, Raphael, Columbus; colored reproductions of some of the Italian masters; posters.

Spanish Room. Flags and coats of arms of Spain and all the Hispanic countries; Mexican baskets, hats, and pottery; costumed dolls; models of Don Quixote and Sancho Panza, the Alhambra; photographs of important South American cities.

An artistic swinging sign can also be displayed outside the door to indicate that it is the *Sala Española, Deutsches Zimmer,* and so on. Entrance and exit doors can be labeled as such in the foreign language. A nice touch is added by having "Welcome" in the foreign language on the door.

Care should be taken, however, that there is no overloading and that everything is in good taste. The author once entered a room in which the teacher had displayed several French newspapers on the walls. Right in front was a copy of *Gringoire* with a leading article in large type entitled "L'Homme nu"! In another French room the "cultural" exhibit consisted of ten neat models of guillotines made by the youngsters.

Slides. With a little ingenuity, homemade slides can be prepared. There are, however, so many excellent commercial sets and so many opportunities to borrow them from loan collections that this is really not necessary. They are best used in the teaching of civilization, although there are also sets that are based on reading texts (for example, *Immensee*).

When slides are mentioned, most people think of the teacher illustrating a prepared talk with them. This results in passive learning with no active pupil participation. To secure participation, the teacher may ask a pupil to prepare the talk. Or—and in this way wider participation can be secured—each slide is discussed briefly by a different pupil who has prepared a few sentences in the foreign language. The teacher lets each pupil who is to talk look at his slide a few days in advance. After the pupil has worked out his text, the teacher corrects it. On the day of the presentation, the pupil delivers it from memory.

Flash cards, charts, pictures, and slides are all visual material. Let us now consider some auditory materials.

Phonograph Records. After its invention in 1877 by Thomas A. Edison, the phonograph record was used chiefly as a medium of entertainment. Vocal and instrumental music was primarily recorded. It took some time before the potentialities of the record were realized as a teaching device and particularly as an extremely valuable technique in learning a foreign language. It was the Army Specialized Training Program that popularized the use of the language record. Through its introduction of the pause, which permits the hearer to repeat, it transformed the disc from a device for passive (aural) learning into active (oral) learning. Later developments, such as magnetic recording, the long-playing record, and tape recording, have vastly increased the effectiveness of the record. Many basic language textbooks are now supplied with records.

Despite radio, film, and television, the record is still a very useful teaching device in foreign languages. Contrasted with scheduled programs on radio and TV, it possesses a number of advantages. The pause after each sentence makes possible two-way communication. It can be used at any time convenient to the teacher or the learner. It can be stopped at any point for the teacher to ask questions, to comment, and to clarify. It can be played over any number of times. And it can be heard in advance by the teacher and evaluated. In other words, it is a medium that is under close control.

The number of recordings has expanded so greatly that there is a vast range of material available—basic records for language learning, recordings for literary appreciation, phonetic exercises, and the whole galaxy of vocal and instrumental records. Here is an inexhaustible treasury from which we can draw for the enrichment of language teaching. As Elton Hocking expresses it, "Sound brings language to life, and life to language."

Tape Recorder. An extremely valuable device for learning a foreign language is the tape recorder. Since the learner's voice is recorded while he speaks, it can be played back for correction and criticism. Tapes are practically indestructible and can be used almost indefinitely. The recordings are easily made, they are portable, they can be edited, they can be stored without difficulty, and they can be relayed without losing quality.

The tape recorder can be used very effectively for the recording of basic dialogues, vocabulary, and grammatical structures. Space should be provided for pupil repetition or response. The tapes may be stored; they can be used repeatedly.

The tape recorder can also be used advantageously for testing comprehension. New selections can be presented or material based on what has already been learned.

For testing and recording each pupil's oral production, the tape recorder is particularly useful. The pupil's speech should be tested at given intervals. A diagnosis will reveal weaknesses and errors. Corrections should then be made and further drill provided.

Musical selections can be taped, especially such as will be used in connection with songs in the classroom. In fact, any type of material integrated with the work of the classroom can be taped. All the language skills can be practiced with tapes, although their primary usefulness is to develop understanding and speaking. With reference to the pupils' span of attention, it is wise to limit the presentation of taped material to ten or fifteen minutes. A longer exposure may lead to boredom and inattention on the part of the pupils.

The making of a tape is not difficult; on the other hand, certain cautions should be observed. It is highly recommended that the room in which the recording is done be a quiet one or at least that noises from the outside be shut out.

The teacher should acquaint himself with the operation of the tape recorder. They all work on the same principle, although there are little mechanical differences between various types. It is, of course, assumed that the teacher has prepared a script, that is, a dialogue, a descriptive piece or a narrative.

The selection should be read clearly, at normal speed. A playing back of the tape may reveal deviations or errors that should be corrected. Revisions can easily be made since the recordings may be erased without difficulty.

141

Directions on the tape should be clear and brief. At the earlier stages they can be given in English. To aid the pupils in comprehension, pauses between sentences are recommended. The beginning and the end of a selection should be indicated, as well as the time allowed.

The pauses for pupil repetition or response should be adequate. That is, they should be longer—only slightly so—than the original production. As brevity is the soul of wit, it is also one of the elements in effective learning. Taped exercises should not be long; fifteen minutes should be the limit.

Radio. The radio, accessible in home and school, store and office, is undoubtedly the most universal form of audio-communication. In larger metropolitan areas there are frequently daily programs in a half-dozen foreign languages. Many school systems have their own station from which they broadcast educational programs to the classrooms. The radio has proved a valuable device for practice in hearing a foreign language.

Its obvious advantages are its immediacy, its realism, its conquest of time and space, its authenticity, and its emotional impact. The dramatic aspects of a program are valuable not only as entertainment but also as pedagogy. The voice charged with feeling and conviction certainly makes a deeper impression on the learner than the printed page.

Nevertheless, there are several handicaps. Radio is a medium that requires highly concentrated attention; it is one-way communication; it may be inconveniently timed; and it cannot be reviewed in advance.

The advantages, however, outweigh the disadvantages. Since radio appeals to one sense only, it does make for concentration of impression. If it is a live program, one can listen in on the event itself. If it is being described by an announcer, his voice may make the event far more impressive than the account of the newspaper reporter. Feeling and emotion can be conveyed; attitudes can be changed. In fact, there is no more effective way of reaching people than through the human voice.

Motion Picture. The motion picture is a very effective teaching medium, for by its very nature it compels attention. Since distractions are cut off, the film provides an intensive experience.

Its effectiveness is increased by the fact that by editing the film one can emphasize certain aspects of a subject. The motion picture can bring the distant past as well as the immediate present into the classroom.

The motion picture builds a common denominator of experience. It reaches even those who can neither read nor write. Because of its esthetic values, it offers a pleasurable experience.

Loop Film. The loop film has the added advantage that it can be shown continuously without rewinding. In learning pronunciation, the student sees the formation of the speaker's mouth while he hears the sound. This is an important side of language learning which the purely auditory techniques neglect.

Value of Films. Experiments have shown that with the use of the film in the classroom there is more learning in less time and there is better retention of what has been learned. Films should be used in combination with other instructional materials. Furthermore, it is not sufficient merely to project a film; the student must be instructed in what to look for. Discussion and evaluation should follow.

Television. The latest medium of mass communication which is now universally used is television. It surpasses all previously devised media in effectiveness, since it combines the advantages of radio and motion pictures. The programs fall into two categories, live telecast—the action taking place at the time—and transcribed telecast.

Since television engages both the eye and the ear, it brings the observer into contact with the event in an exciting manner. The limitations of time and space compel succinctness and clarity of explanation.

However, like radio, television is one-way communication. The teacher on TV has no rapport with the students; he cannot tell what effect his words and actions are having on them. The student can ask no questions; the teacher can give no answers.

It is obvious, then, that as in the case of other audio-visual devices, the teacher is indispensable. There must be preparation before the program goes on; there must be a follow-up after it is over.

The Foreign Language Laboratory. The most effective instrument, however, that has been devised for the practice of the audio-lingual aspects of a language is the foreign language laboratory. In the laboratory the student can listen to the foreign language spoken by natives at normal speed and can engage in much imitative and repetitive drill—an activity that is impossible in the ordinary classroom. The laboratory will be discussed in the next chapter.

Visual Material. It is obvious that there is perforce a far greater use of audio than visual material in the language laboratory. This is due to the fact that learning a language is based on hearing and speaking, rather than on seeing.

Visual materials, however, are a great aid in evoking a foreign atmosphere. This is true of the simplest pictures and objects, as well as of the motion picture. Besides giving information about the foreign country, they can be used as the subject of conversation or of composition.

The effectiveness of visual material—in fact, of all teaching aids—depends on the way the teacher prepares the students for it and the degree to which he strengthens their experience by stimulating questions and comments.

All auxiliary materials must be related to the student's present activities and should stimulate him to further endeavor. Audiovisual materials are an aid in teaching; they should, however, be an integral part of the course and not merely something incidental. Their effectiveness depends primarily on what the teacher does with them. They can be extremely productive, but even the most elaborate mechanical device cannot replace a well-informed, enthusiastic, and vibrant teacher.

Illustrative Lessons

LESSON WITH A PHONOGRAPH RECORD
(Spanish)

This was a third-term Spanish class. The basis of the lesson was disc No. 1 of the Spanish Linguaphone series. The teacher had written the complete text of the record on the front board, so that the pupils could follow it as the disc was played.

The selection was a description of the Lopez family—father, mother, children, grandmother, and so on—and their respective activities in the living room. It was given in clear, simple Spanish in the present tense. A number of questions followed, all of which were answered by the speaker.

The teacher played the record a number of times, each time indicating a different aim, that is, pronunciation, vocabulary, content. The pupils listened intently. After each playing, the teacher practiced the particular feature she wished to emphasize. By the time the questions on the content were asked, the pupils were so familiar with the material that they were able to reply fluently.

The teacher then continued the conversation by asking similar questions about the family of the pupil called upon. She expanded the subject by adding additional factors—a dog, a cat, a neighbor. This increased the interest considerably. New words were written on the board by the teacher.

Comments. This was an excellent demonstration of how a record may be used in the language class. The selection of particular phases for special stress increased its effectiveness. The expansion of the subject by questions with a personal reference showed the resourcefulness of the teacher.

DIALOGUE WITH THE USE OF TAPE RECORDER AND FILM

(French)

This was a fourth-year class in high school. Several pairs of students were called to the front of the room to carry on a dialogue about changing money in a travel agent's office and preparing for a trip to France. They had memorized a script that had been prepared previously. The best one of the several pairs of student dialogues was selected and recorded by the teacher on a tape recorder.

Next, the screen in the front of the room was pulled down and a short film, "Courses et Achats," was projected. It was accompanied by the students' voices which had just been recorded.

The class, which had been provided with mimeographed sheets of the script, repeated each phrase group softly after the tape recording. This was done at the normal speed of French speech.

Since the teacher had insisted on expression and intonation as well as correct pronunciation, the verisimilitude was heightened.

Problems

1. List the advantages of the tape recorder for teaching foreign languages.

2. In teaching a given structure tell what types of exercises you would use on tapes for reinforcement.

3. Outline a plan for recording students' oral performance on tapes at given intervals.

4. Plan a culture lesson with slides and tell how you would secure maximum pupil participation.

5. With regard to room decorations, indicate what problems might arise in connection with a Russian room.

X ' The Language Laboratory

What Is a Language Laboratory? A language laboratory is a room especially equipped with electronic devices so that students may hear the foreign language, record their own imitation of what they have heard, and play back the spoken materials. Each student is seated in a separate booth, or station, which contains a set of headphones, a microphone, and a tape recorder.

The teacher is stationed at a longer desk or counter, called the "console," in the front of the room. It is equipped with a microphone, earphones, one or several tape recorders, a playback machine, and facilities for channeling in radio programs. Buttons and levers constitute the control panel from which the teacher directs the activities of the students. Through wires connecting the console with the student stations, prerecorded lesson materials on tape or discs are transmitted.

Each student station consists of a semi-isolated booth with acoustically treated separating panels. The front is open so that the student sees and can be seen by the teacher.

Procedures. The teacher sends recorded lesson material from the console to the booths, where each student receives it through headphones. A lever permits him to control the volume according to his needs. The microphone amplifies the sound of his voice, so that he hears it clearly and distinctly through the headphones. By pressing the proper button, the student can set the tape recorder so that his own responses will be recorded. At the completion of the exercise, he can rewind the tape and play back the entire performance. This is done so that he can compare his imitation with the model or his responses with the correct ones on the tape.

The Console. The teacher's sending station is usually equipped with several channels for program distribution. There may be three tape decks, a record player, headphones, and a microphone.

The teacher may channel material to the students from a phonograph disc or from a tape. The same tape or disc may be sent to the entire class, or different selections may be sent to different students. The teacher can control the selections by operating the various switches on his control panel. Communication may be established with each student separately. The teacher can listen in and make corrections and comments, and the student may reply. A two-way conversation can thus be carried on without interrupting the work of the rest of the class. Some consoles are so equipped, too, that the utterances of students in the booths may be recorded at the sending station.

Visual Techniques. Although the language laboratory is primarily equipped for auditory practice, visual learning may also be introduced. The blackboard and charts in the front of the room may be used. The room can be darkened for showing of slides or a film.

Part of the visual equipment—which is constant—is the set of charts in the front of the room, on which the positions and the purposes of the various switches are shown. A reduced copy of these diagrams is in each student's booth.

Uses of the Language Laboratory. As stated above, the primary purpose of the language lab is to provide much opportunity for systematic listening and speaking. Practically all of the phases of language learning, however, can be taught in the laboratory. The mechanical equipment may be used for

1. Pronunciation or phonetic drills
2. Corrective work in pronunciation
3. Practice in the use of grammatical forms
4. Aural comprehension

148

5. Dictation
6. The teaching of songs
7. Oral self-expression, original conversation
8. Aural-oral testing.

Effectiveness of the Language Laboratory. The optimum effectiveness of the lab is attained if the following standards are observed:

1. The tapes and discs should be of good quality.
2. The student must participate constantly.
3. Multivoiced records with different speakers are preferable.
4. The tone of the voices should be warm and enthusiastic.
5. Material should be played at normal speed.
6. Material should be varied in order to hold the attention of the listener.
7. The purpose of each exercise should be clear to the learner.

What is not possible in the average classroom can be done in the laboratory. It provides regular practice in listening to model voices and makes it possible for the student to engage in much imitative and repetitive drill. This sort of practice strengthens the learner's ability to understand the spoken language at normal speed. It also helps considerably in building up the student's vocabulary and thereby increases his ability to speak.

In the past, speaking, but not understanding, was emphasized. This led to the ludicrous situation where an American was able to ask questions correctly, but could not understand the foreigner's answers. In fact, one of the most difficult skills is rapid, instantaneous comprehension of the spoken language. To acquire it endless practice in listening is essential. The student must learn to think and react immediately in the foreign language, as he would in the foreign environment where he would have unlimited access to native speakers. The language laboratory is the best device in the way of a contrived experience.

Skills To Be Developed. The language laboratory makes it possible to expose the student to a much greater volume of spoken language than is possible in the ordinary classroom. He is also able to hear many different native voices. Audio-lingually the laboratory is an excellent arrangement, for the learner gets the meaning of foreign language utterances directly from the sound. The fact that material can be repeated and listened to as often as necessary increases the learning possibilities even for the slow learner.

The aim of the work in the language laboratory is to develop the student's ability

1. To readily distinguish sounds and structures, and to get the meaning by sound
2. To constantly improve his pronunciation by purposeful listening and careful imitation
3. To articulate fluently the common speech patterns of the foreign language
4. To answer questions without hesitation and to make the proper responses to commands and directions.

Constant practice in listening and imitating good, clear models should build up the student's fluency of articulation, make his responses automatic, and give him confidence and competence to express his own thoughts with acceptable standards of correctness.

Aims of Laboratory Experiences. All of the four linguistic skills may be strengthened and developed by the language laboratory. Primarily, however, it is to be used to build up audio-lingual facility. Specifically, the aims are:

1. To provide perfect models of pronunciation and intonation for the student to imitate
2. To give the student ample opportunity to imitate and repeat what he hears
3. To practice the structural patterns learned in the classroom
4. To build up the student's competence in rapid comprehension
5. To provide adequate practice in giving immediate responses in the foreign language
6. To make the student critical of his own speech
7. To strengthen the student's ability to express himself freely in the foreign tongue.

Coordination with the Classroom. The language laboratory is really a room for practice rather than a laboratory. (The Germans call it *Uebungsstelle*—place for practice.) It serves as the place for drill and reinforcement after the lesson has been initiated in the classroom. It provides the space and the equipment for the intensive practice necessary to automatize a structure or a pattern. The laboratory affords conditions that make for maximal use of time for listening and speaking. The aural is stressed here, whereas in the traditional classroom the emphasis is mainly on the visual.

Individual Learning. The language laboratory is particularly conducive to the individualization of learning. The teacher can group students according to interests and abilities. In fact, he can provide individual programs for special students.

Although the classroom and the socialized recitation have distinct advantages, the single student in the semi-isolated booth enjoys special opportunities that favor language learning. These are:

1. He hears only correct speech; he does not have to listen to the mistakes made by his classmates.
2. He practices all the time; he does not listen passively while another student recites.
3. Since his utterances are not heard by his classmates, he is not embarrassed in his attempts to imitate the model nor when he is corrected by the teacher.
4. He can always repeat what he has not understood completely.
5. His opportunities to speak are vastly increased. In a normal classroom he may be called upon once during an entire period.

Tests have definitely proved that the student who uses the laboratory acquires a better pronunciation, greater fluency in speech, and keener audial comprehension than the student who is taught in the regular classroom.

Types of Laboratory Lessons. Even though the laboratory is primarily used for drill in listening and speaking, all of the language skills may be practiced in the booth. Various kinds of lessons may be given, such as those described in the following section.

1. Intonation drills of progressively increasing length and speed, to train the student in sustained listening and to require greater memory span.

2. Auditory comprehension exercises, also of increasing length and difficulty, leading up to passages lasting ten minutes. The presentation of the selection should be followed by questions or multiple-choice exercises.

3. Brief talks in the foreign language, first with notes, then without notes (in the upper years). The student is to prepare himself in advance and then speak more or less extemporaneously into

the microphone, without any guiding phrases or questions from the teacher. The talk can be recorded and played before the class at its next meeting.

4. Reading lessons to accelerate silent reading and to provide a model to imitate in oral reading. A selection is played on the tape or spoken into the microphone by the teacher while the students listen with their books open before them. Next, they repeat, after the teacher or the tape. Then the pupils close their books, listen silently, and try to understand purely by ear. Finally, the teacher asks five questions based on the text, pausing for the response, giving the correct answer, and waiting for a repetition of the correct response.

5. Verb drill for a brief, five-minute lesson. The teacher speaks all of the forms of the present tense of a given verb, for example, *aller,* in sentences. He pauses to let the students repeat. Next, the teacher gives merely the pronoun; the students complete each sentence. Various persons are now practiced in completion exercises, for example, "Il va . . ." Students complete the sentence with *à l'école, au théâtre, au cinéma, à l'église,* and so on. The same is done with other persons like *nous allons, ils vont.* Practice is then given in the interrogative and in the negative.

6. Poetry selections can be presented in the laboratory, both for appreciation and for memorization. The line-by-line repetition of a poem recited by a native speaker will help the student to improve his pronunciation and intonation.

7. Pattern drills can be practiced effectively in the laboratory. Each tape will present an example of the structure to be drilled. The model sentences are followed by pauses so that the student may imitate each one. Suitable exercises are changing the tense of a sentence, changing from negative to affirmative, or vice versa, contraction drills, expansion drills, completion drills.

8. Even culture can be taught in the laboratory. The use of visual materials is highly desirable. A film or slides can be shown. The tape may give a description of each slide, providing related information.

Reading in the Laboratory. The special advantages of using a tape in connection with reading are the following:

1. In ordinary reading only the eye is used. By hearing the text spoken

the visual stimulus of the printed page is reinforced by the auditory stimulus.

2. The spoken version enlivens the printed page. The correct intonation and the presentation in thought groups often gives a clue to the meaning of a word or phrase.
3. Being obliged to listen, the student is trained to read at a given speed. He does not hesitate or stop on encountering a new word.
4. If the text is read by a native speaker with a pleasing voice, the enjoyableness of the learning situation is increased. The student's literary appreciation is also heightened.

Content and Form of the Reading-Lesson Tape. (From the *Foreign Language Revision Program for Secondary Schools,* Spanish, Level III, Board of Education, City of New York.)

The reading lesson tape is directly related to the text read by the class. The lesson tape deals with a selected portion of the text, perhaps a chapter or a part of a chapter, or an entire short story, stopping at a logical point. The story value, or the idea value, should be maintained.

The lesson tape may begin with an introductory statement designed to orient the listener-reader to the content of what will follow, or it may begin with the presentation of the text, with advance explanation and repetition of new or difficult words and phrases.

The passage should consist of approximately two minutes of consecutive reading, fluently but not speedily paced.

The student is directed to the page and line where the reading will begin and is told to follow along in the textbook as he listens.

After the first reading, a part of the text is reread in word groups, spaced according to the sense, each word group being followed by a pause timed to permit the student to imitate what he has heard. The student is instructed to imitate not only the pronunciation but also the intonation of the speaker. The passage reread for imitation is selected for liveliness of content; it may be a vivid description or an interesting conversation. There generally follows an exercise in word study and usage. Important and useful words are selected from the text. These words are spoken twice in the foreign language and once in English and then are presented in a brief, usable sentence. The students repeat the word in the foreign language only, and then the sentence containing the word. As a variation, students are sometimes directed to write the word.

Other exercises require sentences to be restated with antonyms or synonyms of the words being studied and true-or-false sentences to be repeated if true, corrected if false. Questions based on the text are so structured that the responses are easily supplied by the student.

The lesson concludes with a brief summary of all or of a part of the lesson in the form of dictation (which may then be used for brief oral repetition) or some other writing exercise.

It is standard procedure in tapes that, for any exercise requiring a response other than direct imitation of a model, the correct answer is provided immediately after the student has given his response. This re-enforces the student's response if it was correct or provides correction if it was erroneous. An important feature in the learning experience is the presentation of the correct form immediately after the student has constructed a response. The student knows immediately whether his answer has been right or wrong, and incorrect learnings have less chance to persist.

What follows depends upon the type of equipment at hand. In laboratory stations containing recorders, the students have recorded the part of the text that they had imitated. At this point they rewind the tape and play back the model reading and their imitation, taking mental or written note of the parts that they recognize as less than satisfactory imitation of the model. They may rewind and listen to the tape several times.

The value of this part of the work is in proportion to the student's understanding that the comparison of the model speech and his imitation depends upon his power of discriminating among sounds and upon his repeated attempts to imitate correctly. The teacher guides the students in this part of the work through monitoring and intercommunicating. Of course, if the student station is not equipped with an individual tape recorder, the student listens and repeats, but cannot review and compare the model and his imitation of it.

Problems

1. Tell how the language laboratory is unusually effective for audio-lingual activities.

2. Indicate what problems, both pedagogical and technical, might arise in connection with the use of the language laboratory and suggest solutions.

3. In connection with a specific lesson, tell what procedures you would use in the classroom and how you would follow them up in the laboratory.

4. Tell how you would organize "library" sessions in the laboratory for a class on the third level.

5. Describe the presentation in the laboratory of an important news item.

XI ⸄ Pupil Activities and Projects

Learning Should Be Pleasant. Learning is essentially an active process. Its success depends upon the learner's readiness and upon the satisfaction that he derives. From the practical point of view this means arousing the pupil's interest, so that he will engage in an activity with eagerness and manage that interest so that its satisfying elements are maintained throughout.

We have gotten far away from the idea, once prevalent, that "La letra entra con sangre." We must, however, recognize that there are certain knowledges and skills that can be learned only through drill, practice, and constant application. Words must be memorized, paradigms drilled, and grammatical rules applied. There is no reason, however, why these activities may not be skillfully motivated and managed, so that they become pleasant and satisfying to the learner.

Such satisfaction can be secured in the daily lesson in a number of ways. Where the teacher is by nature a vivacious and interesting personality, gifted with resourcefulness, that is not difficult.

Today, more than ever, stress is placed on pupil activity. The learner is to plan and carry out as much of the work as possible, with the teacher acting merely as the guide and counselor. There is always the danger, especially in the case of the eager and well-

156

informed teacher, to dominate the lesson and to talk too much. Restraint must be exercised, for it is the pupil who needs the oral practice and not the teacher.

Pupil Self-direction. Sometimes the teacher can withdraw to the background or sit among the pupils and permit a student to assume the direction of the class activities. This may be for five or ten minutes, as in the asking of questions, leading in the singing of a song, or presenting a report; or for a whole lesson, as in the conduct of the home-room or club period. Permitting pupils to assume control of the situation gives them a feeling of power, satisfaction, and pleasure. It also affords an excellent opportunity for them to express themselves in the foreign tongue and to undertake something original.

Games. For lively, snappy oral work permitting much activity on the part of the pupils there is nothing superior, especially in the lower grades, to the game. To have its full value it should be educationally sound: it must adequately drill the facts to be reviewed; it must be brief; the whole class must be able to participate; and the elements of fun and good-natured competition should not be lacking.

Some games like "Buzz" are a useful device for drilling one particular item, in this case, numbers. Other games, like the guessing game, are more comprehensive activities and may involve considerable vocabulary.

The game can be employed to enforce verb forms, points in grammar, idioms, and vocabulary. When groups of pupils or rows of pupils compete with one another, interest is heightened by keeping score and occasionally awarding a prize.

Singing. One of the most enjoyable activities of the foreign language classroom is singing. It is something which pupils never tire of and it is an excellent means of establishing a spirit of well-being in the room.

Besides the pleasure that the pupils derive from it, singing is a useful exercise for improving pronunciation and increasing vocabulary. Furthermore, many songs provide splendid opportunity for the presentation of cultural material. This would be true of the content as a whole, of individual expressions, and of the music.

If properly taught, the song in the foreign language provides immediate pleasure and remains a cultural treasure of lasting value.

Often, all that pupils are able to recall of their language course—and recall with delight—are the rhymes, verses, and songs that they learned.

The words and music, of course, should be simple. Folk songs, popular airs of the past and present, operatic selections, and national airs furnish a good selection.

In teaching a song the teacher may use the following method: After a brief explanation of the background of the song (perhaps a word about its composer, if distinguished), the teacher reads the words. The class repeats in concert and then individual pupils read. The text is then studied for the content. A few stimulating questions by the teacher should serve to bring out the meaning of the selection. If the song consists of a number of verses, one stanza may be taken at a time. If the song does not appear in a book that the pupils have, the teacher may distribute mimeographed copies or write it on the board, from which the pupils copy it into their notebooks.

The teacher may feel that his voice is not adequate for singing or that he cannot carry a tune. In that event he can let a pupil with a good voice take over. Or, a phonograph record of the song may be played.

Often a pupil can be trained to lead his classmates in singing. After the class has acquired a repertory, the choice of what they wish to sing may be left to them. The singing of a song always rounds out the end of a period nicely. It is something to which the pupils look forward and it is an added incentive for them to finish their assigned tasks.

Songs may also be used very effectively for practice in vocabulary, idiom, and grammar. For example, "Alouette" lends itself splendidly to teaching the parts of the body. The pupils point to them as they occur in the selection.

"Carmencita," with its refrain "Me gustan todas, me gustan todas," is ideal for practicing the impersonal verb *gustar*. In fact, the teacher can also bring in gender by letting the girls sing to the boys "Me gustan todos" and by referring to "el rubio" instead of "la rubia."

An example of a song by which verb forms, specifically the subjunctive, may be practiced is the German folksong, "Treue Liebe," in which each verb in the second stanza is in the subjunctive.

Wär' ich ein Vögelein,
Wollt' ich bald bei dir sein,
Scheut' Falk und Habicht nicht,
Flög' schnell zu dir.
Schöss' mich ein Jäger tot,
Fiel' ich in deinen Schöss,
Säh'st du mich traurig an,
Gern *stürb'* ich dann.

With a little thought, many songs may be found that are delightful to sing and that contain useful words and expressions. There is no pleasanter way to learn. "En s'amusant, on apprend tout."

The Foreign Language Club. The foreign language club serves a number of useful purposes, especially if it is a more or less spontaneous organization on the part of the pupils and if the faculty adviser is an enthusiastic and resourceful teacher.

Through the club those cultural activities for which there is little or no time in the classroom may be carried on. These include

1. Visits to museums, churches, cinemas, cultural centers, restaurants, theatres, concerts, and the opera
2. The giving of concerts and plays
3. Talks in the foreign language by distinguished guests
4. The collecting and displaying of postcards, magazines, tickets, stamps, coins, books, etc.
5. Additional singing of more difficult songs
6. The presentation of films and slides.

As much as possible, the activities of the club should be carried on in the foreign language, especially the more formal part of the meeting with its set phrases and expressions. The skillful teacher can do a good deal of incidental teaching in the most natural way, so that the pupil learns unconsciously. He must never feel that he is in the classroom or even in school.

Foreign-born children may be chosen as officers of the club because of their superior language facility, but the average student should not be excluded because he does not possess this ability. Any pupil who shows genuine interest ought to be admitted, so that the influence of the club may become as widespread as possible.

159

The wealth of cultural knowledge which the students acquire "painlessly" through club work is astounding. The freedom from the restraints of the classroom and the informality of discussions, visits, and excursions create an atmosphere conducive to pleasurable learning.

The gifted student has the opportunity to follow a special bent or to engage upon unusual projects. The resourceful teacher will soon discover the interests of her pupils and utilize them in the best possible manner.

Glee Clubs. One of the finest specialized extracurricular activities is the foreign language glee club. This will primarily attract pupils who are musical or have good voices. It provides an interesting activity for many pupils whose class work is not brilliant but who do enjoy the cultural phases of foreign language studies.

The glee club may be organized as a special group—quartet, sextet, and so on—of members of the foreign language club or as a larger, separate organization. What is possible along this line is evidenced by the splendid achievements of the Inter-High School German Glee Club of New York. This group, composed of four hundred high school students, met voluntarily every Saturday afternoon under the direction of L. Leo Taub for ten years. Its annual concerts, which were finally given in Carnegie Hall, were attended by approximately three thousand persons. An enterprise of this kind is a wonderful example of voluntary student activity in the field of foreign languages.

Projects. The basic principle of all projects is pupil activity. Each pupil should contribute whatever he can, his contribution being in line with his own interests and capacities. The teacher will merely guide, direct, and suggest. The project may be undertaken by one pupil or by a group of pupils.

If the project is based on foods, the following activities may be carried on:

1. Gathering menus from foreign restaurants and steamships
2. Studying the sources of foods
3. Drawing pictures and labeling them with foreign names
4. Listing foreign language terms that have been introduced into American cookery
5. Preparing some of the foreign dishes in home economics classes
6. Bringing to class, if possible, samples of food products.

A project in folk costume and modern dress would involve

1. Collecting illustrative postcards and foreign catalogues
2. Making dresses for dolls
3. Making sketches of costumes
4. Making costumes for use in assembly and club programs
5. Bringing in fashion magazines and books on costumes
6. Making lists of foreign language terms applied to clothing
7. Visiting museums and stores.

In a project in geography the pupils will engage in

1. Drawing maps in colors (showing cities or rivers or mountains)
2. Making relief maps in clay or soap
3. Making pictorial maps
4. Making jigsaw-puzzle maps
5. Studying the relationship between physical conditions and occupations
6. Studying the relationship between climate and products
7. Indicating on blank outline maps agricultural and mineral regions, industrial centers, and the like
8. Preparing travel maps.

Some topics or projects will have to be developed by the teacher, who will impart the necessary information, especially on such topics as customs, ways of travel, and so on. Thus he may

1. Draw upon his personal experience or studies
2. Invite teachers from other departments, or persons from outside the school, to contribute
3. Show views by means of postcards, slides, stereopticons, and films
4. Arrange exhibits of realia gathered, when possible, with the help of pupils.

Foreign Stamps. Postage stamps may be used as the basis for many interesting projects in cultural studies. They may be used for teaching colors, the monetary system of the given country, abbreviations, geography, famous buildings, famous men, and important events in history. Dealers in stamps will arrange collections under given categories such as animals, flowers, famous men. Each pupil is to be encouraged to keep his own collection and to do individual research. A lifelong interest may be built up this way.

Games

GEOGRAPHY GAME
(French)

After making a few preliminary announcements in French, the teacher assigned the names of various cities, mountains, and rivers of France to a number of pupils.

"Cohen, vous êtes Bordeaux; Quinlan, vous êtes les Pyrénées; Meyer, vous êtes le Rhin; Patti, vous êtes Paris." As each pupil arose, he stationed himself on the side of the room corresponding to the part of France where his particular item was located. The front of the room was north, the rear south, and so on.

The pupil leader, a boy who stood in the center of the room, made a general statement about the location of France and its boundaries. Then, as he pointed in a given direction, each of the other pupils made a statement or two about the river, town, or mountain he represented. Each one began "Je m'appelle . . ." and then added a sentence or two, as:

> Je m'appelle Lyon. J'occupe un beau site au confluent du Rhône et de la Saône.
> Je m'appelle les Alpes. Je suis le système de montagnes le plus important d'Europe.
> Je m'appelle la Seine. Je prends ma source dans la Côte d'Or et me jette dans la Manche. Je suis le plus régulier des fleuves de France. J'en suis le plus navigable.

Occasionally, the teacher interjected a question like, "Pourquoi êtes-vous bien connu?"

ALPHABETICAL GAME

This is a good way to review vocabulary. Each pupil in turn is asked to give a word in alphabetical order, for example,

Arbe, banc, canif, dame, eau, faim, garçon
Apfel, Baum, Carl, Dach, Essen, Feuer, Garten

This game works best with nouns. The letters *x, y,* and *z* may be omitted.

GOING TO SCHOOL

(German)

This is effective for reviewing classroom or school vocabulary. Each pupil in turn varies the sentence and introduces a different noun or describes a different action.

Ich gehe in die Schule und bringe mein Heft mit.
Ich gehe in die Schule und bringe mein Buch (meine Feder, mein Heft, meinen Imbiss) mit.
Ich komme in die Schule und sehe den Lehrer.
Ich komme in die Schule und setze mich (trete in das Klassenzimmer, nehme den Hut ab).

SHOPPING

(Spanish)

Each pupil in order or volunteers at random "go to the store" to buy something. The vocabulary belonging to each particular kind of shop can thus be reviewed. For example,

Voy a la camisería y compro una camisa (una corbata, un cuello, un pañuelo, etc.).
Entro en la carnicería y compro un pollo (carne de vaca, carne de carnero, etc.).
(Girls) Voy a la tienda de Wanamaker y compro una blusa (una falda, paño de lana, un sombrero, un vestido, etc.).

PRODUCTS

This is useful for reviewing the products of countries, provinces, and cities. Pupils say in the foreign language,

A ship is coming from Le Havre loaded with silk (laces, perfumes, jewelry, hats, dresses, etc.).

A train is coming from Nuremberg loaded with toys (pencils, pens, books, Christmas cakes, etc.).

JUMBLED LETTERS

The teacher writes the letters of a given word on the board in mixed order. The pupils are told that the letters, if properly assembled, spell the name of a country, an author, an animal, a vegetable, and so on. The first pupil guessing correctly wins.

The teacher can review a certain vocabulary group this way, giving, for example, only the names of countries or languages or foods. Example: parts of the body—*beamj, huxeecv, sbar, solilere*. These would be solved as *jambe, cheveux, bras, oreilles*.

The same can be done with sentences. Example: "zeonnd-oim al lmepu—Donnez-moi la plume."

TELEGRAMS

Each pupil writes ten letters on a slip of paper. He passes this slip to his right-hand neighbor who must write a ten-word telegram, beginning the words with each one of the ten letters on his paper. The letters can be used in any order. The teacher can simplify the game and remove the difficulties by working out possible telegrams in advance and assigning the appropriate letters. These can be put on the board and the whole class may work on the solution.

BOTTLE

The pupils are seated in a circle with a bottle lying on its side in the center. The first player asks a question and spins the bottle. The pupil toward whom the neck of the bottle is pointing must give the answer. He in turn asks a question and spins the bottle. If a pupil fails to answer, he is out.

WORDS

The first pupil gives a certain word. The next player must begin his word with the last letter of the preceding word. Sides may be chosen. The words may be limited to a specific group.

ADVERTISEMENTS

A number of advertisements of American products in foreign magazines are mounted and displayed about the room. Each picture is numbered. At a given signal, the pupils are permitted to look at the advertisements and to identify them by number on a sheet of paper. The pupil identifying the greatest number of advertisements correctly wins. (If the name of the article appears in the illustration, it may be blotted out with ink or covered with paper.)

INNKEEPER

One pupil is the innkeeper. Each of the others, who are the travelers, chooses a letter of the alphabet. Each traveler in turn applies at the inn. The innkeeper asks a number of questions. Each question must be answered by the traveler by employing words commencing with his letter. (Certain letters, of course, are valueless. In French, for instance, *k, w, x, y,* and *z* may be omitted.) Examples:

—Comment vous appelez-vous?
—Pierre.
—D'où venez-vous?
—De Paris.
—Quelle est votre profession?
—Peintre.
—Que désirez-vous pour votre déjeuner?
—Petits pois et pommes de terre.

* * *

"Wie heissen Sie?"
"Ich heisse Franz."
"Woher kommen Sie?"
"Ich komme aus Frankfurt."
"Was ist Ihr Beruf?"
"Ich bin Färber."
"Was wünschen Sie zum Mittagessen?"
"Feine Fische und frische Feigen."

WORD FAMILIES

A word is given to the class. Each pupil writes as many related words as he can in a given time. The pupil producing the greatest number of words wins. Examples:

écrire, écrit, écriteau, écritoire, écriture, écrivain
Bauer, Baumeister, bauen, Gebäude, Baustil, Umbau, Nebenbau,
Baumaterial
Carne, carnicería, carnicero, carnívoro, carnoso, carnuza

ALPHABET

Two sets of cards are prepared, each card containing a letter of
the alphabet, with separate cards for the accented letters. The class
is divided into two teams, standing in parallel lines about four feet
apart. About two feet beyond the first two pupils a chalk line is
drawn. After the cards have been mixed thoroughly, each line of
pupils gets a set. The cards are placed face down. The leader calls
out a word from a list. The two pupils holding the first letter of the
word run to the chalk line. The one arriving first and facing
the pupils and displaying his letter wins. The two pupils holding the
following letter must not start until the defeated first letter is back
in his place. This is continued until the word is spelled. The players
then resume their places in line. The side having the most letters
in the word wins.

GUESSING IDENTITY

On the back of each pupil is pinned a card or paper bearing the
name of some writer, musician, hero, flower, animal, province, or
city. No pupil is aware of what his own card says. In turn, or alphabetically, each pupil must guess the inscription of his card by asking
questions of his classmates, who answer only Yes or No.

BASEBALL

The class is divided into two teams, with a batter and captains.
The players take their places on a baseball diamond marked out for
them. From a prepared list the pitcher gives out a word that must
be translated, defined, or spelled. If the batter gives the correct
answer he proceeds to first base. If he fails, he is out. Score is kept
as in baseball.

REVIEW OF IDIOMS AND PROVERBS WITH KEY WORDS

The teacher lets individual pupils select a card each from a pack. Each card—which may be cut in the shape of a key—contains a key word for an idiom or a proverb the class has learned. As soon as the pupil has picked his key, he must give an appropriate idiom (or proverb, if these are being reviewed). If the same key reappears, the pupil must give a different idiom.

REVIEW OF IDIOMS AND PROVERBS WITH PICTURES

The class is divided into two teams lined up on opposite sides of the room. The teacher exposes flash cards containing pictures. Each pupil in turn must give the idiom (or proverb) that the picture illustrates. If he gives the wrong idiom, or states it incorrectly, he is out.

GUESSING

One pupil leaves the room while his classmates determine upon some object to be guessed in the room.

When the pupil who left returns, he asks his classmates various questions in the foreign language until he guesses the object chosen. "Is it abstract or concrete? Living or inanimate? Large or small? Black, white, yellow, blue, red, or green? Of wood, paper, glass, metal, cloth? Square, round, oval? On the floor, the wall, or the ceiling?"

This game, if properly used, will give excellent practice in a rather extensive vocabulary of useful words.

The guessing may be made somewhat easier by indicating the first letter of the name of the object selected.

GUESSING WHO SPOKE

A pupil volunteers to go to the front of the room. Facing the blackboard and covering his eyes he tries to guess the name of the classmate who says, "Good morning," or some other greeting. The guessing pupil asks, "Who is it?" and the one who spoke, changing his voice somewhat, replies, "It is I."

This game occasions considerable fun although it really practices only a limited number of expressions *(c'est moi; ich bin es).*

VERB RELAY RACE

The teacher writes the infinitives of as many verbs on the board as there are rows in the room (usually five). The pupils in each row then go to the board, in regular order and as quickly as possible, to complete a given tense of the verb assigned to the row. When they have finished, the teacher or a monitor checks the work and indicates the winning row.

REVIEW OF VOCABULARY BY CHAIN

(Spanish)

The class is divided into two teams on opposite sides of the room. The first pupil begins by saying a sentence. His opponent must give a sentence that contains a word (other than an article, pronoun, or preposition) used in the previous sentence.

Every time the first pupil's turn comes, he starts off with a new sentence. Example:

Tengo un libro rojo.
El libro está en la mesa.
La mesa es de madera amarilla.
La madera viene de los árboles en el bosque.
En la primavera los árboles son hermosos.

REVIEW OF VOCABULARY BY OPPOSITES

The pupils of two teams are expected to give the opposite of a word given by the previous pupil.

The same game can be played with cognates in the modern languages and with derivatives in Latin.

168

Clubs

UNIQUE FUNCTION OF A LANGUAGE CLUB
(Italian)

This particular Italian Club has engaged in most of the activities that are interesting to language clubs in general, but it has gone beyond the language clubs' usual limits into a social field rich with opportunities and worthwhile undertakings. It has built up a sympathetic bond between the school and the home and among the students themselves. Parents are invited to frequent entertainments and exhibits; students are assisted in their school difficulties. Members of the club help their classmates after school in other subjects as well as in Italian. These after-school periods are supervised in a friendly way by the faculty adviser, who keeps a sympathetic eye on the young people and guides them when the occasion demands. This clearing house of student knowledge and student help creates a spirit of good fellowship and sportsmanship among the members of the club.

An attendance committee investigates and reports on cases of excessive absence, visiting the absentee's home and explaining to the parents, in Italian if necessary, the importance of regular attendance at school.

The club also provides for the social needs of its members, engaging in such enterprises as the teaching of social dancing. With the aid of an old phonograph and a few records, a considerable degree of proficiency has been attained. The musical members of the club have formed a trio and a glee club, which have been very successful.

Funds of the club are used to provide two prizes every term for the best students in Italian classes. Books on Italy have also been purchased for the school library.

TERM PROGRAM FOR A FRENCH CLUB

Clubs are extracurricular forms of supposed diversion. Therefore, only "good times," planned for twenty weeks, will keep our fickle admirers with us. The club must be made attractive. In a junior high school a resourceful teacher planned a program for the term and posted it on the bulletin board one week before registration:

> Le Cercle Français hopes that its prospective members will find the program for the ensuing term interesting and entertaining. It welcomes any recommendations pertaining to the activities that you may care to suggest. Prizes are offered to the winners on contest days.

PROGRAM

Week of September 13. Organization meeting; election of officers; method of procedure [including all of the essential French terminology, such as names of officers and elementary terminology involved in parliamentary procedure].

Week of September 20. Let's See What the French Are Doing! [Discussion by the class from *Le Petit Journal*.]

Week of September 27. Report on Louis XIV. Film: *The Sun King and His Palace at Versailles*.

Week of October 3. Contest day: Word Game. [Books are necessary.]

Week of October 10. Song day: the story of "La Marseillaise." [The use of the piano or harmonica is suggested where phonograph records are not available.]

Week of October 17. Slides on the Riviera.

Week of October 24. Contest day: original crossword puzzles.

Week of October 31. Visit to the newspaper plant of *L'Amérique*.

Week of November 7. Talk: "Normandy, the Garden of France; Brittany, the Fishing Province."

Week of November 14. Visit to a French steamer.

Week of November 21. Talk: "Touring the Gold Coast Towns of France." Film: *Nice, Cannes, and Monte Carlo*.

Week of December 5. Discussion: "Vive la France" [customs]. Song day.

Week of December 19. *La fête de Noël. Joyeux Noël et Bonne Année.*

Week of January 2. French plays: (1) *L'Apprenti du Barbier;* (2) *Un Tour de Gascogne* [dramatized and acted out by more advanced students with a preliminary English synopsis].

Week of January 9. Let's Travel! Talk by the children. Slides.

Week of January 16. Visit to the French Museum.

Week of January 23. Report: "Scenes in Paris." Slides: "Highways and Byways of Paris."

Week of January 30. Last meeting. Party with refreshments in the cafeteria. Singing, dancing, and tableaux.

The above program proved most interesting and effective. It secured an unusual amount of pupil interest and activity, correlated the work in culture with several departments, and made learning about the foreign country and its civilization a pleasure and a delight.

PARLIAMENTARY EXPRESSIONS

(French)

Je déclare la séance ouverte. L'ordre du jour. M. le secrétaire, voulez-vous bien faire l'appel (lire les noms)? M. le secrétaire, voulez-vous bien faire la lecture du procès-verbal? Y a-t-il des rectifications? des additions? Le procès-verbal est adopté. La parole est à M. . . . Passons à l'ordre du jour. M. le président, je propose que . . . Est-ce que quelqu'un veut appuyer la proposition (motion) de M. . . . ? Je l'appuie volontiers. Voulez-vous discuter cette proposition? Je vais le mettre aux voix. Que ceux qui approuvent la motion lèvent la main (droite). Maintenant, ceux qui sont de l'avis contraire. . . . Que ceux qui veulent adopter la proposition l'indiquent en disant "Oui." Que ceux qui sont de l'avis contraire disent "Non." Il y a seize voix pour. . . . Il y a huit voix contre. . . . Il n'y a pas d'opposition. La proposition est adoptée (à l'unanimité). La motion est donc votée (rejetée, repoussée). La séance est levée.

(German)

Der Vorsitzende eröffnet die Versammlung. Der Schriftführer verliest das Protokoll. Hat jemand etwas einzuwenden? Der geschäftliche Teil der Versammlung. Unerledigte Geschäfte. Berichte von Ausschüssen. Einen Antrag stellen, unterstützen, besprechen, zurückziehen, einem Ausschuss überweisen. Ums Wort bitten; das Wort haben. Ueber einen Antrag abstimmen; dafür oder dagegen stimmen. Die Abstimmung geschieht durch Ja oder Nein. Der

171

Antrag wird angenommen oder abgelehnt. Die Gegenprobe. Die Stimmenmehrheit. Die Stimmengleichheit. Die geheime Abstimmung; Stimmzettel. Der Vorsitzende ruft den Redner zur Sache. Vertagung der Versammlung. Der Ausschuss erstattet Bericht. Der Bericht wird angenommen, abgelehnt. Der Vorsitzer ernennt einen Ausschuss. Der Ausschuss schlägt die folgenden Kandidaten vor. Die Versammlung schliessen. Die Vertagung der Versammlung beantragen.

(Italian)

Si apre la seduta. Il segretario (la segretaria) passerà alla lettura del verbale della seduta precedente. Ci sono correzioni di fare al verbale letto? Il verbale si dichiara approvato.

Il primo argomento all' ordine del giorno è . . . Ci sono altri argomenti da trattare? Rapporti dei comitati. Si prega il presidente (la presidentessa) del comitato di fare la sua relazione.

Fare una proposta; presentare una mozione. Proporre di. . . . Prendere una deliberazione; approvare l'ordine del giorno. La proposta è approvata, rigettata. Mettere ai voti. Si apre la discussione sulla proposta fatta. Ritirare la deliberazione, l'ordine del giorno. La proposta è affidata al comitato.

Un socio (socia) domanda la parola. Ha la parola. I soci votano sull'ordine del giorno. Il voto è favorevole, contrario; opporre, sostenere. Chi è favorevole alla proposta alzi la mano; chi è contrario dica di "No."

La proposta è approvata. La maggioranza. La proposta è accettata ad unanimità.

Il comitato propone, nomina, i seguenti candidati. Proporre di chiudere la seduta. Si dichiara chiusa la seduta fino a. . . .

(Spanish)

Abrir la sesión. Nombrar una comisión. Los que estén por la afirmativa digan sí. Los que estén por la negativa digan no. Se aprueba la moción. Presentar una moción. Tener la palabra. Secundar la moción. Poner la cuestión a votación. Ha sido propuesto y secundado. La moción no ha sido aprobada. Proceder al nombramiento de empleados. El primer asunto de la lista. ¿Hay otros asuntos de que tratar? Proponer que se suspenda la sesión. Poner el asunto en carpeta. Corregir la constitución. Aceptar una resolución. Desechar una proposición. Retirar una moción. Posponer. Se resuelve que. Pedir la palabra para una moción de orden. Llamar al orden. Reconsiderar el voto. Un quorum. El secretario dará al acta de la sesión anterior. Pedir la palabra. Los que aprueban el acta se servirán indicarlo levantando la mano derecha. Los de opiniór contraria se serviran indicarlo de la misma manera. El acta está aprobada por mayoría de votos. Cerrar la discusión. ¿Alguno de los miembros desea presentar alguna proposición a este respecto? Proponer que se levante la sesión. Se levanta la sesión.

SUITABLE NAMES FOR SCHOOL PAPERS

(French)

Le Petit Journal, L'Étudiant Français, Le Français, L'Abeille, La Vie, La Voix, Le Courrier, Cocorico, Le Petit Canard, La Petite France, L'Oriflamme, Çà et Là, Nous Autres, Le Clairon, Le Petit Courrier, Chanticler, Le Rapporteur, Petite Revue.

(German)

Der Postillon, Der Trompeter, Das Echo, Das Deutsche Eckchen, Das Plaudermäulchen, Der gute Kamerad, Das Kränzchen, Alt Heidelberg, Kunterbunt, Allerlei, Der Ausrufer, Der Wächter, Unter Uns, Der kleine Beobachter, Der Deutsche Bote.

(Italian)

Preludio, Il Classico, Lo Studente Italiano, L'Eco, La Voce.

(Spanish)

El Faro, El Chismoso, La República, Rojo y Oro, El Correo, El Estudiante de Español, El Eco, La Luz, La Voz Estudiantil. Las Noticias, El Jefe, Adelante, La Prensita.

Illustrative Lessons

EXAMPLE OF PUPIL SELF-DIRECTION
(French)

A ninth-grade class was being conducted entirely by the pupils themselves. A girl stepped to the front and, assuming the chairmanship, announced in turn the title of each selection and the name of the pupil who was to present it. She prefaced her announcement with a little introduction in French, describing the program of the afternoon and extending a cordial welcome to the supervisor.

Nine pupils—boys and girls alternating—addressed the class in French, relating narrative and descriptive material of their own choice. Among the items were "Le Chien et le cheval," "Notre-Dame," "Marie et sa famille," "Ma bicyclette," "Pierre," "La Tempête," and "La Bibliothèque de l'école."

The pupils presented these fluently and effectively. At the close of each selection the chairman arose and inquired, "Avez-vous des corrections ou des compliments?"

Various pupils then raised their hands and offered, from notes they had made while the selection was being given, corrections in pronunciation and syntax. Occasionally the teacher, who sat in the back of the room as one of the audience, offered a correction, especially if the criticism was unjustified or entirely wrong. Sometimes, too, as in the case of the word *rue,* the teacher had a pupil point out on the pronunciation chart words illustrating this sound, and had the class read the word in concert.

Most of the pupils' comments—and there were from six to ten after each selection—were corrections of supposed mispronunciations. Each one was introduced by the expression, "Vous avez dit . . . au lieu de . . ." Sometimes a compliment was given in the form, "Vous avez bien fait."

After all the selections had been given, the teacher conferred with two pupil secretaries, who had rated each recitation and struck an average. The chairman, meanwhile, expressed her appreciation of the attention and interest of the class.

Comments. This whole activity was conducted by the pupils in the foreign language. Perhaps some of the expressions used by the pupil critics could have been less stereotyped, but the use of standardized expressions undoubtedly aided their fluency. From one third to one half of the class participated actively. It was all quite interesting and well planned. It certainly afforded much opportunity for individual oral expression, with a minimum of interference by the teacher. It is worth noting, too, that no questions were asked.

IMPROVISED DRAMATIZATION

(Spanish)

The teacher informed the class that a number of shopping scenes were to be enacted. Eliciting the Spanish words for various articles, the teacher listed them on the front board. Colors and the names of fabrics were reviewed. Expressions such as "It does not fit me," "I would like something cheaper," "I don't like this style" were added.

After a few brief introductory remarks in Spanish—with a touch of humor—the teacher called on a number of students to enact a scene between a salesman and a customer.

This was varied by a conversation between two women customers, one with the manager of the store, and the dramatization of a "nylon line." The students who participated spoke in a fairly fluent and lively manner, entering into the spirit of the occasion. Now and then the teacher, who was in the back of the room, would make a comment or a suggestion.

In instances where several articles were purchased by one customer, it was necessary to do a little addition in Spanish and to make change. This provided additional practice with numbers.

Comments. This was a lively and interesting lesson which afforded practice in many useful words and expressions. There was a maximum of pupil participation and a minimum of teacher domination. The conversation was improvised and spontaneous. It could have been improved, possibly, by a planned outline of each scene. Also, the use of a few props would have lent an air of verisimilitude to the dramatizations.

Problems

1. Select a given song in the foreign language and tell how you would teach it.

2. Prepare a series of programs for a foreign language club.

3. Describe a class project that will allow for individual differences.

4. Prepare a list of supplementary reading texts in English for a second-year group.

5. Organize a class project based on stamp collecting.

XII ˊ Culture

Although there is nothing new about teaching pupils some facts about the foreign people whose language they are learning, the systematic and organized presentation of cultural material in connection with modern language instruction is of recent development. The Modern Foreign Language Study brought out the fact that the texts most widely used in French and Spanish really contained extremely little cultural information, and that even this little consisted in the main of a mere mention. Furthermore, what did receive mention was often of comparatively little importance. In the case of the French texts, for example, the most frequently occurring item was marriage customs.

Inadequate Earlier Procedures. The earliest attempts to overcome this deficiency in foreign language teaching resulted in the employment of realia and the presentation of numerous facts. These were readily memorized by the pupil and easily tested through completion or true-false tests. The pupil learned the names of ten cities and what each was famous for, ten authors and a work of each, and so on. In German he matched Heine with Lorelei; in French he wrote Rouget de Lisle after "Marseillaise"; in Spanish he identified *picador*, Cervantes, and *puchero*. This was unfortunate, for it emphasized the acquisition of factual knowledge, was entirely unrelated to the pupil's life, and gave him nothing to do. It was mere book knowledge learned by rote. Little time was devoted to this instruction, because it was considered of comparatively minor importance.

A long step was taken forward with the introduction of a number of texts that attempted to portray foreign life interestingly and accurately. Some of these collections, in the foreign language, consisted of a series of articles on the chief phases of the nation's history. Others were comprised of brief extracts from the works of modern authors, of different points of view, so as to present various aspects of a given subject. For advanced classes there are, of course, historical readers and histories of literature in the foreign language.

Despite its indifferent treatment in the past, the teaching of culture is of paramount importance. The linguistic phase comes first, of course; the cultural follows close behind. In fact, it forms an integral part of the language teaching, for language is the chief vehicle of culture.

The Nature of Culture

In the final analysis, we do not teach foreign languages so that students may order a meal in French or write a letter in German or use the subjunctive correctly in Spanish but rather to introduce them to some of the more important characteristics of the foreign culture.

This introduction to the life of the foreign people should provide the basis for better understanding and appreciation. It should lay the foundation for permanent life interests. The presentation should, of course, be full of warmth and human interest. The listing of lifeless and unrelated facts is the very antithesis of this and defeats the purpose in view.

In its broadest sense the culture of any people or country may be viewed from a number of different aspects. There is the sociological phase; there are the artistic contributions; and there is the anthropological aspect. The sociological or social science aspect of culture comprises the history, geography, and the economic and political development of a country. Under the arts are literature, painting, sculpture, architecture, and music. From the anthropological point of view, the human behavior of a people is considered, that is, its folkways, religion, customs, typical reactions, psychological traits, daily life, standard of living, and so on.

In the past, the first two categories largely provided the material for the study of the culture of a foreign people. The student was taught facts about the geography, history, and government of the foreign nation. An attempt was made to develop an appreciation of the major contributions in literature, art, and music. Everyday activities of the foreign people were not overlooked, but they were not emphasized particularly.

Changed Emphasis

With the introduction of the new method of foreign language instruction, the attitude toward the teaching of culture has changed radically. (It is interesting to note that the term "civilization" was dropped in favor of "culture"—the original designation for this area of study.) Emphasis is placed on the way of life of the foreign people —their everyday activities—rather than on their political development or creative achievements. The point of view of the cultural anthropologists is accepted. According to them, language is the most typical and the essential element in any culture; language and culture are not separable. The daily life of a people reflects the character of any culture. The anthropologists reject the so-called refinement culture—literature, art, and music—as a phase of language instruction, asserting that books, pictures, and films concerned with a culture have presented "little more than the colorful, the quaint, and the inoffensive."

Anthropological Culture

The teaching of culture should be tied up directly with the language; "knowledge of culture is best imparted as a corollary or an obbligato to the business of language learning." [1] A daily five-minute presentation at the beginning of each language period is recommended.

Brooks offers sixty-four topics concerned with culture, with suggested questions, covering almost six pages. Examples of some of these "hors d'oeuvres," as he calls them, follow.

[1] Nelson Brooks, *Language and Language Learning* (New York: Harcourt, Brace & World, Inc., 1960), p. 86.

179

Greetings, friendly exchange, farewells. How do friends meet, converse briefly, take their leave? What are the perennial topics of small talk? How are strangers introduced?

Expletives. What words and intonation patterns are commonly used to enliven one's speech by way of commentary upon one's own feelings or actions, those of the person addressed, or the nature or behavior of other elements in the immediate situation?

Verbal taboos. What common words or expressions in English have direct equivalents that are not tolerated in the new culture, and vice versa?

Discipline. What are the norms of discipline in the home, in school, in public places, in the military, in pastimes and in ceremonies?

Pets. What animals are habitually received into the home as pets? What is their role in the household?

Personal possessions. What objects are often found decorating the bureau and walls of a young person's bedroom? What articles are likely to be discovered in a boy's pocket or a girl's handbag?

Cleanliness. What is the relation between plumbing and personal cleanliness? What standards of public hygiene and sanitation are generally observed?

Cosmetics. What are the special conditions of age, sex, activity, and situation under which make-up is permitted, encouraged, or required?

Tobacco and smoking. Who smokes, what, and under what circumstances? What are the prevailing attitudes toward smoking? Where are tobacco products obtained?

Soft drinks and alcohol. What types of nonalcoholic beverages are usually consumed by young people and adults? What is the attitude toward the use of beer, wine, and spirits? What alcoholic drinks are in frequent use at home and in public?

Cafés, bars, and restaurants. What types of cafés, bars, and restaurants are found and how do they vary in respectability?

Races, circus, rodeo. What outdoor events are in vogue that correspond to our auto or horse races, circuses, and similar spectacles? [2]

Anthropological vs. Refinement Culture

The above are some of the items of daily living that the cultural anthropologist would have the teacher present to the student of a foreign language. "It is culture in this technical, scientific sense that

[2] Brooks, pp. 86–92.

has been so misunderstood and so inadequately presented in our classrooms."

More conservative teachers may ask whether the pupil does not get a better insight into French culture by being told of the contents of the Louvre rather than of the handbag of a young Parisienne!

The topics listed by Brooks unquestionably cover many details of daily life, especially in urban areas. Whether they are all important or significant enough to be taken up within the limited time of the average foreign language course is to be questioned. The list of topics is so extensive that it must dismay the teacher who has struggled in the past with the vast body of refinement culture. Fortunately, there are several factors that relieve the burden. The first and foremost of these is the fact that the dialogues and the newer basic materials are primarily concerned with daily activities. They contain, then, the cultural data—or at least some of it—that is to be integrated with the language. Forms of address, degrees of intimacy, social customs, the names of foreign dishes, habits of eating, dress, sports, school life, and festivities are all presented. They provide plenty of factual data as well as an insight into the psychology of the foreign people.

Procedure

In order to make sure that the various items are being covered, the teacher should make a list of the idioms, model sentences, and expressions in the dialogues, and after each one indicate what cultural element it contains. This compilation will serve as a checklist of the culture to be taught during the prereading period.

In most of the newer basic books, the first dialogues are quite sure to contain references to the following items:

greetings and farewells	proverbs and sayings
polite expressions	classroom expressions
forms of address	telephoning
sports	eating and drinking
introducing persons	birthdays
numbers	festivities

The above topics are to be taken up during the prereading period, directly linked to the language activities. Gesture and dramatization will aid greatly to the verisimilitude of the situations. In some instances, as in telephoning or eating, simple props can be used to enliven the conversation. Cultural contrasts and comparisons can be brought out by reference to the pupils' own experiences.

The Teacher Paramount. The important factor, however, as in all phases of instruction, is the teacher. He must be thoroughly imbued with a knowledge of the foreign land and of its cultural achievements. In the case of the ideally prepared teacher this knowledge will be vivified by travel abroad. A teacher who has had this preparation ought to be able to give his students a coherent, sympathetic, and accurate picture of the foreign country. He will be able to arouse the interest of his listeners and stimulate them to engage in projects and research by themselves. The teaching will consist not of the memorizing of unrelated facts but rather of the presentation of opportunities for vicarious, enriching experiences.

Pupil Participation and Activity. In studying foreign civilizations the student should be active, not passive. There are many interesting and instructive things that can be done. For the resourceful teacher and the enterprising pupil the possibilities are unlimited. Pupil activity is to be utilized and maintained. How can this be done?

This can be done by training pupils to collect and organize illustrative material, to prepare scrapbooks, models, and collections, to develop projects planned by the class and the teacher, to read books in English on the foreign land, to consult books of reference, and to write in good English brief and simple reports on their reading; by having them visit ships, museums, libraries, churches, stores and shops, cultural centers, foreign quarters, concerts, and the opera; by having them report upon films and radio programs given in the foreign language. In a word, while the teacher should always guide and direct, he should at the same time stimulate as much as possible the initiative and active participation of the pupils.

Desirable Outcomes. If culture is properly taught it will enhance and enrich foreign language instruction and establish it as a significant social study. Some of the more desirable outcomes may be listed:

1. The increase in knowledge of
    a. the geography, climate, natural resources, and products of the foreign country
    b. the history, cultural achievements, social development, and international significance of the foreign people

    c. the contributions of the foreign people to American civilization.
2. The development of skill in
    a. the preparing of reports
    b. the collecting and organizing of material
    c. the use of library facilities and reference works
    d. the carrying on of individual research
    e. the preparing of projects and the construction of models.
3. The building up of attitudes of
    a. open-mindedness
    b. friendliness toward foreign peoples
    c. tolerance.
4. The growth in appreciation of
    a. the beauties of the art, music, and literature of a given foreign nation
    b. the beauties of art, music, and literature in general
    c. the fundamental process in the development of civilizations and humanity.
5. The inculcation of ideals of
    a. fairness
    b. humanity
    c. democracy.

Again, the effectiveness with which knowledge, skills, attitudes, appreciations, and ideals are taught will depend largely upon the character and personality of the teacher. In fact, in connection with the teaching of civilization, *the attitude of the teacher is more important even than his scholarly equipment. He must bring enthusiasm to his task.* "Enthusiasm" means, etymologically, "filled with the spirit of a god," and it is this conflagration that is needed to light the ready torches of the young.

As Briggs once said, it would be better that literature or music or science of a relatively superficial kind be taught with contagious enthusiasm than that Shakespeare and Beethoven and the physics of a Millikan or a Bohr be presented with mechanical dullness that creates permanently hostile attitudes toward them and their kind.

When To Teach Culture. The cultural phase of foreign language work may be carried on directly, in special periods, or indirectly, in connection with the reading. Incidental teaching has the advantage that it does not separate the linguistic from the cultural and permits the latter to arise in the most natural way from the text. Specific teaching of culture, on the other hand, has the advantage of making it possible to provide for a more complete treatment of a logical sequence of topics. A judicious combination of both incidental and specific teaching will probably prove most effective.

Incidental Teaching of Culture. Cultural facts and topics may be discussed in connection with current events, national holidays, festivals, or with their occurrence in the reading text.

In Connection with Current Events. The cabinet has fallen in Paris. A pupil has brought in a clipping from the newspaper. The teacher puts it on the bulletin board together with a picture of the new premier. The name of the new prime minister is pronounced and is written on the board. A brief discussion of the government of France and a comparison with that of the United States follows. The teacher may give a few notes under the title, "How France Is Governed."

The purchase of a Raphael is announced by the city art museum. The teacher or a pupil brings in a photograph of the new acquisition. Perhaps the teacher has a colored reproduction to show the class. The importance and significance of Raphael are discussed. Reproductions of some of his major works are passed around. Several pupils are asked to bring in reports on the artist's life and works.

An Organization of American States Conference takes place in Lima. Since this event is of considerable international importance and is featured for a week in the papers, it may be used as the basis of a number of projects. The bulletin board is given over wholly to news clippings and pictures concerned with the conference. Reports are brought in on the geography and history of Peru, the situation and importance of Lima, the Incas, the Pan American movement. The latter is, of course, considered the main topic.

In Connection with Holidays and Festivals. Christmas and Easter celebrations may form the basis of interesting projects. If several foreign languages are taught in a school, groups representing each may stage little dramatizations, including song and dance, in the auditorium, to show how these festivals are celebrated in the foreign country. The anniversaries of historic figures such as Columbus, Louis XIV, Joan of Arc, Lafayette, Cervantes, Goethe, Beethoven, and so on should also be observed in the respective foreign language class. A literary or historical calendar on the teacher's desk not only acts as a reminder of the anniversary but also presents a picture of and some important facts concerning the eminent man.

184

Occurrence in the Text. The treatment of civilization in connection with the reading depends largely upon the type of text used in the class. If a historical reader, like Hills and Dondo's *La France,* or a travel text, like Spink and Millis's *Aventures de la Famille Gautier,* is being read, there is no special problem, since the cultural material is presented in sequence and in considerable detail.

We are concerned here, instead, with cultural references in readers not specifically designed to present a civilization. Here some ingenuity is required to apportion time and attention properly and to prevent the mere accumulation of a mass of disconnected items. In some instances the selection may be such that it can be used as the basis of a topic in civilization; in other instances a single word may have to be expanded to build up a theme.

In *Pas à Pas* the first story, "Les Souliers de Noël" lends itself to a discussion of French Christmas customs; "La Laitière" to a presentation of peasant life; "Mon Premier Examen" to a comparison of school life in France and in America; "Le Chien de Brisquet" will lead to the topics "Normandy" and "Le Bûcheron."

In *Emil und die Detektive,* mentions of Berlin, Bahnof Friedrichstrasse, Kaiser-Friedrich-Museum, Bahnhof Zoo, Eisenbahnfahrplan, Café, Radfahrer, Untergrundbahn, and so on can be easily expanded.

The teacher must plan rather carefully and distinguish between words that require but a brief comment and those that are to be used as the starting point for a longer discussion. For example, the mention of a European railway compartment may be given a brief explanatory comment, or it may be used as the center of a discussion on railways and transportation in the foreign country. The treatment will depend upon the importance of the subject and how well it fits in with the syllabus in culture.

Teaching Culture in Special Periods. A civilization can be treated more fully if special time is allotted to it and a detailed plan is followed. This calls for a kind of auxiliary syllabus to accompany the regular work in language instruction.

The topics to be covered will include geography, history, transportation, chief cities, the peasant, family life and customs, schools, the foreign language, important cathedrals and other buildings, outstanding achievements in art, science, literature, and music, and the contribution of the foreign people to American civilization.

General Plan for Teaching Culture

In the *Course of Study in Modern Languages and Latin for the Secondary Schools,* issued by the Board of Education of New York City (1956), an outline of a general plan for the cultural phase of language teaching is provided. This outline is recommended for use in connection with all the modern languages. It is as follows:

I. Why should we be interested in the study of the country?
   A. Relation to the United States
      1. Foreign place names, districts in the city, areas in the U.S.
      2. Names in American history
      3. Influence on our language, food, dress, furniture, architecture, music, the arts
      4. Contributions to the American way of life
   B. Personal interests
      1. Vocational
      2. Avocational

II. We take a trip to . . . [name of country].
   A. Preparations
      1. Steamships, air service
      2. Passport, visas
      3. Currency
   B. First impressions on arrival
      1. Landscapes, streets, buildings, stores, farmlands
      2. People
      3. Architecture
      4. Means of transportation

III. We visit a home in . . . [name of country].
   A. The family
   B. Types of dwelling, rooms, furnishings, occupations, schools attended, typical meals, amusements
   C. Life in the city, in the country

IV. In developing the above topics, the teacher will plan to incorporate and correlate the relevant geographical aspects, historical background, and social and economic factors such as:
   A. Physical features of the country
      1. Geographical location
      2. Topography—rivers, mountains, lakes
      3. Climate

B. Historical background
  1. Important events and dates
  2. Holidays
  3. Outstanding personalities
  4. Form of government
C. Social and economic factors
  1. Cities
      a. Capitals, important cities, and seaports
      b. Medieval centers
  2. Industries and commerce
  3. Resources
  4. Institutions
D. Arts and sciences
  1. Music
  2. Arts
  3. Literature
  4. Science

Culture in the New York State Syllabus for French

A more recent plan for teaching culture—specifically, French culture—is that suggested in the New York State curriculum bulletin entitled *French for Secondary Schools* (Albany, 1960). It will be noted that there is no basic difference from the New York City plan; both begin with the immediate and proceed to the remote; both start with the concrete and go to the abstract.

Theme I. France in the Contemporary World
  I. The influence of France on American culture
    A. Contemporary culture
      1. French products imported
      2. English language, social customs, etc.
    B. The American heritage
      1. The role of France in early discovery
      2. Place names
      3. Areas where French is spoken
      4–6. Contributions of Frenchmen to the American scene.

  II. Areas of the world where French is the official language

  III. France, the nation
    A. The geography of France

B. Paris
C. The economic geography of France
D. Widely known social customs

IV. The community: important areas

Theme II. The France of the French

I. The French way of life
   A. Daily life in France
      1. Houses and apartments
      2. Family life
      3. Education (11 items)
      4. Recreation (11 items)
      5. The French worker (11 items)
      6. French holidays and customs
      7. French cuisine
      8. Transportation and communication
      9. The money system
     10. The metric system
     11. Religion

II. Highlights in the history of France
   A. Early invaders
   B. Great personalities of French history
   C. Outstanding events in French history

III. The historical monuments of France
   A. In Paris and its environs
   B. In the provinces

IV. The French language

V. The government of France

Theme III. France in the Development of Civilization

I. French contributions to civilization
   A. Literature
   B. The arts (painting, sculpture, architecture)
   C. The dramatic arts
   D. Music (7 items)
   E. Science (9 items)

II. The French community
III. Institutions to promote the spread of culture
IV. Democratic ideas and institutions
V. Institutions to promote research and to set standards

There are six and a half pages more detailing "Some Basic Values of the French People" under the headings Family Life; Education; Ethics and Personal Relations; Beauty, Art, and Esthetics; General Knowledge; General Conduct; Respect for French Heritage; and Language. (In their enthusiasm for presenting an attractive picture of French character, the authors of the syllabus overpraise somewhat certain French traits at the expense of American habits.)

Correlation. No other school subject provides so many opportunities for correlation with other departments as culture. The departments of English, social sciences, art, and music can all be of service in aiding the student. Correlation in the work of two or three departments can be definitely planned for a week or for a whole term. If the German classes are studying Beethoven, the music department, in its appreciation courses, can pay special attention to the works of this composer. If Spanish classes are taking up Velasquez, the art department can feature reproductions of his paintings on bulletin boards. Exchange of displays and materials should be provided for—records in music and pictures in art.

The art department can also help by supervising the work of students who are making sketches, illustrations, maps, and proverb cards for the foreign language room. The music department can render invaluable service in preparing vocal and instrumental selections for foreign language assemblies and in coaching glee clubs.

Cooperation of this sort would help to remove the barriers that seem to separate the various subjects from one another, encourage mutual helpfulness and understanding among teachers and pupils, and help to integrate the educational process.

To make research and supplementary reading feasible, the school library should definitely set aside part of its funds for the purchase of foreign language books and books in English about foreign countries. Useful reference works and collections of art reproductions should also be included.

Illustrative Lessons

READING LESSON WITH STRESS ON THE CULTURAL PHASE

(German)

A Reading Lesson. The text was "Friedrich der Grosse und Mendelssohn" in Remy & Roessler's *German Reader*. It was the familiar anecdote of Frederick the Great who placed beside the plate of the tardy philosopher Mendelssohn a note reading: "Mendelssohn ist ein Esel. Friedrich II."

The teacher began by remarking: "Heute lesen wir eine interessante Geschichte auf Seite . . . Wie ist der Titel?"

"Friedrich der Grosse und Mendelssohn."

"Wer war Friedrich der Grosse?"

A pupil who had an index card which the teacher had given him before class raised his hand. The card contained three typewritten sentences in German which the pupil read aloud:

"Friedrich der Grosse war der berühmteste König von Preussen. Er lebte zur Zeit von George Washington. Er war nicht nur ein grosser General, sondern auch ein kluger König."

The teacher said, "Sehr gut!" and then commented on Frederick's unhappy youth, his love for things French, his severe father, his admiration for Washington, his sympathy with the American cause, and the fact that he sent his sword to Washington at Mount Vernon with the words, "From the oldest general in the Old World to the bravest general in the New World." Also, reference was made to Frederick's enlightened despotism, his tolerance, and his broadmindedness. The teacher displayed good pictures of Frederick, of Sans Souci, and of Potsdam. Mention was made of Jannings in the excellent film *Der alte und der neue König*.

"But we have another name in the title. Who has heard of Mendelssohn? Watch the spelling of his name!"

A pupil volunteered, "He was a composer."

"Ja, das ist richtig, Felix Mendelssohn war ein Komponist. Also, wer war Felix Mendelssohn?"

The pupil who had the appropriate index card read aloud:

"Felix Mendelssohn, der Komponist, komponierte viele schöne

Stücke. Er wurde in Hamburg geboren. Schon mit siebzehn Jahren shrieb er die Musik zu Shakespeares Sommernachtstraum."

"That is correct; the music of the *Midsummer Night's Dream* is well known. But which one of Mendelssohn's compositions is even more universally known—one which all you girls hope some day to hear when you go to the altar?"

"The Wedding March."

"That's correct. There is another one, that goes like this [the teacher hummed]. Who composed that?"

"Wagner."

"Richtig. Wagner war auch ein Komponist. Was ist ein Komponist?"

"A composer."

"Nennen Sie etliche Komponisten."

The pupil read from the card, "Berühmte Komponisten waren Bach, Mozart, Beethoven, Wagner."

The teacher meanwhile wrote the words *der Komponist* on the board.

"Now just to show you what sort of music Mendelssohn composed, I will play several selections for you."

On the portable phonograph the teacher then played selections from the overture to the *Midsummer Night's Dream*. After getting the pupils' reaction to this, the teacher remarked,

"Mendelssohn composed music for a number of Shakespeare's plays. Here is 'Who is Sylvia?' " She played the record.

"Mendelssohn was one of the famous composers of *Lieder*, like Schubert and Schumann. Here is a very well known one, entitled 'On Wings of Song.' You must have heard it innumerable times on the radio." She played the record.

"How do you like this music? What is its characteristic quality?

"Now this music was composed by Felix Mendelssohn. The Mendelssohn of our story, however, was the philosopher Moses Mendelssohn. Also, wer war Moses Mendelssohn?"

The pupil read, "Moses Mendelssohn war ein Philosoph. Er war der Grossvater des Komponisten Felix Mendelssohn."

The teacher wrote *der Philosoph* on the board.

"Was ist ein Philosoph?"

"A philosopher."

"And what is a philosopher?"

"A philosopher is a man who has worked out a definite system of thought or a definite view of life. Famous philosophers of ancient times were Socrates, Aristotle, and Plato. A famous English philosopher was John Locke. Some very famous German philosophers were Kant, Fichte, Schopenhauer, and Nietzsche."

"Can anyone name an American philosopher? . . . Well, there is John Dewey and also Santayana, who wrote a novel, *The Last Puritan*." The teacher made a few comments on Dewey's influence on education.

"Now, in our story another famous man is mentioned—Lessing. Wer war Lessing?"

The pupil read, "Lessing war ein berühmter deutscher Dichter. Er schrieb *Nathan der Weise*, ein Drama, das die Toleranz lehrt."

Meanwhile, the teacher wrote on the board *der Dichter, das Drama, die Toleranz*. The meanings of these words were skillfully elicited.

"Well, now, here we have an unusual situation: the rather severe, aristocratic Prussian king and the little middle-class Jewish philosopher. Both sit down together at an evening meal in the beautiful royal palace, Sans Souci. Because of the philosopher's lateness in arriving, the king has left a brusque note at his plate. But the philosopher is quick at repartee. How many of you would like to read the story and hear what the witty reply was that the little Jewish philosopher gave the mighty Prussian king?"

The class now read the story silently while the teacher wrote on the board another dozen words and idioms from the text. After the silent reading had been completed—within a few minutes—the teacher asked simple questions in German on the text. Meanwhile, six pupils with index cards had been sent to the board to do exercises based on the text. These brought out and reviewed grammatical points occurring in the text.

The board work was corrected as soon as the oral work was finished. The teacher commented on the exercises, getting the pupils to point out briefly what was involved. Finally, volunteers were called on to go to the front of the room and summarize the story in simple German. About five pupils did this, the class offering suggestions and pointing out errors.

Comments. This lesson was particularly rich in cultural content. It shows what can be done when the teacher considers himself not merely a language teacher but an educator in the widest sense of the word.

A wealth of information was presented within the framework of the lesson built up on a simple anecdote about Frederick the Great. This was possible because the lesson had been carefully planned and because the teacher used the device of supplying certain pupils with index cards containing the information asked for. In this way no time was lost and attention was concentrated on the points selected for study. There was, as will be noted, a minimum of word study, pronunciation, and drill. The emphasis was on the cultural side.

At the close of such a period the pupil should be able to define *Philosoph, Komponist, Dichter,* and *König,* and give examples of each; he should have some idea of the character and significance of Frederick the Great; he should have some appreciation of the beauty of Mendelssohn's music and of the palace of Sans Souci. The ideals of tolerance and understanding and his sense of humor should have become strengthened; an interesting anecdote should have been added to his repertory; and his fluency and command of German should have increased. Not to be overlooked are such incidental references as those to John Dewey and Santayana, which connect the simple little story of the eighteenth century with the present time. The anecdote is an especially apposite one in these days of racial prejudice and intolerance. The lesson becomes an emotional and moral experience as well as a language exercise.

CULTURAL LESSON ON NOTRE DAME AND THE LOUVRE

(French)

Aim

To teach some facts about Notre Dame and the Louvre, and to arouse an interest in, and appreciation of, these buildings. Also, to teach an appreciation of some works of French painting and sculpture.

Text

Huebener & Neuschatz's *Parlez-vous Français?* pp. 352–55, "A Famous Cathedral and a Famous Museum."

Materials

Photographs, pictures, or slides of Notre Dame, Sainte-Chapelle, the Louvre, the Bastille Column. Reproductions of several famous works of art in the Louvre, for example, the "Venus de Milo," the "Winged

Victory," the "Mona Lisa," paintings by Millet, David, Watteau, Greuze, Monet, Cézanne.

Assignments and Preparation

The class has read at home "A Famous Cathedral and a Famous Museum." Five pupils have been asked to look up and bring in reports on

1. Gothic architecture
2. the description of Notre Dame in Victor Hugo's *The Hunchback of Notre-Dame*
3. Millet
4. a summary of the taking of the Bastille from *A Tale of Two Cities*
5. works of art in the Louvre.

For (1) and (3) the pupils can be referred to the encyclopedia; for (2) and (4) they should consult the actual novels; for (5) any popular work on art can be used. *Paris* by Pierre-Gauthiez (available in French and English, and profusely illustrated) is to be recommended.

Procedure

The teacher motivates the day's lesson by saying, "Now today, *mes enfants*, we will pay a flying visit to Paris. What buildings or structures come to mind when we hear Paris mentioned?"

"Notre Dame and the Louvre."

"Yes, perhaps above all the Arch of Triumph, where the Unknown Soldier is buried, and the Eiffel Tower. But today we will visit the beautiful cathedral and the famous museum. Here is a picture of Notre Dame; notice the tall square towers, the large rose window, the three immense entrances. . . . What style of architecture is this?"

"Gothic."

"That is correct. And what do we understand by that? William, read your report on Gothic architecture."

William goes to the front and reads his report. Being an enterprising youngster he has also brought in some pictures of famous Gothic cathedrals and mentions some Gothic churches in the vicinity of the school.

"Excellent. But let us hear more about Notre Dame. Elizabeth, what does Victor Hugo tell us about it in his famous *Hunchback of Notre-Dame?*"

After the reading of the report, the teacher presents her pictures or slides of the cathedral, with interesting comments. Having been in Paris last summer, she brings in some colorful personal reminiscences. The Sainte-Chapelle comes in for incidental mention.

The Louvre is treated in the same way. Care must be taken not

194

to yield to the temptation of presenting too much. About a half dozen French artists and ten works of art should be treated. The teacher may introduce a few more by incidental mention.

Problems and Questions for Discussion

1. Discuss the problems involved in presenting controversial topics in the foreign language classroom.

2. List the places and institutions in your locality that would be of interest to your students in connection with given topics in civilization, for example, a Gothic church—architecture; an art museum —painting; a foreign restaurant—cooking, and so on.

3. Using a given reading selection as the basis, indicate what cultural references you would exploit incidentally.

4. Outline a culture lesson on a given topic for a fourth-level class.

5. Discuss the difficulties involved in testing the desired outcomes from the teaching of culture.

XIII ʹ Foreign Languages in the Elementary School

History. The teaching of foreign languages in the public elementary schools is not new. In a number of cities of the Midwest (Cincinnati, Milwaukee, and St. Louis), as well as in Buffalo, German was taught during the latter half of the nineteenth century. French was offered in some elementary schools in San Francisco and in several cities in New England; Spanish was taught in the rural schools of New Mexico. At the turn of the century both French and German were taught in the eighth grade of New York City's grade schools. Interest, however, waned, and because of highly aroused emotions during World War I, such instruction was dropped.

After the war some attempts were made to restore it. French was introduced in 1921 in the elementary schools of Cleveland as part of the enrichment program for superior children in grades 1 to 6. In 1924 the same language was begun in the sixth grade in Oakwood-Dayton, Ohio. Some other projects of this kind—all in French —were set up in Niagara Falls, New York (1930), Breaux Bridge, Louisiana (1932), P.S. 99, Brooklyn (1934), P.S. 208, Brooklyn (1936), and Detroit (1935). This tendency was accelerated by the renewed interest in foreign languages brought about by World War II. Smaller classes were organized, the conversational aim was set up, and mechanical aids were employed. Particular stress was placed upon the importance of beginning foreign language instruction earlier.

Foreign Languages in the Elementary Schools (FLES). These efforts were more or less sporadic until they were officially recognized by Earl J. McGrath, U.S. Commissioner of Education. In a stirring speech in St. Louis, in 1952, he gave the idea such impetus that it became a country-wide movement. The following year he called a conference in Washington on the "Role of Foreign Languages in American Schools," which was attended by 350 educators. In 1951 nine new programs had been introduced; by 1953 there were 65 new projects in this area. Within a few years 300,000 children were receiving instruction in a foreign language in grades 1–6. Over three fourths of the enrollment was in Spanish, about one fifth was in French, and the rest was in German or other languages.

An active and enthusiastic champion of the movement was Professor Theodore Andersson of Yale University, who was serving as director of the country-wide foreign language study of the MLA. This organization gave the matter a great deal of attention and, under the direction of Dr. Kenneth Mildenberger, developed much useful material for the classroom teacher. For the sake of brevity the movement was named FLES (Foreign Languages in the Elementary Schools).

At first the idea took root in smaller rather than in larger communities. The movement was slow in reaching the big cities. Although New York had had some foreign language classes in the grades since 1934, no official action was taken until 1958. In that year French and Spanish were introduced as part of an enrichment program for intellectually gifted children.

Pro and Con. Although the movement has been making steady headway over the years, many educational administrators are not fully convinced. In fact, there are language specialists who are opposed. The arguments in favor of the earlier start are generally the following:

1. Only by an early start can language mastery be assured.
2. Preadolescents can learn a foreign language without self-consciousness. They are free of the inhibitions of the adult learner.
3. The early start instills respect for other people and fosters tolerance.
4. Appreciably more children will be eager to study a foreign language later on.
5. The student who began early will be much further along in high school and in college.

Those who are skeptical of the value of the early instruction reply:

1. The teaching of a foreign language in the grades requires time and money. We cannot afford to sacrifice essential learning to a subject of doubtful value.
2. Peace may be furthered by the knowledge of a foreign language, but few attain a sufficient facility to make it useful. Furthermore, to further peace we should study Russian and Chinese, rather than French and Spanish.
3. There are few teachers on the elementary level who have mastery of a foreign language.
4. Dependable research is insufficient to indicate conclusively that the preadolescent has greater ability to learn a language.
5. Bilingualism tends to interfere with the learning of the vernacular.

Problems. Despite the objections expressed above, FLES has been growing year by year. Colleges, too, have faith in the movement, for more and more courses are being organized to train language teachers for the grades.

A number of problems still remain to be solved, however. Among these are the following:

1. In what grade is instruction to begin?
2. Is it to be for all children or only for the bright?
3. Is it to be offered only for enrichment or as a foundation for later language study?
4. If it is to be a foundation, how will it be linked with courses in the junior and senior high school? What credit is to be given?
5. Which one, or ones, of the four most widely taught foreign languages shall be offered?
6. Exactly what are the objectives to be attained?
7. Is the classroom teacher or a specialist to conduct the session?

There is no agreement, even among language experts, on the above questions. If the movement is to succeed, aims and norms must be agreed on and materials and procedures must be worked out. A steady supply of trained teachers must be available. It is of the utmost importance, too, that the course of study be cumulative and sequential, so that a firmer foundation is laid for formal language study in high school.

In most cases the teaching of a foreign language to younger children is done informally. Formal instruction is avoided. Incidental learning, however, is ineffective in the long run and the teacher soon realizes that the laws of learning apply for the very young as they do for the older pupil. The basic principle of learning, especially in the case of a language, is repetition.

Repetitio Mater Studiorum. The same word, the same expression, must be practiced many times before it becomes automatic. With younger children the amount of repetition must be increased.

Continued repetition, however, leads to monotony and a killing of interest. The teacher must, therefore, be resourceful in devising ways and means of introducing variety. The same material must be reviewed in different ways.

How is this to be done? Largely by varying the questions, introducing new activities, using different kinds of illustrative material, and employing new devices.

Another basic principle in language learning is imitation. Children will imitate readily and will acquire the sounds of another language, but they must hear them correctly. In the beginning much chorus response will be used. There is danger here that not all pupils will be pronouncing accurately. This may be overcome by calling on individual pupils and by spot checks.

The foreign language should, of course, be used as much as possible, but it is no crime to use the vernacular occasionally. In fact, it is economical and sensible to make brief comments in English. Use of the foreign language exclusively may lead to misunderstanding, loss of interest, and frustration.

The tempo of the lesson should be brisk; the tone should be cheerful. To maintain interest at high pitch there should be a variety of activities. In fact, no activity or exercise should go on for more than ten minutes.

Since younger children are physically active, it is important to employ activities that require moving about or the use of hands and arms. The action series is especially useful in this respect, since it combines the spoken word with the appropriate action. Games, too, are very good. Much action can be secured by giving commands to individual pupils or to the whole class. Dialogues and little dramatizations are very effective.

At every session at least one song should be sung. It has been found that leadership by the teacher or by a pupil with a good voice is preferred by the class over the playing of a record. In some instances the song can be dramatized or combined with actions (for example, "Alouette," "Sur le pont d'Avignon").

Objectives. In New York City the foreign language program in the elementary schools is confined to some two hundred classes of intellectually gifted children. Several foreign languages are offered; instruction in them is given three times a week or ninety minutes in all. The program begins in the fourth grade and continues through the fifth and sixth grades. Articulation with the junior high schools is provided.

According to Curriculum Bulletin No. 13, *French in the Elementary Schools, Grades 4–5–6,* the objectives of the program are the following:

> The ability to listen to and understand a native speaker in a conversational situation within the child's experience
>
> The ability to express himself in the foreign language using the correct sound system in a conversational situation within his experience
>
> The ability to read aloud (using the correct sound system) and to read silently (with comprehension and without recourse to English translation) material that has been mastered audio-lingually
>
> The ability to copy material that has been mastered audio-lingually and to write it from dictation, and the ability to do simple written exercises based on the structures learned
>
> In addition, it is hoped that the children . . . will gradually develop an understanding and an insight into the behavior and thought processes of the people whose language they have been studying . . .

It is evident that the objectives are practically identical with those posited for the secondary school level.

Basic Considerations. In any well-organized FLES program provision is, of course, made for articulation with the upper years. The guiding principles and basic procedures are therefore bound to be almost alike. Almost, but not quite, for we are dealing with younger children and maturity and experience do make a difference. The everyday life situations of the elementary school pupil are different from those of the high school student. Classroom devices and games that appeal to the little child are likely to bore and seem ridiculous to the teen-ager, whereas extended drills and exercises are out of place on the lower level.

This means that in working out the content of the topics the situations will be somewhat different. Pattern drills will be modified and not used a great deal. In fact, exercises will be varied and kept brief so as to maintain interest. Even the all-important dialogue will not be the core of every lesson.

A big difference between the lower and the upper years will be the use of the familiar pronoun. This cannot be avoided, if the situations and conversations are to be authentic.

On the other hand, the same basic principles of language learning that occur on the secondary level will be observed in the elementary classes, namely:

1. As far as possible, the foreign language will be the language of the classroom. English will be used sparingly.
2. The teacher will speak clearly and distinctly, but at the normal rate of speed.
3. Listening and speaking will precede reading and writing.
4. Structures are to be learned by imitation and repetition.
5. Words and sentences are to be associated with actions, pictures, objects, and persons. Translation is to be avoided.
6. New words are taught in context and not in isolation.

The Dialogue. As stated above, the dialogue is not quite as important on the elementary level as in the upper classes. It may be introduced at the beginning of a period or may summarize a series of lessons. In the latter case the children will be using functionally words and structures they have learned. Dramatization will add to the liveliness of the situation.

The approach is slightly different from that used at the high school level. After having given a brief explanation of the content of the dialogue in English, the teacher acts out the parts herself. If they are suitable, dolls, puppets, or drawings on the board may be used to enliven the roles. The teacher recites the dialogue two or three times.

The dialogue is then imitated by the class, first in chorus, then in groups, and finally by individual pupils. Only after it has been thoroughly memorized should any attempt be made to dramatize it.

During the choral recitation, the teacher will go about the room to catch mispronunciations. Certain words and phrases may have to be singled out for correct and remedial practice.

Dialogue Adaptation. After the dialogue has been mastered, basic structures will be practiced in different types of pattern drills. The most useful ones will be found to be repetition, question-and-answer, cued responses, relay, substitution, replacement, and transformation. Of course, not all of these will be used in one lesson; possibly three or four will suffice. It is especially important, at this stage, to keep the exercises brief and to have frequent changes from one activity to another.

The pattern drills are useful not only for reinforcing the automatic manipulation of structures but to build up vocabulary. For this purpose the response, repetition, and substitution drills are particularly effective.

Grammar

The teaching of grammar on the elementary level follows the same plan as that on the high school levels, namely, grammatical structures are learned through frequent repetition of model sentences. Constant pattern practice should establish automatic responses. Knowledge of the correct forms, as well as facility in their use, is acquired through repeated practice.

The following points in grammar are suggested for listening comprehension and for speaking.

FRENCH

Grade 4

    Definite and indefinite articles, singular and plural
    Gender and number of nouns
    Masculine and feminine, and plural, of adjectives
    Possessive adjectives

Subject pronouns
Regular verbs of the first conjugation
Irregular verbs: *aller, avoir, être, faire, voir*
Time expressions: days, months, hours of day
Numbers: from 1 to 50
Contractions of *de* and *à*, with article
Voici, voilà, il y a
Weather expressions
Idioms with *avoir*

Grade 5

Possession
Irregular adjectives
Numbers: from 50 to 100; simple arithmetic; dates
Verbs of second and third conjugations
Some irregular verbs
Idiomatic expressions

Grade 6

Possessive adjectives
Telling of time, in detail
Verbs of second and third conjugations
Several more irregular verbs
Adjectives, irregularities
Numerals: 1 to 100, 1000, 1,000,000; dates (years)

SPANISH

Grade 4

Definite and indefinite articles; plurals
Nouns, singular and plural
Masculine and feminine of adjectives; agreement
Possessive adjectives
Subject pronouns
Regular verb of first conjugation
Irregular verbs: *estar, hacer, ir, poner, tener, ser, ver*
Numerals: 1 to 50
Telling time; days, months, seasons
Possession
Contraction of *de* and *al*
Weather expressions
Idioms with *tener*

Grade 5

Numerals: 50 to 100; simple arithmetic; dates
Telling time; minutes
Verbs of second and third conjugations
Some irregular verbs
Idiomatic expressions

Illustrative Lessons

A FIRST LESSON IN FRENCH

The teacher enters the room and says to the class, "Bonjour!" By an encouraging wave of the hand she indicates that the class is to repeat. If the pupils do not catch on, she can say: "Repeat after me," or "Répétez."

Then she will say, "Bonjour, mes enfants . . . and you will say, 'Bonjour, Madame.'"

TEACHER: Bonjour, mes enfants!
CLASS: Bonjour, Madame!

After several repetitions, the teacher circulates and shakes hands with individual pupils, saying: "Bonjour, Georges, Bonjour, Robert," and so on. Pupils will reply, "Bonjour, Madame."

Then the teacher says, pointing to herself: "Je m'appelle Mme Jones." Pointing to a pupil she says, "Comment t'appelle-tu? . . . I'm asking you for your name . . . Answer, 'Je m'appelle . . .'" Various pupils give their names. The teacher says, "Très bien, très bien . . . Chester, what do you think I said?"

As a pupil answers, the teacher gives him the French equivalent of his name, if there is one. "Now you will ask one another for your names." A chain drill follows.

A game is now played. One pupil faces the board and tries to guess who is speaking. "Bonjour, Alain!" "Tu t'appelle Robert." "Non, je m'appelle Jean." The pupil whose name is guessed correctly then takes the place of the one at the board.

The third person is introduced by the teacher's pointing and remarking, "Il s'appelle Henri," and asking the question, "Comment s'appelle-t-il?" For girls, of course, *elle* will be used.

204

At the close of the period, the teacher will say, "Au revoir, classe!" and the class will say, "Au revoir, Mme Jones!"

A SECOND LESSON IN FRENCH

What was learned in the first lesson will be repeated. "Bonjour, mes enfants!" "Bonjour, Mme Jones!" Names will be asked for by the teacher and in chain drill. The teacher will note absentees.

"Ah, où est Robert? . . . Il est absent . . . Où est Marie? Elle est absente." These expressions will be practiced and will be followed by "Il est malade," "Elle est malade," and "Quel dommage!"

Pointing to herself the teacher will say, "Je suis le professeur," and pointing to a pupil, "Tu es un élève." The pupils will be taught to answer, "Je suis un élève (une élève)" in answer to the question, "Qui es-tu?"

This expression can be developed into "Es-tu le professeur?" and the answer, "Non, je suis un élève." The pattern can be reinforced with chain drill. Another question to ask will be, "Qui es-tu?"

If time permits, extra drill can be given on "est-il absent?" and "est-il malade?" The negative will, of course, have to be avoided for the time being.

At the close of the period, the teacher will say say, "Au revoir, mes enfants," and the class, "Au revoir, Mme Jones."

A THIRD LESSON IN FRENCH

After the expressions learned in the second lesson have been reviewed, the teacher will say to individual pupils, "Comment vas-tu?" and the pupil will be taught to reply, "Très bien, merci, et vous?" to the teacher. He will ask a fellow-pupil, "Comment vas-tu?" in the chain drill. At this point the teacher can explain the difference between the two pronouns. To avoid difficulties, the reply to the question will remain: "Très bien."

To summarize what has been learned, a little dialogue can be worked out. This will assume the following form:

—Bonjour!
—Bonjour!

—Qui es-tu?
—Je suis un élève.
—Comment t'appelle-tu?
—Je m'appelle _____
—Comment vas-tu?
—Très bien, et tu?
—Très bien aussi. Au revoir!
—Au revoir!

The dialogue should always be kept short, but if time permits and the class is bright, a few more items may be added such as:

—Robert est absent.
—Pourquoi?
—Il est malade.
—Quel dommage!

The dialogue will be recited in chorus, in groups and individually. Two pupils can act it out before the class.

In each of the three lessons different drill patterns can be used. This will constitute the so-called dialogue adaptation. The simplest is, of course, the repetition drill, which merely requires the pupil to repeat what the teacher says. The next step is the response drill —questions and answers, first between teacher and pupil and then between pupil and pupil. The latter leads to the relay, or chain drill. The same thought may sometimes be expressed in several ways: "Je suis le professeur. Et tu?" "Je suis un élève (une élève)." "Es-tu le professeur?" "Non, je suis un élève." "Es-tu un élève?" "Oui, je suis un élève." In the directed dialogue the teacher instructs the pupil: "Demandez à Robert s'il est le professeur." This can be expanded to ". . . le professeur ou un élève."

A GEOGRAPHY LESSON WITH BRIGHT SIXTH-GRADE PUPILS

(French)

The teacher asked questions in French about France and its neighbors. After each pupil had answered, he wrote his sentence on the board. Some of the statements were: "L'Espagne est en Europe."

"Voici la carte de France." "La France est en Europe." "L'Italie est en Europe." "L'Angleterre est en Europe." The two maps in the front of the room were continually referred to.

The teacher continued her questioning along the following lines: "Nomez quelques pays en Europe . . . Comment s'appellent les habitants de l'Italie? de l'Espagne? de l'Allemagne? de la France? . . . Voici un autre pays en Europe: la Suisse. Montrez-moi l'Allemagne . . . Quels sont les pays qui sont voisins de la France?"

Next, surrounding bodies of water and the various rivers of France were taken up. In connection with the English Channel, the teacher said, "Voici La Manche. Une manche, qu'est-ce que c'est?" She pointed to her sleeve. "Montrez-moi votre manche. Why do you suppose it has this name?"

The teacher skillfully "unlocked" new words by circumlocution or gesture, as when she remarked, "Un océan est un grand étendu d'eau," and made a sweeping gesture to indicate expanse.

She also elicited definitions from pupils by asking such questions as "Quelle est la différence entre un fleuve et une rivière?"

Questions on various rivers of France followed. Cities, too, were located on the map.

The lesson closed with the singing of a number of songs which referred to French regions and cities, such as "Ma Normandie" and "Paris."

Comments. With a little skill, as in the lesson described above, the teacher can combine the teaching of geography with the learning of French in an interesting manner. The entire lesson was well organized, even the songs contributing to the topic.

ORAL COMPOSITION WITH FIFTH-GRADE PUPILS

(French)

After copies of the textbook Le Français Vivant had been distributed, they were opened to page 13. The teacher introduced the story, "Jacqueline a une poupée," with a few simple sentences in French. This led to questions in French, "Qui a une poupée? Comment s'appelle-t-elle? Avez-vous une poupée?" When a boy was called on, the class burst into laughter. The boy, however, rose to the occasion by answering, "Je ne suis pas une fille." The teacher then inquired, "Avec quoi jouez-vous?"

The teacher now read the selection sentence-by-sentence. The class repeated it in concert. When black hair was mentioned, the teacher pointed at a child with black hair, at another with blonde, and at another with red hair. She also distinguished between the words *rouge* and *roux*.

Then the teacher remarked, "Now let us make up a story about something—about your doll, your family, or yourself." Various members of the class contributed about twenty sentences, ranging in length from three words to thirteen. They mentioned the members of their family, their toys, their friends, the color of their hair, what they ate, and so on. Occasionally, the teacher stimulated the pupils by a question or two in French. At the end of the exercise she remarked, "I think we have a very nice story. How many children would now like to sing?"

The teacher brought out a record player, and while it played "Frère Jacques" the class sang. When the machine broke down, a boy was called to the front to lead the class in the singing of three additional songs. Each child had a notebook in which the words of a number of songs had been copied.

Comments. A good deal of the pleasurableness of this lesson was due to the personal note that the teacher introduced in her questions. This made the conversation seem perfectly natural.

A LESSON WITH FOURTH-GRADE PUPILS

(French)

The teacher began the lesson by greeting the class in French and asking a few simple questions. The class answered these in concert and then several pupils answered individually.

Next, the teacher explained the reason for the vocabulary that appeared on the front board and that was entitled "La Cuisine Française." She had written the chef of the restaurant Louis XIV for a bill of fare and for some recipes. The chef had sent these and now the class was making a study of the menu.

As the teacher pointed to each word she pronounced it and the class repeated it in concert. In a number of instances she brought in very interesting cultural references. In connection with *bouilla-baisse* she elicited that this soup was made in Marseille, the largest port in southern France, from which ships sailed to Africa. One pupil was called upon to explain just what *crêpe suzette* was.

Next, various pupils were called on to point out objects in the room and to perform simple actions. A boy went to the door, opened it, closed it, and sat down again. The class showed the teacher their rulers, their pencils, their notebooks, and so on. The teacher employed such expressions as *montrez-moi, touchez, où est, donnez-moi*.

The masculine and feminine forms of the definite article were distinguished. The teacher also asked, "From what language does French really come? What kind of Latin did the Roman soldiers speak?" Then she introduced the class to a little elementary etymology, explaining the derivation of *tête* from the Latin *testa* (bean), the humor in back of the word, and the significance of the circumflex accent. She also elicited the relationship of French to English.

The form *j'ai* was then reviewed. A lively exercise in oral composition resulted when the pupils were asked to say something about their family. Many of them contributed, beginning their sentences with *j'ai*. The teacher then used the blackboard to illustrate the use of *a* as the third person of the verb, without, however, using any grammatical nomenclature. She used the model sentence, "Marie a une mère." While paper was being passed out, six pupils were sent to the front board and six to the rear. The teacher dictated three sentences as follows:

Je m'appelle _____.
J'ai un père et une mère.
Qui a trois livres?

The sentences on the board were quite correct except for the last word. Evidently the pupils were not yet familiar with the plural. The teacher explained it to them. After going over the board work and commenting on the significance of the apostrophe and the grave accent, the teacher had the class sing a French song.

Comments. The teacher's lively manner and her skill in employing a wide variety of exercises made this a very interesting lesson. Precision in pronunciation was insisted on, although the teacher did not demand too much in this regard. Grammatical terminology was dispensed with. The children learned forms and constructions as if they were vocabulary.

DRAMATIZATION WITH A CLASS OF BRIGHT CHILDREN

(French)

This selected group consisted of pupils from 4B through 6B.

A little girl went to the front of the room and inquired, "Quelle chanson voulez-vous?" One pupil suggested "Frère Jacques." The class sang this song while two pupils acted it out in the front of the room.

This was followed by the singing of the "Marseillaise." At the words *marchons, marchons,* the children tramped in march time. The teacher, who had been standing on one side without intervening, inquired, "Does anyone want to tell us about this song?" A little girl arose, went to the front, and related in lively and fluent English how the "Marseillaise" was written.

Next, the teacher suggested a game and twelve pupils lined up in front of the room. One youngster explained the story which they were about to enact, namely, "Notre Ane." Each pupil in turn told of some ailment from which the donkey was suffering and the cure that was attempted. The whole group sang a refrain after each pupil's recital, accompanying the singing with expressive gestures. Two boys took the role of the donkey.

This was followed by the acting out of a street scene in which four women meet and chat.

Next, five girls danced in a ring and sang the song, "Savez-vous planter les choux?" The whole class then sang, with accompanying gestures, the little ditty, "C'est comme ça."

A somewhat more pretentious dramatization now followed. A dozen pupils went to the front of the room and acted out "The Three Little Pigs" while several pupils told the story in fluent French. Next came a little dramatization of "The Three Bears" and then a simplified version of "The Bluebird."

Then came some conversation. A little girl in the front of the room asked some of her classmates questions and gave them orders

210

to carry out. As they did so, she told in French what was being done. Then another pupil pointed to one of his classmates and designated him as a given animal ("Vous êtes un chien," for example). The pupil pointed to would then emit the sound made by the animal.

Comments. The children in this group had memorized an amazing amount of French and rattled it off in the most natural manner. Their repertory of little dramatizations and songs was extensive. The teacher had to make corrections less than half a dozen times. No grammatical terms were employed. The speech was as natural as the vernacular, and it was made more effective and meaningful by the accompanying gestures.

Problems

1. Write a refutation of the five objections to teaching foreign languages in the elementary schools, given on page 198.
2. Make a list of the differences between an elementary school child and a high school student that would be significant factors in planning the teaching of a foreign language.
3. Prepare a lesson for a fifth-grade class on Christmas.
4. Prepare a lesson for a fourth-grade class on Thanksgiving.
5. Tell how a visit to the zoo might be made the basis of an interesting and effective language unit in the sixth year.

XIV ' Evaluation

Measurement. Learning is measured primarily for purposes of administration and supervision, and for the purpose of evaluating the effectiveness of instruction. Pupil achievement may be judged by an estimate of classroom performance or on the basis of examinations. The former is the informal, subjective method of teacher judgment; the latter is the more formal, objective method.

In foreign languages it is necessary to measure the skills and the knowledge the pupils have acquired in each of the various phases of language learning. The test may be employed for diagnostic or prognostic purposes. It may also have as its aim the stimulation of the pupil to his best effort. Depending upon its construction, a test may have a favorable or an unfavorable influence on the learning situation.

Since the measurement movement in education began, efforts have been made to appraise every kind of educational outcome statistically. There is hardly a subject in the whole curriculum for which tests have not been devised. Everything from such humble skills as sewing and woodworking to character traits like honesty and ambition have been measured.

An accurate appraisal of any educational outcome requires a statistically correct measuring device and an intelligent interpretation of the resultant figures. The devices consist of two kinds: the test and the scale. The standardized test is an examination in which the materials, the time, the conduct, and the scoring are rigidly prescribed. The norms of the test have been standardized. The objective test, on the other hand, is unstandardized and consists merely of new-type questions.

The measuring scale is an arrangement of the test results or scores in such a way as to indicate a series of steps in ability ranging from zero to a maximum degree, by units or steps. The scale is a fixed standard with which any individual or group of individuals may be compared.

A test must possess two fundamental qualities: validity and reliability. A test is valid to the degree to which it measures what it purports to measure. It is reliable to the degree to which it measures what it does measure. The reliability of the test on the basis of a comparison between two tests is termed the coefficient of correlation. The comparison may be made with other measurements of the same ability—other test scores, teachers' marks, and so on. If the correlation is below .80, it is low and unreliable.

There are different types of tests for different purposes: prognostic, to discover the presence of certain abilities; diagnostic, to locate specific weaknesses in the pupil's learning; achievement, to measure the amount that has been learned. The latter is also known as a survey test. To achieve its real purpose a diagnostic test should suggest remedial measures for the individual weaknesses. Basic, however, in all educational measurement and of prime importance for prognosis is the general intelligence test.

Achievement tests are also employed to measure the pupil's degree of mastery of a given section of a textbook. These may be designed to test as frequently as every three lessons, with special review tests for every eight or nine lessons.

Information is relatively easy to measure, but the ability to think and reason is not so easily appraised. Most difficult of all to measure are the emotions and character traits. It is not possible to measure all human reactions; only the narrower products of education can be appraised statistically.

The chief value of measurements and standardized tests has been a decrease in the element of subjectivity and an increase in that of objectivity in evaluating the results of learning. The use of tests and scales has also made it possible to appraise the pupil in terms of his own capacity, so that each pupil's work may be placed on a sounder and fairer basis. Adaptations to individual differences can be more effectively achieved. Furthermore, diagnostic tests have made possible the location of special difficulties and weaknesses, permitting the more effective use of remedial measures. Also, some progress has been made in the use of prognostic tests, so that pupils may be properly guided in their choice of courses and subjects.

Purposes of Testing. It is undoubtedly true that many teachers still think of testing as a probing, by means of a written examination, into the pupils' fund of accumulated knowledge, for the purpose of assigning a rating. Actually testing is an integral part and a continuous function of teaching. In fact, the rating or mark is a minor factor; the test serves far more important functions. There are:

1. The diagnosis of individual, or group, weaknesses, deficiencies, and errors in learning
2. The selection, grouping, and placement of students
3. The better organization of instruction
4. The review of knowledge acquired
5. The adaptation of procedures to meet individual needs
6. The motivation or incentive for increased effort
7. Practice in the taking of tests and examinations.

The rating or score will, of course, be significant, for it is a measure of achievement at a given point. The carefully constructed test will, however, not only provide a rating but will influence the teacher's teaching practices and the pupils' learning habits.

There is a great variety of tests, ranging all the way from the brief daily quiz—frequently oral—to the written final examination. Even more formal are the printed comprehensive tests, from other agencies, such as the College Entrance Board Comprehension Tests and the New York State Regents Examinations. We are concerned here mainly with the type of test prepared by the teacher or department head.

Principles of Test Construction. The longer comprehensive examination is generally designed to measure all four foreign language skills, that is, listening, speaking, reading, and writing. It is more scientific, however, to measure the various skills individually. This is especially to be recommended in the case of auditory comprehension and oral production. Separate tests may also be employed to measure pronunciation, vocabulary, structural control, or culture. In order to provide the teacher with a good overview of the students' performance, the test should consist of a fair sampling of items and an appropriate choice of different types of questions.

To secure optimum effectiveness, a test should be characterized by the following:

1. Instructions to the pupil should be clear and brief. They should be simple if given in the foreign language. A model of question and answer should be supplied.
2. The test should be based on a fair sampling of what has been taught.
3. The relative weights of questions should correspond to the importance of the skill measured.
4. The types of questions should be those used normally in the classroom.
5. As far as possible, everything should be in the foreign language.
6. Vocabulary, grammar, and idioms should be tested in context.
7. No incorrect forms should be presented.
8. As far as possible, questions should be arranged in ascending order of difficulty.
9. Translation into English should be used sparingly—in fact, only in advanced courses.
10. Translation into the foreign language is to be avoided.
11. Sufficient time should be allowed for the completion of the test.
12. The test should be so organized that it is easy to administer and to rate.

In order that the students may be perfectly at ease, they should have had previous practice in answering the types of questions that appear on the test. A test should be a satisfying, not a frightening, experience. The pupils should know what is expected of them and they should be given every opportunity to demonstrate their ability.

The questions appearing on a test should present no difficulty to the pupil, at least as far as form and construction are concerned, for they will be of the same nature as the drills employed in the daily lesson. The transformation, replacement, restatement, completion, and expansion patterns are as useful for testing as for teaching.

The Construction of a Test. Care must be taken that every phase of the unit to be measured is included. The easiest questions should come first, the moderately difficult ones next, and the difficult ones last. For the pupil's sake every precaution should be taken to insure definiteness, clarity, and ease in answering. Directions should be clear and succinct. A model answer should precede all types of questions, with the possible exception of comprehension questions. Sufficient space should be provided for the writing of the answer. Objectivity is increased by making only one answer possible. The test should be multigraphed or mimeographed.

Forms of new-type questions that may be employed in constructing an achievement test are the *completion exercise,* the *true-false statement, multiple-choice,* and *matching.* A number of variations of each are possible, depending upon whether vocabulary, grammar, or comprehension is being tested.

The completion exercise may require the insertion of an ending or a word or a phrase.

> Marie est notre amie; aidons-_____.
> Les enfants jouent _____ piano.
> Quel âge ont-ils? _____ seize ans.

To maintain perfect objectivity care must be taken to frame the statement or question so that only one answer is possible. For example in

> J'ai trouvé mon livre et _____ plume,

the examiner obviously expects *ma* in the blank, but *la, ta, sa, notre, votre, leur,* and *une* would be equally correct. A difficulty of this kind can be overcome by placing the English of the required word in parentheses.

> Avez-vous (too much) _____ sucre?
> Quand (will they be) _____ à la gare?

Some teachers prefer doing this throughout an exercise of this type. Then, however, it becomes an exercise in translation, rather than in comprehension.

The completion exercise may be used to test both vocabulary and grammar. Variations for vocabulary testing are:

Write the opposite of

> 1. grand _____
> 2. riche _____

216

3. lentement _____
4. sous _____

Write a synonym for

1. laufen _____
2. rasch _____
3. herrlich _____

Write an English cognate for

1. scappare _____
2. biblioteca _____
3. magnifico _____

Write the Spanish for

1. to fall _____
2. a horse _____
3. to look at _____

The completion type of question is also useful in testing knowledge of a foreign civilization.

1. _____ est le Premier de la France.
2. Les _____ séparent la France et l'Espagne.
3. La "Mona Lisa" est dans le _____.

The multiple-choice type of exercise can also be employed to test knowledge of grammar or vocabulary. It is quite objective, guessing is minimized, and it requires merely the underlining of a word or phrase.

Underline the related word:

Poisson 1. légume 2. eau 3. mère 4. soupe
Tante 1. fille 2. frère 3. femme 4. cousin

Underline the correct cognate:

Dach 1. that 2. dash 3. thatch 4. death
Ohr 1. or 2. oar 3. our 4. ear

Multiple-choice may be combined with completion.

Underline the word or phrase that best completes the meaning of the sentence:

Cuando tengo sed . . . 1. bailo   2. bebo   3. como   4. corro   5. me acuesto

Me gusta tomar el café con . . . 1. sal   2. pimienta   3. leche   4. limón   5. agua

This type of question may also be used for testing knowledge of a foreign civilization.

Pompei è presso . . . 1. Bologna   2. Napoli   3. Milano   4. Palermo.

La Cavalleria Rusticana é . . . 1. una novella   2. una poesia   3. un'opera   4. una commedia

Matching is useful in testing vocabulary, idioms, and knowledge of a foreign civilization.

Select from column I the items that match those in column II. Put the number in parentheses:

1. Roma	( ) gran porto
2. Appennini	( ) sede del papa
3. Genova	( ) generale
4. Vaticano	( ) scultore
5. Garibaldi	( ) poeta
6. Arno	( ) isola
7. Firenze	( ) catena di monti
8. Sardegna	( ) città eterna
9. D'Annunzio	( ) culla della arti
10. Michelangelo	( ) fiume

Guessing can be minimized by having two or three items more in column I than in column II.

Comprehension may be tested aurally by reading a passage aloud and asking a number of questions in the foreign language. The pupils write their answers after listening to two readings.

Or, the passage is presented in print to the pupil and he is asked to answer a number of questions, in either English or the foreign language. Probably the best way to guard against guessing or copying without actual comprehension is to require the pupil to translate his answer.

Read the following passage; then answer each question in Spanish, translating your answer into English.

Un juez examinaba a una señora como testigo y le preguntó a ella:
—¿Cuántos años tiene usted?
—Treinta, respondió ella.
—Treinta, observó el juez. Hace tres años que declaró usted la misma edad en este tribunal.
—Es, contestó ella, que yo no soy de esas personas que hoy dicen una cosa y mañana otra.

1. ¿Qué hacía un juez?
(Spanish) _____
(English) _____
2. ¿Qué le preguntó a la señora?
(Spanish) _____
(English) _____
3. ¿Cuántos años tenía la señora?
(Spanish) _____
(English) _____
4. ¿Qué observó el juez?
(Spanish) _____
(English) _____
5. ¿Cómo respondió la señora?
(Spanish) _____
(English) _____

In a simple passage like the above it is easy to frame the questions so that only one answer is possible. In the use of more complicated passages this is not so easy, especially if questions requiring judgment are asked. Greater objectivity can be secured by employing true-false or multiple-choice questions. Whenever several equally correct answers are possible, the key should supply these.

Finally, there is the *true-false* type of question. This lends itself to the testing of comprehension and knowledge of a foreign civilization.

Before each of the following statements place a check (√) if it is true and a cross (×) if it is false:

_____ 1. La rumba es un baile cubano.
_____ 2. La mantilla no se usa en España.
_____ 3. Sorolla fué un famoso pintor.

219

The true-false type of question is not very satisfactory for testing comprehension; it is not easy to construct statements of sufficient difficulty, since often clue words cannot be avoided and since guessing cannot be precluded.

Testing Aural Comprehension. Comprehension of the spoken word may be tested as an individual skill or in connection with other skills. The major aim is to determine the student's facility in understanding the foreign language, at normal speed, spoken by a native speaker.

True-False Test. The simplest test of aural comprehension is the true-false test. The teacher says or reads a number of statements in succession, saying each one twice. On a sheet, after the corresponding number, the pupils will indicate by a check mark whether the statement is true or false. Sample statements in Spanish might be:

1. Seis y cuatro son once.
2. El burro es un animal.
3. Hace calor en el invierno.
4. No oye; es ciego.
5. El primo es el hijo del tío.

Action Responses. Action responses are especially suitable for testing auditory comprehension, since they involve dramatization. Common classroom commands can be used for this purpose; for example:

Levántese Vd.	Vuelva a su asiento.
Vaya a la pizarra.	Siéntese Vd.
Vaya a la puerta.	Muéstreme un lápiz.
Abra Vd. la puerta.	Muéstreme una pluma.
Cierre Vd. la puerta.	Abra Vd. su cuaderno.

Multiple-Choice Items. Multiple-choice questions are also very useful for testing aural comprehension. Of course, the pupil will also have to know how to read the foreign language in order to indicate his answer.

The students' ability to discriminate sounds can be tested by letting them look at a series of words or phrases, while the teacher pronounces only one of them twice. The students indicate by a check mark or number which one the teacher uttered. For example:
como, come, coma, comen   cabo, caoba, acaba, a capo

In another type of test, the student checks the statement that is the correct answer to the question he hears. For example:

Cuando una persona dice: ¡Felices vacaciones! ¿Qué contesta Vd.?
1. No hay de qué.
2. Igualmente.
3. Sírvase.
4. Ya lo creo.

In a third type of test the student completes a sentence. He is to choose the correct word or sentence from those in the test booklet. For example:

Juan come porque
1. tiene sed
2. tiene sueño
3. tiene hambre
4. está perezoso

A more expanded type of auditory-comprehension test requires the student to select the correct answer to a question based on a brief passage. For example:

Un mendigo está a la esquina de una calle, pidiendo limosnas. Dice a los peatones: ¡Una limosna para el ciego!

¿Qué quiere el mendigo?
1. Él quiere limones.
2. Él quiere piedad.
3. Él quiere una moneda.
4. Él quiere un cigarro.

A variation of the reading passage test eliminates reading. The student merely indicates by letter or check mark which of the four statements that he hears is correct. For example:

Juan vuelve de la escuela a las tres y media. El bebe dos vasos de leche y entonces va a jugar beisbol con sus compañeros.
Cuando Juan vuelve de la escuela, el   (a) tiene sed, (b) está fatigado,   (c) está triste,   (d) quiere dormir.

In all of the tests described above, writing by the student has been kept at a minimum, since auditory comprehension was the chief item involved. The two skills can, however, be combined. For example, in the test based on a passage, the answers, instead of being merely checked, are written out by the student. It is customary to read the questions as well as the passage twice. This holds also for the dictation exercise, which more properly comes under the category of writing.

Testing Reading Comprehension. In the beginning, that is, before writing has been introduced, reading comprehension can be tested orally. Very soon, however, formal tests will have to be used and these will be of the objective type. The student will be required to indicate by letter or number the correct answer among four multiple-choice items or to complete unfinished sentences.

At present the most widely used type of objective reading-comprehension test consists of a reading selection followed by a series of statements or questions, and four or five completions, one of which the student is to choose.

The question below, taken from the Spanish III Regents Examination of June, 1962, may serve as an example.

Un vecino pobre iba todos los sábados al monte a cortar leña, que traí después en su burrito y vendía en el pueblo cuando estaba seca. Uno de tantos sábados se perdió en el monte, y lo cogió la noche sin poder dar con la salida. Cansado de andar por aquí y por allá, resolvió subir a un árbol con la esperanza de dormir allí sin peligro. Ató el burrito, y subió hasta la copa. De repente vió a lo lejos una luz. Bajó y se encaminó a ella. Al acercarse vió una casa iluminada, donde se oían música, cantos y risas. Sin hacer ruido, entró en la casa y se escondió detrás de una puerta.

21. El pobre se dirigía al monte para

    1. recoger madera
    2. visitar un vecino
    3. cortar el camino
    4. llegar a la aldea

22. ¿Qué le pasó al leñador un sábado?

    1. Vendió su asno.
    2. Se le perdió el burrito.

3. Padeció de sed.
4. Se desorientó.

23. ¿Por qué subió al árbol el pobre?

 1. Quería encontrar a su burro.
 2. Quería protegerse.
 3. Tenía que cortar un ramo.
 4. Esperaba esconderse.

24. ¿Qué notó el pobre a lo lejos?

 1. unos cuantos cantantes
 2. las muchas estrellas del firmamento
 3. una vivienda donde había luz
 4. un carnaval donde se oía mucha risa

25. Al entrar en la casa, ¿que hizó el hombre?
 1. Empezó a cantar.
 2. Dió gritos.
 3. Se ocultó
 4. Rió a carcajadas.

It will be noticed that the completion statements, in most cases, do not repeat the exact words of the passage, but rather reproduce the idea. The student has to know that *se desorientó* is the equivalent of *se perdió* and that *se ocultó* is the same as *se escondió*. The obvious is avoided; also the absurd, which could be eliminated by the reader without actual comprehension. It is of interest to note that 50 per cent of the credit on this Regents examination is given to reading comprehension.

In addition to testing the student's ability to grasp the basic ideas and the details of a reading passage, this type of question may be used to test vocabulary, idioms, and structures. The student is required to choose appropriate synonyms and antonyms, related words, definitions, the word that describes a particular situation or person and so on.

Although the true-false exercise is used liberally in the beginning, for obvious reasons, the completion and particularly the multiple-choice type of question predominate later on. On the Regents Examination presented, above 80 per cent of the paper consists of multiple-choice items.

223

MLA Tests

The MLA Cooperative Foreign Language Tests are entirely in consonance with the new method of language instruction. They consist of a series of tests of competence in French, German, Italian, Russian, and Spanish. They can be used in college as well as in high school. Listening, speaking, reading, and writing are measured separately at two levels of achievement.

These tests were prepared as a cooperative project of the Modern Language Association of America, the Educational Testing Service, and the U.S. Office of Education, Department of Health, Education and Welfare. The eighty different tests were prepared by committees of language teachers from high schools and colleges.

The tests measure the four language skills separately.

Listening. Taped material is run off, to which the student listens. He answers multiple-choice questions based on single utterances, brief conversations, passages read by one person, telephone conversations, and dramatic scenes enacted by two, three, or four speakers. The speakers are natives of the foreign country. Individual students or groups may be tested. The responses in the test booklet are scored objectively by using the appropriate answer key.

Speaking. The student receives his instructions from a master tape. He responds by speaking into a microphone; his performance is recorded. The test presents both verbal and visual stimuli. The student is expected to repeat what he hears, read aloud, answer questions based on pictures, and describe pictures presented singly or in sequence.

The student listens to the stimulus material through earphones and then responds by speaking into a microphne. His responses are recorded on tape and are evaluated later by the teacher, who is supplied with an evaluation form.

Reading. The student's facility in reading is tested by means of questions involving four choices. Completion sentences measure the student's comprehension of words and idiomatic expressions. Passages taken from periodicals and literary sources are used to test the student's discrimination of words and phrases and his ability to get the main thought and some of the details.

Writing. The student is asked to write structured and free responses. He demonstrates his understanding of the correct usage of articles, pronouns, verbs, and prepositions by filling in blanks. Some simple idioms are also introduced. The student is also required to rewrite sentences, making the necessary changes in tense, gender, number, person, and word order. He writes or rewrites paragraphs and short dialogues based on verbal stimuli. The structured paragraphs and dialogues are rated on a five-point scale. Completeness, word and sentence structure, clarity, coherence, and idiomatic usage are considered.

Since the four skills are tested separately, the tests may be administered independently. The time allowance for testing a skill is the same for all five languages. There are, however, variations in time for the different skills, namely: listening, twenty-five minutes; speaking, ten minutes; reading, thirty-five minutes; and writing, thirty-five minutes. Except for directions, no English is used in any of the tests. In no instance is the student asked to translate.

There are four test booklets available for each of the five languages: lower level forms LA and LB and higher level forms MA and MB. The A and B forms at each level may be used alternately.

The weakest part of the new MLA tests is the testing of speaking competence. This part requires an audio-active laboratory in which pupils can record at all stations. The various phases of speaking ability to be rated are much too complex for practical purposes. In addition, the time needed for scoring is excessive.

Foreign Language Tests

MLA Cooperative Foreign Language Tests in French, German, Italian, Russian, and Spanish.

Test Booklets (units of 10) contain materials to be used in evaluating listening, speaking, reading, and writing. $5.00 per package.

Listening Comprehension Tapes. Contains stimulus material for Listening Test. $7.00 each.

Speaking Test Tapes. Instructions for the Speaking Test. $7.00 each.

Scoring Keys for Scoring Test Booklets. One free with each order. Additional keys 25¢ each.

Directions for Administering and Scoring. Single booklet for all MLA tests. Additional copies $1.00 each.

Manual for Interpreting Scores. Separate manual for each language. $1.00 each.

Technical Report. Single Technical Report for all languages. $1.00 each.

Standards of Teaching

In order that the language teacher may determine whether he is growing professionally, it is well for him to consider from time to time whether or not he is observing the best teaching procedures and practices. Such a self-evaluation is particularly important for the young beginner. It is advisable, however, even for the veteran to measure his work against a set of standards. *Dum docemus, discimus.*

The daily classroom lesson is, of course, the most essential part of the teacher's job, and on the basis of it his effectiveness must be judged.

The following standards are an attempt to provide reasonable and pedagogically sound criteria by which to appraise the quality of a lesson in a foreign language. They may be used by the teacher to evaluate his effectiveness. They may also be used as a check list by the supervisor.

STANDARDS FOR
THE FOREIGN LANGUAGE LESSON

I. Physical conditions
  A. The room
    1. There should be adequate light and ventilation.
    2. The floor should be free from paper and refuse.
    3. Cleanliness and tidiness should be predominant.
    4. The desks should be free from inscriptions.
  B. Blackboards
    1. The blackboard should be free from the exercises of the previous class.
    2. All written work on the board, whether done by the teacher or by the pupils, should be neat, legible, accurate, and in sequential arrangement.
    3. All exercises written by the pupils should have a brief heading in the foreign language ("My name is . . ." and the date).
  C. Illustrative material
    1. Carefully selected illustrative material should be put on display in every foreign language classroom, whether

it is used exclusively by the foreign language teacher or not. This will consist of posters, pictures, photographs, pupils' drawings, lettered proverbs, and travel folders. The material should be selected on the basis of its attractiveness and its representativeness of the foreign culture.

2. Every foreign language room should contain a good map of the foreign country.

3. Every foreign language classroom should contain a bulletin board for the display of news items and pictures of current interest. The display should be changed frequently.

4. To the above may be added dolls in foreign costume, carvings, models made by pupils, a calendar in the foreign language, and so on.

5. Pictures and other illustrative material should be neatly labeled in the foreign language.

II. The lesson

A. Definiteness of aim and procedure

1. Every lesson should be a planned lesson. The written plan should include the aims, the scope, and the classroom activities.

2. An important feature of the plan is the proper allotment of time to the various activities. The lesson should be so planned that it can be taught within the period.

B. Motivation

1. Every lesson should be properly motivated, so that the interest of the pupils is aroused and so that they feel the need for all that follows. Each step and each exercise should be accompanied by a brief explanatory comment.

C. Economy in procedure

1. The distribution of books and materials, going to the board, collecting homework, and so on, should be routinized so that no time is lost.

2. Economy in routine demands uniformity. This is particularly true of rising when reciting, going to the front of the room to give an oral report, and so on. Pupils should know exactly what is expected.

3. That exercise or procedure should be chosen which bests suits the pupils, the subject, and the occasion.

4. The use of mimeographed sheets is far more economical than copying from the board.

5. Other activities should be carried on by pupils at their seats while board work is being done.

6. Conducive to good classroom management is well-organized monitorial assistance.

D. Questioning

1. Questions should be put to the class.

2. Time should be allowed for thinking.

3. Pupils should be called upon by name.

4. Questions should be so distributed that all have an opportunity to recite.

5. Normally, the teacher should avoid mechanically repeating the pupil's answer. If the teacher does repeat, it should be done with the obvious intent of stressing the word or expression.

6. As a rule, although not always, answers in complete sentences should be required.

7. Questions should be clearly formulated.

8. Answers may frequently be written on the board.

9. Whenever possible, questions should be sequential.

E. Methods and devices employed

The teacher should test the procedures employed by asking himself:

1. Are they modern or antiquated?

2. Are they economical?

3. Are they interesting and stimulating?

4. Do they make a multiple-sense appeal?

5. Do they make for self-activity?

6. Are they adequate?

7. Has sufficient practice been given?

F. Psychological factors

1. Motivation, continual and subtle, must lubricate the gears of the lesson.

2. Interest, genuine and sincere, in what is being done should prevail on the part of the teacher as well as the pupils.

3. Personal elements should enter into the questions and exercises to give them warmth. An absolutely objective attitude makes for coldness.

4. Humor and pleasantry should be a feature of the lesson.

G. Individualization of instruction

1. The difficulty and scope of the question should be adjusted to the intelligence and character of the pupil.
2. Special talents (drawing, singing, ability to play an instrument) should be utilized by the teacher whenever the occasion arises.
3. A pupil whose native language is being studied should be used for reading aloud, correcting oral work, dictating, giving summaries in it, and so on.
4. Remedial instruction should be given the weaker pupil or the one who has fallen behind.
5. Homework assignments should frequently be differentiated at three levels to provide for the slow, the average, and the superior.

H. Summarizing and testing
1. Before the close of the period, the teacher should have the main points of the lesson summarized briefly, in writing or orally.
2. A few minutes of testing, either oral or written, should reveal whether the aims of the lesson have been achieved.
3. The written test can be given at the beginning of the next period.

I. New assignment
1. Modern procedure requires that the homework assignment be given at the beginning of the period, or that it arise out of the day's lesson.
2. The teacher should make certain that every pupil knows what is to be done.
3. The assignment should be motivated, should be of reasonable length, and should not involve unusual difficulties. Sufficient explanation should be given to enable the average student to prepare successfully.

J. Creating life situations
1. As far as possible the foreign tongue should be the language of the classroom. It should be employed for all routine classroom commands and brief comments right from the start. In advanced classes it should be used almost exclusively.
2. The pupil should not only participate in the lesson but also play a definite role. The teacher is to be the director, the stage manager, the prompter, the guide and helper—not the doer.

3. The verisimilitude of the situation will be enhanced by the teacher's freedom from the textbook. Lively, improved, spontaneous exercises are preferable to the sentences in the book. The latter should be a guide and a help to teacher and pupil—not a taskmaster.
4. Cultural references in the text should be exploited. The extent to which this is done will depend upon the nature of the reference and the time available.

III. The pupils
  A. Attentiveness
    The pupils should maintain an attitude of interest and attention.
  B. Participation
    1. As far as possible, the participation of every pupil in the room should be enlisted—each one according to his abilities.
    2. The class should bear the burden of the work. The teacher is to initiate, stimulate, guide, correct, and criticize the activities.
    3. The participation of the pupils should be natural, voluntary, and spontaneous.
  C. Posture and behavior
    1. Correct posture in sitting, standing, and walking should be required of the pupils.
    2. Courtesy toward the teacher and fellow-pupils should prevail.
    3. An attitude of mutual helpfulness should be maintained.
  D. English and voice
    1. Correct and precise English should be required of the pupils.
    2. A clear and pleasant voice quality should be encouraged. Recitations should be loud enough for all to hear.
  E. Classroom standards
    1. Neatness on the board and in all written work should be taken for granted.
    2. Reciting, going to the board, addressing the class, and distributing material should be so routinized that every pupil knows what is expected.

IV. The teacher
  A. Appearance

1. The teacher's attitre should be neat, dignified, and in consonance with his age and position.
2. The teacher should set a good example to the class in posture.
3. As a guide and leader, the teacher should endeavor to present a radiant, vital, and stimulating personality to the class.

B. Manner
1. The teacher's attitude should be courteous, friendly, and cheerful.
2. He should set a good example in such traits as patience, generosity, broadmindedness, and humor.
3. The teacher should exemplify the ideals of scholarliness, tolerance, and fairness.
4. He should endeavor to maintain a spirit of good fellowship with the pupils without, however, descending to undue familiarity or cheap humor.

C. Voice and English
1. The teacher's voice should be clear, of sufficient volume, and of pleasant tone.
2. Excessive talking—the weakness of many a good teacher—should be avoided.
3. The teacher's English should be correct, precise, well-chosen, and pleasing. It should be a model for the class.
4. The same holds true of the foreign language.

D. Professional attitude
1. The alert teacher will belong to at least one language association.
2. He will read and contribute to professional literature.
3. He will welcome visitors to the classroom and will be eager for constructive supervision and criticism.
4. The dedicated teacher will look upon teaching as one of the most important vocations, and upon education as the most significant contribution to our social life. The daily lesson will be a gratifying experience, a happy contact with developing young minds and spirits.

In short, the teacher with ideals will consider himself primarily an educator of American youth and only secondarily a teacher of a specific language. This involves keeping constantly in mind the incidental learning, the imponderables and intangibles, and the outcome of the educational process as a whole. It means giving one's best to the pupils, endeavoring daily to be an inspiring leader and a sympathetic guide. It means cultivating vigor of thought and expression, self-confidence, good judgment, cheerfulness, a sense of humor, and tact. It means aiming to develop in the pupils habits of observation and discrimination, sustained effort and application. It implies inculcating ideals of open-mindedness and tolerance, emphasizing the beautiful and the noble.

One who sets out to do this will be not merely a teacher of French, German, Italian, or Spanish, but a true educator and a rich personality, contributing toward a better world.

Problems

1. Using a given passage, prepare multiple-choice exercises to test reading comprehension.

2. What would you add to and eliminate from the standards suggested?

3. List ten economies in classroom procedure that would apply to most language lessons.

4. Evaluate one of your own lessons on the basis of the criteria offered, checking those items that you might improve.

5. On the basis of lessons observed, indicate those items you believe many teachers to be weak in.

Bibliography

General

Belasco, S., and D. Cardenas (eds.), *Applied Linguistics: Spanish. A Guide for Teachers*, D. C. Heath & Co., Boston, 1961.

Brooks, Nelson, *Language and Language Learning*, Harcourt, Brace & World, Inc., New York, 1960, Second Edition, 1964.

Conant, James B., *The American High School Today*, McGraw-Hill Book Company, Inc., New York, 1959.

Foreign Language Revision Program for Secondary Schools

French, Levels I and II	French, Levels III and IV
German, Levels I and II	German, Levels III and IV
Hebrew, Levels I and II	Hebrew, Levels III and IV
Italian, Levels I and II	Italian, Levels III and IV
Latin, Levels I and II	Latin, Levels III and IV
Russian, Levels I and II	Russian, Levels III and IV
Spanish, Levels I and II	Spanish, Levels III and IV

Board of Education of the City of New York, Bureau of Curriculum Research, New York. Levels I and II, 1962; Levels III and IV, 1963.

French for Secondary Schools, Bureau of Secondary Curriculum Development, New York State Education Department, Albany, 1960.

German for Secondary Schools, Bureau of Secondary Curriculum

233

Development, New York State Education Department, Albany, 1962.

Spanish for Secondary Schools, Bureau of Secondary Curriculum Development, New York State Education Department, Albany, 1962.

Huebener, Theodore, *Why Johnny Should Learn Foreign Languages,* Chilton Co., Philadelphia, 1961.

Huebener, Theodore, *Opportunities in Foreign Language Careers,* Universal Publishing & Distributing Corp., New York, 1964.

Johnston, Marjorie C., *Modern Foreign Languages in the High School,* U.S. Office of Education, Government Printing Office, Washington, D.C., 1958.

Modern Foreign Languages in the Comprehensive Secondary Schools, National Association of Secondary School Principals, Committee on Curriculum Planning and Development. The Association, Washington, D.C., 1959.

O'Connor, P., and W. F. Twadell, "Intensive Training for an Oral Approach in Language Teaching," *Modern Language Journal,* II, 2, 1962.

O'Connor, P., *Modern Foreign Languages in the Secondary Schools: Pre-Reading Instruction,* U.S. Office of Education, Bulletin 1960, No. 9, Government Printing Office, Washington, D.C., 1960.

Ollmann, M. J. (ed.), *MLA Selective List of Materials.* Modern Language Association of America, New York, 1962. For use by teachers of modern foreign languages.

Parker, William R., *The National Interest and Foreign Languages,* rev. ed. Sponsored by the U.S. National Commission for UNESCO and the Department of State. Government Printing Office, Washington, D.C., 1962. Discussion outline and work paper.

Politzer, R. L., *Teaching French: An Introduction to Applied Linguistics,* Ginn & Co., Boston, 1960.

Politzer, R. L., and C. N. Staubach, *Teaching Spanish: A Linguistic Orientation,* Ginn & Co., Boston, 1961.

Starr, W., M. Thompson, and D. Walsh, *Modern Foreign Languages and the Academically Talented Student.* National Education Association and the Modern Language Association of America, New York, 1960.

Valdman, A., and S. Belasco (eds.), *Applied Linguistics: French, A Guide for Teachers,* D. C. Heath & Co., Boston, 1961.

Elementary Schools

Andersson, Theodore, *The Teaching of Foreign Languages in the Elementary School*, D. C. Heath & Co., Boston, 1953.

Cioffari, Vincenzo,"The Teaching of Foreign Languages in the Elementary School—A Realistic Analysis of the Present Movement," *The Modern Language Journal*, March, 1954.

Curriculum Bulletin. 1961–62, Series No. 13, *French in the Elementary Schools*, Grades 4–5–6, Board of Education, New York City, 1963.

Curriculum Bulletin. 1961–62, Series No. 14, *Spanish in the Elementary Schools*, Grades 4–5–6, Board of Education, New York City, 1963.

Keesee, Elizabeth, *References on Foreign Languages in the Elementary School*, Circular No. 495, Government Printing Office, Washington, D.C., 1960.

Méras, Edmond A., *A Language Teacher's Guide*, Harper & Brothers, New York, 1962.

Mildenberger, Kenneth W., "Foreign Language in the Grades," *The American School Board Journal*, October, 1956.

Modern Language Association of America Foreign Language Program, *FLES Packet*, Modern Language Association, New York, 1960.

Selvi, Arthur M., *Foreign Language Instruction in Elementary Schools*, Northeast Conference on the Teaching of Foreign Languages, Committee Reports, 1954.

Sister Georgiana, S.P., "Teaching Foreign Languages in the Elementary Schools," *The Catholic School Journal*, November, 1953 and December, 1953.

Audio-Visual Materials and Techniques

Archer, John B., chairman, "Report of the Committee on the Philosophy of the Language Laboratory," in *Reports of the Working Committees of the 1957 Northeast Conference on the Teaching of Foreign Languages*, Massachusetts Institute of Technology, Cambridge, Mass.

Eddy, Frederick D., chairman, "The Secondary School Language Laboratory: Some Observations on Present Practice and Long Range Possibilities," in *Reports of the 1956 Northeast Confer-*

ence on the Teaching of Foreign Languages; Margaret Gilman, editor, Bryn Mawr, 1956.

Eddy, Frederick D., and Elton Hocking, "Language Learning Today," *Audio-Visual Instruction,* September, 1959.

Fulton, Renée, "Language Laboratory Develops the Listening Ear," *Modern Language Journal,* May, 1959.

Gaudin, Lois, "The Language Laboratory," *French Review,* February, 1952.

Hirsch, Ruth, "Audio-Visual Aids in Language Teaching," Monograph Series on Languages and Linguistics, Georgetown University, Washington, D.C.

Hocking, Elton, and Robert S. Merchant, "The Fabulous Language Labs," in *Educational Screen and Audio-Visual Guide,* April, 1959.

Huebener, Theodore, *Audio-Visual Techniques in Teaching Foreign Languages,* New York University Press, New York, 1960.

Johnston, Marjorie C., and Catherine C. Seerley, *Foreign Language Laboratories in Schools and Colleges,* U.S. Dept. of Health, Education and Welfare, Office of Education, Bulletin No. 3, 1959.

Marty, Fernand, "Language Laboratory Techniques," *Educational Screen,* February, 1956.

Modern Language Association, "The Language Laboratory," Foreign Language Bulletin 39.

Modern Language Journal, May, 1959. This issue is devoted to the language laboratory.

Pleasants, Jeanne Varney, chairman, "Report of the Committee on Teaching Aids and Techniques," in *Report of the Working Committees of the 1957 Northeast Conference on the Teaching of Foreign Languages,"* Massachusetts Institute of Technology, Cambridge, Mass.

"Using Laboratory Techniques in Teaching Foreign Languages in New York City Schools," Curriculum Research Bulletin, Board of Education, New York City, 1961.

"Using the Tape Recorder," Curriculum Bulletin 1952–53, Series No. 6, Board of Education, New York City.

Index

Elementary school (*Cont.*):
    tive lessons, 204–11; objectives, 200–201; problems, 198–200
Evaluation, 212–32
Expansion drill, 21
Extra-curricular activities, 159–60

Film: *See* Pictures, Motion pictures.
Flash cards, 133–34
FLES movement, 197–98
Foreign languages: cultural value, 1, 10, 24, 59–60; political value, 3; practical value, 2; sociological value, 3

Games, 157, 162–68
Geography, 162
Gesture, 69–70
Glastonbury method, 11
Grammar, 98–117; analysis, 99–100; drills, 100–102; in elementary schools, 202–204; structure, 102–17
Graphic symbol, 13, 14
Guided writing, 78

Hagboldt, Peter, 7
Herbartian scheme, 120
History, in elementary schools, 196–97
Homework. *See* Assignments.

Idioms, 42–44, 167
Imitative writing, 76
Inference, 90–91
Integration drill, 22

Language, 14
Language laboratory, the, 127, 143–44, 147–55; coordination with classroom, 150–51; individual learning, 151; problems, 154–55; procedures, 147–48; skills to be developed, 149–50; types of lessons, 151–54
Langue, 14
Learning: aspects of, 7–11; laws of, 5; results of, 5–7
Lesson, the, 118–31, 226–32; the assignment, 125–29; devices in, 122–24; laboratory, 151–52; the recitation, 124–25; standards, 226–32

Lesson plans, 118–20, 129–31
Linguistics, 11, 14–16
Listening, 7, 10 27–30. *See also* Language laboratory.

McGrath, Earl J., 197
Measurement of learning, 212–14
Mildenberger, Kenneth, 197
MLA tests, 224–25
Morpheme, 15
Motion pictures, 142–43, 145
Motivation, of reading, 51–52

National Defense Education Act, 3, 11

Oral activities, 61–62. *See also* Speaking.

Pantomime, 69–70
Papers, school, 173
Parliamentary expressions, 171–73
Parole, 14
Pattern drills, 19–22
Phonation, 14
Phoneme, 14, 15
Phonograph records, 140, 144–45
Pictures, 135–37; compositions based on, 82–83
Prereading phase, 127. *See also* Listening, Pronunciation.
Projects, 160–61
Pronunciation, 27, 30–33

Questioning, techniques in, 120–21

Radio, 142
Reading, 7, 8, 10, 48–74, 128; comprehension, *see* Comprehension; illustrative lessons in, 64–74; in language laboratory, 152–53; principles of, 50–53
Recitation, 124–25
Rejoinder drill, 21
Repetition, 199–200
Repetition drill, 19
Replacement drill, 19
Response drill, 19
Restatement drill, 19

Index of Illustrative Lessons